Concentrate online study and revision support

D0316743

Visit our online resource centre at:

www.oup.com/lawrevision/

Take your learning further:

- ➤ Multiple-choice questions
- ➤ An interactive glossary
- ➤ Outline exam answers
- ➤ Flashcards of key cases

➤ Download our free ebook, *Study and Exam Success for Law Students*, which includes:

- • Guidance on how to approach revision and prepare for exams
- • Guidance on how to use a statute book

'I always buy a Concentrate revision guide for each module and use the online resources. The **outline answers are particularly helpful** and I often use **the multiple choice questions to test my basic understanding** of a topic'

Alice Reilly,
Cardiff University

'The Online Resource Centre has been **exceptionally useful**. In my first year, I used the resources to **quiz myself**, to **test my knowledge and understanding** of cases, and **to pick up extra pointers that could give me a few extra marks**'

Kelly Newman, University of Exeter

consolidate knowledge › focus revision › maximise potential

New to this edition

Fully updated with recent developments in the law, including:

- A valuable reminder in *Blue Monkey Gaming Ltd v Hudson & Others* (2014) that the responsibility for identifying and proving title to goods under a retention of title clause falls solely on the seller and not the administrators dealing with an insolvency.

- Although there are benefits to sellers incorporating retention of title clauses into their contracts, there are also dangers. *FG Wilson (Engineering) Ltd v John Holt & Co (Liverpool) Ltd* (2014) illustrates how sellers can be denied a claim for the price under the contract by virtue of trying to protect themselves with a retention of title clause.

- Another case on the meaning of 'disposition' for the purposes of the *nemo dat* exception under **s 27 HPA**. *VFS Financial Services Ltd v JF Plant Tyres Ltd* (2013) held that the taking of property in lieu of a debt does not constitute a disposition under **s 27 HPA** and that 'disposition' was limited to the specific types of transaction mentioned in **s 29(1)**, which requires the transfer of a vehicle in return for money.

- A reminder by the Court of Appeal in *Samarenko v Dawn Hill House Ltd* (2013) that the requirement to pay a deposit, including the time for payment, will ordinarily be a condition of a contract for sale of land and time will be 'of the essence' in relation to the date for payment.

- Updated chapter on Consumer Credit to take account of the many significant changes in this area of law, including:

  - An examination of the new regulatory regime for consumer credit which now falls under the **Financial Services and Markets Act 2000** by virtue of the **Financial Services and Markets Act 2000 (Regulated Activities) (Amendment) (No 2) Order 2013** and the new terminology that is now used.

  - A Supreme Court decision which held that where a consumer rescinds a sales contract that had been financed by credit he was also entitled to rescind the credit agreement, although not as a result of the 'like claim' provision in **s 75(1)** but via an altogether different and less obvious route of an implied term (*Durkin v DSG Retail Ltd and HFC Bank Plc* (2014)).

  - *Nram plc v McAdam* (2014) on the position where a lender represented that an unsecured loan of more than £25,000 was regulated by the CCA 1974. In such a case, the rights and remedies available under the CCA were imported into the (unregulated) agreement.

  - The first Supreme Court decision on the meaning of unfair relationships for the purposes of ss **140A–D CCA** (*Plevin v Paragon Personal Finance Ltd* (2014)).

Commercial Law
Concentrate

3rd edition

Eric Baskind

Senior Lecturer in Law,
Liverpool John Moores University

OXFORD
UNIVERSITY PRESS

OXFORD
UNIVERSITY PRESS

Great Clarendon Street, Oxford, OX2 6DP,
United Kingdom

Oxford University Press is a department of the University of Oxford.
It furthers the University's objective of excellence in research, scholarship,
and education by publishing worldwide. Oxford is a registered trade mark of
Oxford University Press in the UK and in certain other countries

First edition 2012
Second edition 2013

Impression: 1

Public sector information reproduced under Open Government Licence v2.0
(http://www.nationalarchives.gov.uk/doc/open-government-licence/open-government-licence.htm)

Published in the United States of America by Oxford University Press
198 Madison Avenue, New York, NY 10016, United States of America

British Library Cataloguing in Publication Data
Data available

Library of Congress Control Number: 2015931985

ISBN 978–0–19–872971–6

Printed in Great Britain by
Ashford Colour Press Ltd, Gosport, Hampshire

Contents

Table of cases

Table of cases

✳✳✳✳✳✳✳✳✳✳

Table of cases

✳✳✳✳✳✳✳✳✳✳✳

Table of legislation

Table of legislation

Table of legislation

****

#1

Introduction to contracts of sale of goods

Key facts

- English law has different legislative regimes for certain kinds of contractual relationships.

- A contract of sale of goods is a special kind of contract defined by **s 2(1) of the Sale of Goods Act 1979** (hereafter referred to as the **SGA**).

- Essentially this is a contract by which the seller transfers or agrees to transfer the property (this means ownership) in the goods to the buyer and where the consideration is satisfied by money.

- This distinguishes it from other forms of contract, some of which may also be regulated by statute.

- As we will see in Chapter 2, 'Statutory implied terms', p 8, certain terms are implied into contracts of sale of goods by operation of law that, for example, require them to be of satisfactory quality and fit for purpose.

- For this reason, it is important to know whether or not a contract is one of sale of goods.

- Some other statutes also imply certain terms into other types of transaction.

Chapter overview

This chapter provides a general introduction to sale of goods law. It explains:

- what a sale of goods contract is;
- why there is a different framework for these types of contract; and
- the specific legislation for contracts of sale of goods and other relevant transactions.

Key definitions used in the SGA

There are several important definitions contained in the SGA that you need to know. The first is, what is meant by a **contract of sale** of goods?

Contract of sale of goods

This is defined by **s 2(1) SGA** as:

> a *contract* by which the seller transfers or agrees to transfer the *property* in *goods* to the buyer for a *money consideration* called the price.

This definition calls for the words in italics to be defined:

Contract

This is not defined in the SGA and (apart from consideration) takes an identical meaning to a contract at common law: **offer, acceptance, consideration,** and an intention to create a legal relationship.

Property

Property means ownership. So, to *transfer the property in goods* simply means to transfer ownership in them.

Goods

Goods are defined in **s 61(1) SGA** as including 'all personal chattels other than things in action and money'. A 'personal chattel' is something physical such as a chair, television, or hat. Note that land and houses are not personal chattels but are 'real property'. However, industrial growing crops and things attached to or forming part of the land which are agreed to be severed before sale or under the contract of sale are deemed to be goods. A 'thing in action' is an intangible right enforceable by legal action. It has no intrinsic value—its value derives from the right to sue in respect of it. Examples of things in action include cheques, shares in companies, patents, and copyrights. By way of illustration, a cheque for £100 has no intrinsic worth in the sense that it is not worth £100, but it gives the recipient the right to sue for the money if unpaid.

The Mayor and Burgesses of the London Borough of Southwark v IBM UK Ltd [2011] EWHC 549 (TCC)

This case considered whether the sale of software is a contract of sale of goods. The contract stipulated that title, copyright, and all other proprietary rights in the software remained vested in the manufacturer. The purchaser merely had a licence to use it. The court held that there was no transfer of property in goods for the purpose of the **SGA**. Therefore, the **SGA** did not apply to the contract. As Akenhead J explained [at paragraph 95]:

> A preliminary question to consider is whether the . . . contract was a contract for the sale of goods at all. That involves a consideration first as to whether under section 2(1) there was to be a 'transfer' of 'property in goods' and secondly whether 'goods' were being sold. I have formed the view that there was here no 'transfer' of property in goods for the purposes of the 1979 Act. What was provided by IBM was in effect a licence . . . to use the software and, therefore, there is no transfer of property . . . [The contract] specifically talks about 'title, copyright and all other proprietary rights in the software' remaining vested in [the manufacturer]. Because copyright is identified as a specific right being retained, the use of the words 'title' and 'other proprietary rights' suggests strongly that ownership rights are retained.

But is computer software 'goods' for the purposes of the SGA? Akenhead J stated (*obiter*) that in principle software could be 'goods' for the following reasons:

- although a blank CD is worth very little, there is no restriction in the SGA on any goods being excluded from the Act by reason of their low value. CDs are physical objects and there is no reason why they should not be considered as goods;

- the fact that a CD is recorded so as to add functions and values to it simply gives a CD a particular attribute. Thus, if a customer buys a music CD, it must be 'goods'. There can be no difference if the CD contains software; and

- the definition of 'goods' is expressed to be an inclusive rather than an exclusive one. Put another way, the SGA is not excluding anything which might properly be considered as goods.

✅ Looking for extra marks?

Although in *St Albans City and District Council v International Computers Ltd* (1996) Sir Iain Glidewell said that it is necessary to distinguish between the program and the disk carrying the program, it seems from the decision in *Southwark* that it is important to examine the contractual terms pursuant to which the customer acquires the software. If, as in the *Southwark* case, it is simply a licence to use that is being granted, there may be no transfer of property. However, if the arrangement between the parties can be said to involve the transfer of property to the buyer, →

➡ then there may be no reason why in principle software that is so transferred cannot be 'goods' for the purposes of the SGA.

Money consideration

English law usually requires something known as 'consideration' to render an agreement enforceable as a contract. Unlike an ordinary contract where consideration may be satisfied by something of economic value, a contract of sale of goods requires consideration to be money. A simple exchange where one person exchanges his goods for another person's goods will be the basis of a contract but not one of sale of goods because of the absence of money changing hands. But if the exchange involves some money changing hands, for example because one person's goods are worth more than the other's, then this may be deemed to be two contracts of sale.

Aldridge v Johnson (1857) 7 E&B 885

A farmer exchanged some bullocks for some barley. As the barley was worth more than the bullocks the difference was made up by a payment of cash. The court held that this amounted to two contracts of sale of goods because the parties had given a price to both lots of goods and the consideration was money.

Esso Petroleum Ltd v Commissioners of Customs & Excise [1976] 1 WLR 1

Garages supplied a free gift to motorists for every four gallons of petrol purchased. The House of Lords held that the supply of the free gift did not constitute a contract of sale of goods. The motorist's consideration in return for the gift was not the payment of money but was the entering into of the separate (but linked) contract for the petrol.

Revision tip

When answering a question on sale of goods it is essential to have in mind that the SGA only applies to contracts of sale of goods as defined by s 2(1) SGA. A contract will not be one of sale of goods unless:

1. there is a transfer or an agreement to transfer the property in the goods to the buyer. Therefore, other kinds of contract, such as contracts of hire, **hire purchase**, or contracts to provide services are not governed by the SGA; and
2. the consideration is satisfied by money.

In addition to the definition of a contract of sale, you should also be familiar with the following terms as these are also used in the SGA:

Sales and agreements to sell

Both sales and agreements to sell may be contracts of sale of goods. The difference between these two types of transaction is that with a sale the property in the goods is transferred from the seller to the buyer as soon as the contract is made (s 2(4) SGA), whereas with an agreement to sell the transfer of the property in the goods takes place at a future time or is subject to some condition later to be fulfilled (s 2(5) SGA). An agreement to sell becomes a sale when the time elapses or the condition is fulfilled subject to which the property in the goods is to be transferred (s 2(6) SGA).

Specific goods and unascertained goods

At the time of making the contract the goods will either be specific or unascertained.

Specific goods are goods that are identified and agreed upon at the time a contract of sale is made (s 61(1) SGA). This means that both buyer and seller have identified and agreed upon precisely which goods will be sold under the contract.

Unascertained goods are not defined in the SGA but are in effect all goods that are not specific.

Goods may become **ascertained** as soon as they have been identified and agreed upon after the contract of sale is made.

It will be seen in Chapter 3, 'Passing of property and risk', p 31, that the distinction between specific and unascertained goods is important, as this usually determines the time at which property in the goods is transferred from the seller to the buyer.

Existing goods and future goods

The goods which form the subject of a contract of sale may be either **existing goods** or **future goods**.

Existing goods are goods that are either owned or possessed by the seller (s 5(1) SGA).

Future goods are goods to be manufactured or acquired by the seller after the making of the contract of sale (s 5(1) and s 61(1) SGA).

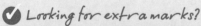 **Looking for extra marks?**

It is important to know whether or not the SGA governs the transaction because this will often determine the type and extent of liability in the event, for example, of the goods being defective. As we will see in Chapter 2, 'Statutory implied terms', p 31, the SGA implies into contracts of sale of goods certain terms (such as they must be of satisfactory quality and fit for purpose) which impose strict liability on the seller. As these terms are implied by statute into all contracts of sale of goods, they do not need to be agreed expressly by the parties. If the SGA does not apply to the transaction, and no other statute applies, then these terms will not be statutorily implied and the liability of the seller will be based on common law and is likely to be fault-based.

Contracts other than of sale of goods

As we have seen, a contract of sale of goods is intended to transfer the property (ownership) in the goods to the buyer. There are many other ways of doing this, for example, by giving away goods as a gift or leaving them in a will, but these are not contracts of sale of goods because one of the essential ingredients (money consideration) contained in s 2(1) SGA is missing.

There are also other ways of transferring possession (but not ownership) in goods, such as contracts of hire. These are also not contracts of sale of goods because, once again, an essential ingredient in s 2(1) is missing—the transfer of ownership in the goods.

These contracts are, therefore, not governed by the SGA but by other statutes. Therefore, in addition to contracts of sale of goods, it is important to consider other types of contracts, governed by different statutes, as these also impose certain implied terms, similar to those contained in the SGA. These are set out in Table 1.1.

Table 1.1 Implied terms in other types of transaction

Type of transaction	Implied terms	Why not SGA?
exchange or barter	**Supply of Goods and Services Act 1982, ss 2–5**	consideration not 'money' as required by **s 2(1) SGA**
hire	**Supply of Goods and Services Act 1982, ss 6–11**	no transfer or agreement to transfer property (ownership) in goods as required by **s 2(1) SGA**
hire purchase	**Supply of Goods (Implied Terms) Act 1973, ss 8–11; Consumer Credit Act 1974**	no obligation by the hirer to purchase goods, hence no obligation to transfer property in them as required by **s 2(1) SGA**
services—including where goods are also supplied (known as work and materials contracts)	**Supply of Goods and Services Act 1982, ss 2–5 and 12–16**	the substance of the contract is the provision of the overall service rather than the transfer of property in the goods as required by **s 2(1) SGA**

⑨ Key debates

Topic	**Time for an English commercial code?**
Author/Academic	Dame Mary Arden
Viewpoint	Discusses the original **Sale of Goods Act** in 1893 which was intended simply to codify rather than alter the common law rules.
Source	(1997) 56 *Cambridge Law Journal* 516

Topic	Software as goods
Author/Academic	Sarah Green and Djakhongir Saidov
Viewpoint	Discusses the decision in *Watford Electronics Ltd v Sanderson CFL Ltd* (2001) as to whether or not software should be classed as 'goods' for the purposes of the SGA.
Source	[2007] *Journal of Business Law* 161

Topic	Software: binding the end-user
Author/Academic	George Gretton
Viewpoint	Discusses the Scottish case of *Beta Computers (Europe) Ltd v Adobe Systems (Europe) Ltd* (1996) where Lord Penrose criticised the idea that software supplied on a permanent medium, such as a disk, would amount to a contract of sale of goods in the same way as, for example, the sale of a book.
Source	[1996] *Journal of Business Law* 524

#2

Statutory implied terms

Key facts

- Having explained what constitutes a contract of sale of goods, this chapter sets out and explains the significance of the terms implied into these contracts by operation of law.

- The **SGA** implies into contracts of sale of goods certain implied terms:

- the seller's right to sell the goods (**s 12(1) SGA**);

- the goods being free from encumbrances and the buyer enjoying quiet possession of them (**s 12(2) SGA**);

- the description of the goods (**s 13(1) SGA**);

- the quality of the goods (**s 14(2) SGA**);

- the fitness for purpose of the goods (**s 14(3) SGA**); and

- sales by sample (**s 15 SGA**).

- The terms implied by **ss 14(2)** and **14(3) SGA** apply only where the seller sells goods in the course of a business. If the seller does not sell the goods in the course of a business then **ss 14(2)** and **14(3)** will not apply but **ss 12, 13,** and **15** will.

- We will also consider the terms implied into other kinds of contract by different statutes.

Chapter overview

Is the transaction a contract of sale of goods and what are the consequences?

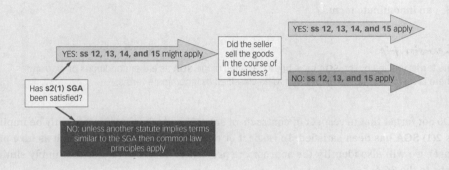

Introduction

The terms of a contract set out the obligations of the parties to it. Contractual terms can either be **express** or **implied**. An express term is one that has been expressly agreed by the parties, either in writing or orally. As well as express terms, further terms may be implied into the contract by the court. A typical example of when a court might imply a term into a contract is when it can be assumed that both parties would have agreed to such a term had they thought about it at the time the contract was made. Terms may also be implied by custom, trade usage, or operation of law.

In this chapter, we will be looking at terms implied by the SGA. As we saw in Chapter 1, 'Introduction to contracts of sale of goods', p 1, the SGA implies certain terms into contracts of sale of goods. These terms will be implied irrespective of the parties' intentions.

Classification of terms

Contractual terms (whether express or implied) will vary as to their importance. For example, if I offer to sell you my car, we might agree on the following terms:

- that the bodywork is in good condition;
- that the tyres are new; and
- that the car will be washed before delivery.

Let us say that I have breached all three of these **express terms** in that the bodywork is full of rust, the tyres are worn out, and I did not wash the car before delivery. Clearly, you will be more troubled by the first two breaches than the third one. It is for this reason that the

****

law classifies terms according to their importance. There are three classifications of a term. It may either be:

1. a **condition**;
2. a **warranty**; or
3. an **innominate term**.

Revision Tip

The terms implied by the **SGA** have been classified in the **SGA** as either conditions or warranties. There is no room, therefore, for them to be classified as innominate terms.

Do not forget that in respect of contracts of sale of goods these terms may *only* be implied if s 2(1) SGA has been satisfied. In respect of other types of transaction (such as **hire purchase**), we will also identify the appropriate provisions in other statutes that imply similar terms to the SGA.

Implied terms as to title—s 12 SGA

Section 12 SGA sets out three different terms as to title:

1. a *condition* that the seller has the right to sell the goods (s 12(1));
2. a *warranty* that the goods are free from any charge or encumbrance (s 12(2)(a));
3. a *warranty* that the buyer will enjoy quiet possession of the goods (s 12(2)(b)).

Section 12(1)—a condition that the seller has the right to sell the goods

This is one of the most important **implied terms** in the SGA as it imposes a duty on the seller to pass a good title to the goods.

s 12(1) SGA:

. . . there is an implied condition on the part of the seller that in the case of a sale he has a right to sell the goods, and in the case of an agreement to sell, he will have such a right at the time when the property is to pass.

Looking for extra marks?

Note that **s 12(1)** does not require that the seller should also be the owner, nor does the section require him to acquire title before transferring the goods to the buyer (*Karlshamns Oljefabriker v Eastport Navigation Corporation* (1982)).

Implied terms as to title—s 12 SGA

✳ ✳✳✳✳✳✳✳✳✳✳

A situation might arise where there exists a doubt as to a person's title to goods. This might happen if, for example, a person finds goods and sells them. A person who finds goods has what is known as a 'possessory title' to them but this is strictly subject to the title of the owner who can reclaim them. A finder who fails to disclose to the buyer that he only has a possessory title to the goods will be in breach of s 12. If he does disclose the true position then he is protected by s 12(3) and s 12(5) which provide that where it appears from the contract or is to be inferred from its circumstances an intention that the seller should transfer only such title as he (or a third person) may have, then there is an implied warranty that none of the following persons will disturb the buyer's quiet possession of the goods and the seller will not be in breach of s 12(1):

- the seller;
- in a case where the parties to the contract intend that the seller should transfer only such title as a third person may have, that person; and
- anyone claiming through or under the seller or that third person otherwise than under a charge or encumbrance disclosed or known to the buyer before the contract is made.

A breach of s 12(1) (being a condition) will entitle the innocent party to treat the contract as at an end. This is subject to the rule in s 11(4) that in the case of a contract of sale of goods a buyer cannot generally terminate the contract for breach of condition once he has accepted the goods (see Chapter 8, 'Acceptance', p 107, for rules on **acceptance**) and can only generally bring an action for damages for breach of warranty. However, in *Rowland v Divall* (1923) Atkin LJ held that the buyer's right to terminate the contract for a breach of s 12(1) was not lost just because he might have accepted the goods by his extensive use of them. In *Rowland* the contract was for the purchase of a car which the seller had no right to sell as, unbeknown to him, it had earlier been stolen. As the entire purpose of a contract of sale is to transfer ownership in the goods to the buyer, there was in this case a total failure of consideration because the buyer could never have obtained title, because the seller had no right to sell. There was therefore no proper **acceptance** even though he had use of the car for several months before the true facts came to light.

✔ *Looking for extra marks?*

The decision in *Rowland v Divall* has been criticised. Notwithstanding the fact that the buyer only had use of the car rather than ownership, which he had contracted for, the result meant that he had several months' use of it for nothing. As a result, the car was worth less when he returned it than when he 'bought' it. Applying this principle to the following situation illustrates the problem. Suppose A buys a case of wine from B and then drinks it before finding out that B had unwittingly bought the wine from a thief. Could it really be said that A has suffered a total failure of **consideration**? According to the decision in *Rowland v Divall* he has, because he could never own the wine even though he has consumed it and would be entitled to the return of the price he had paid to B. The true owner of the wine could sue A or B (or, if he could find him, the thief) for damages in the tort of conversion. If the true owner sues B it will mean that B will be liable to him for the →

➡ value of the wine as well as having to return to A the price A originally paid him, whereas A will have benefited by having had the wine for nothing.

Revision tip

Do not confuse ownership of the goods with the right to sell them. A person may sell goods even if he doesn't himself own them as in the case of an agent (see Chapter 12, 'The creation of agency and the agent's authority', p 171). Conversely, a person may own the goods but not the right to sell them. This can be seen from the following case:

Niblett Ltd v Confectioners' Materials Co Ltd [1921] 3 KB 387

D sold a quantity of tins of condensed milk some of which were labelled 'Nissly'. The buyers were informed by Nestlé that this infringed their trade mark. The buyers brought an action against D for breach of s 12(1). It was held that even though D owned the goods they were in breach of s 12(1) because they had no right to sell them.

Sections 12(2)(a) and 12(2)(b)—warranties that the goods are free from any charge or encumbrance and that the buyer will enjoy quiet possession of the goods

In *Microbeads AG v Vinhurst Road Markings Ltd* (1975) the seller sold some road marking machinery. Shortly after the sale an unconnected company obtained a patent relating to road marking machines which entitled them to bring an action against the buyer to enforce their patent. As a result, the buyer brought an action against the seller for breach of the condition as to their right to sell the machines and also for breach of the warranty of quiet possession. The Court of Appeal held that there was no breach of the implied condition as to the seller's right to sell because that condition related to the time when the contract was made, which predated the third party's patent. The seller therefore had the right to pass good title in the machines. However, there was a breach of the implied **warranty** that the buyer will enjoy quiet possession of the goods as the words 'will enjoy' relates to the future use of the goods.

Revision tip

Don't forget that because the implied terms in ss 12(2)(a) and 12(2)(b) are classed as warranties, any breach of them will not give the buyer the right to treat the contract as at an end, but only to claim damages.

Contracts other than of sale of goods

Revision tip

Don't forget Chapter 1, 'Contracts other than of sale of goods', Table 1.1, p 6, which identifies the corresponding implied terms in other types of contract.

Sales by description—s 13(1) SGA

Where the contract is for a sale of goods by description, there is an implied condition in s 13(1) that the goods will correspond with the description. This condition applies whether or not the seller sells the goods in the course of a business.

What is a sale of goods by description?

There is no statutory definition of the phrase 'a contract for the sale of goods by description' and it is therefore important to look to the ordinary meaning of the words and the decided cases for guidance as to its meaning. There is unlikely to be much difficulty in applying this phrase in the case of a sale of **unascertained** or **future goods** because there can be no contract for the sale of goods of these categories except by reference to a description of some sort.

The difficulty is likely to arise in cases where the sale is of **specific goods**. A contract for the sale of specific goods is *capable* of falling within s 13(1) but, if it is to do so, it has to be a contract for sale '*by* description'.

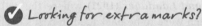 **Looking for extra marks?**

Even though there is no statutory definition of the phrase 'a contract for the sale of goods by description' it is clear from s 13(3) that a sale of goods is not prevented from being a sale by description by reason only that, being exposed for sale or hire, they are selected by the buyer. Therefore, sales of goods in self-service supermarkets could be sales by description.

In *Beale v Taylor* (1991), Taylor advertised his car for sale, which he believed to be a 1961 Triumph Herald 1200. The advertisement read 'Herald convertible, white, 1961 . . .'. Beale bought the car and shortly afterwards found that it was in fact made up of two cars welded together. The rear portion consisted of a 1961 Triumph Herald 1200 model, but the front portion consisted of an earlier 1948 model. The Court of Appeal held that there could be a sale by description of a specific chattel, even where the chattel was displayed and inspected by the buyer, so long as it was sold not merely as the specific thing but as a thing corresponding to a description so that the buyer relied at least in part on a description. When Beale made his offer for the car he relied on the description given in the advertisement and on the badge showing that it was a 1961 Triumph Herald 1200. It was therefore a sale by description. Since the car did not correspond with its description, Beale was entitled to damages for breach of the condition implied by s 13.

In *Beale*, the entire car was not what the description claimed it to be. However, this case should be contrasted with the following case where the car was accurately described as being vintage, but some of its components were not. In *Brewer v Mann* (2012), Mann advertised for sale a '1930 Bentley Speed Six' car. Brewer obtained the car on **hire purchase**. Brewer later argued that the car did not conform to this description because the engine was not an original Bentley engine but a Bentley engine that had been modified to Speed Six specifications. Brewer further argued that the bodywork had been altered. The Court of Appeal held that the description of the car in the hire purchase contract did not require it to be an original 1930 Bentley Speed Six. Consequently, alterations to its engine and bodywork did not constitute a breach of its description. The identity of a vintage car was to be ascertained by the normal customs of the vintage car trade, and, on the evidence of both experts, the car did correspond with its description as a '1930 Bentley Speed Six'.

The description must amount to a term in the contract

Just because a description has been attributed to the goods (either during negotiations or in the contract) it does not necessarily mean that the contract is one of sale by description. A court will only hold that a contract is one for the sale of goods *by* description if it is able to impute to the parties a common intention that it shall be a term of the contract that the goods will correspond with the description (*Harlingdon and Leinster Enterprises Ltd v Christopher Hull Fine Art Ltd* (1991)).

At one time it was relatively easy to reject goods for breach of this condition. This earlier approach can be seen in cases such as *Re Moore and Landauer* (1921), where the sellers contracted to sell a quantity of tinned fruit which were to be packaged in cases each containing 30 tins. The overall correct quantity was delivered, but some of the tins were packed in cases containing 24 tins. The Court of Appeal held that this was a sale of goods by description and that the statement in the contract that the goods were to be packed 30 tins to a case was part of the description. As some of the goods tendered did not correspond with that description the buyers were entitled to reject the entire consignment.

For the description to fall within s 13 it must be a 'substantial ingredient of the identity of the thing sold'

The decision in *Re Moore and Landauer* was doubted by Lord Wilberforce in *Reardon Smith Line Ltd v Hansen-Tangen* (1976), where he described the decision as 'excessively technical'. The dispute in *Reardon Smith Line* concerned a vessel which the contract stated would be built in shipyard Osaka 354, but because of its size the vessel was in fact built in shipyard Oshima 004. By the time the vessel was ready for delivery, the market had collapsed and the charterers sought to escape from their obligation by rejecting the vessel on the ground that the vessel tendered did not correspond with the contractual description in that it was an Oshima 004 rather than an Osaka 354 vessel. The House of Lords held that it was important to ask whether a particular item in a description constituted a 'substantial ingredient of the identity of the thing sold' and only if it did could it be treated as a condition. In the present case, it was plain that the hull or yard number of the vessel had no special significance for the parties so as to raise it to a matter of fundamental obligation.

The description must be relied upon by the buyer

The Court of Appeal held in *Harlingdon and Leinster Enterprises Ltd v Christopher Hull Fine Art Ltd* (1991) that there is no sale by description where it was not within the reasonable contemplation of the parties that the buyer was relying on the description. The buyer must then have placed reliance on the description.

Summary of s 13

See Figure 2.1 and see also Chapter 10, 'Summary of remedies for breach of s 13 SGA', p 139, for the remedies available to the buyer for a breach of **s 13**.

Contracts other than of sale of goods

Revision tip

Don't forget Chapter 1, 'Contracts other than of sale of goods', Table 1.1, p 6, which identifies the corresponding implied terms in other types of contract.

Figure 2.1 Breach of **s 13(1)**

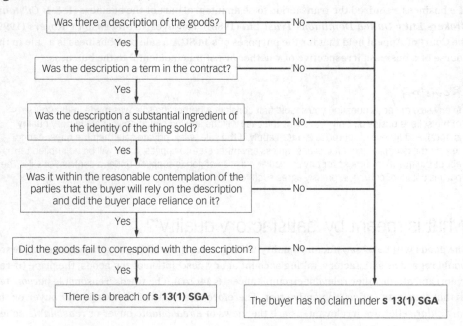

Satisfactory quality—s 14(2) SGA

Where the seller sells the goods in the course of a business, s 14(2) implies a condition that the goods supplied under the contract should be of satisfactory quality.

Revision tip

Don't forget that, unlike the condition implied by s 13 which applies whether or not the seller sells the goods in the course of a business, the condition implied by s 14(2) applies only where the seller sells the goods in the course of a business.

✓ *Looking for extra marks?*

1. Satisfactory quality was, until 1994, known as merchantable quality. The **Sale and Supply of Goods Act 1994** amended **s 14(2) of the SGA**, replacing 'merchantable quality' with 'satisfactory quality'.

2. Liability under s 14(2) is strict and arises if the seller sells goods in the course of a business that are not of satisfactory quality. The seller need not be at fault.

In the course of a business

Albeit for the purposes of the **Unfair Contract Terms Act 1977**, the expression 'in the course of a business' required the transaction to be an integral part of the business (*R & B Customs Brokers Ltd v United Dominions Trust Ltd* (1988)). However, in *Stevenson v Rogers* (1999) the Court of Appeal held that for the purposes of s 14 SGA a sale by a business is a sale in the course of a business irrespective of whether or not it is incidental to the business.

Revision tip

In any sale of goods question you should first consider whether the sale was made in the course of the seller's business. Only if this was the case will the implied conditions of satisfactory quality (s 14(2)) and fitness for purpose (s 14(3)) apply. If the sale was a private sale then the buyer cannot rely on these implied conditions and, unless any other statute applies, there will be no implied terms about the quality or fitness for any particular purpose of goods supplied under a contract of sale. The parties could, of course, expressly agree such terms.

What is meant by 'satisfactory quality'?

The goods will be of satisfactory quality 'if they meet the standard that a reasonable person would regard as satisfactory, taking account of any description of the goods, the price (if relevant) and all the other relevant circumstances' (s 14(2A)). The words 'reasonable person' tell us that this is an entirely objective test. Therefore, the views of the *particular* buyer or the *particular* seller are irrelevant, as are the views of a *reasonable* buyer or *reasonable* seller.

The goods will be satisfactory if a reasonable *person* considers them to be satisfactory having the knowledge of the particular transaction and considering this against s 14(2A) and s 14(2B).

The other factors noted in s 14(2A) are also important. Price is likely to be a relevant factor in many transactions. A reasonable person is likely to expect goods costing more to be of a higher quality than their cheaper counterparts. 'All the other relevant circumstances' would include, where appropriate, the fact that the goods are second-hand rather than new or the fact that the goods were sold for scrap rather than for general use.

Whilst s 14(2A) sets out the general definition of satisfactory quality, it is s 14(2B) that lists five matters that are in appropriate cases aspects of the quality of the goods. These are:

(a) fitness for all the purposes for which goods of the kind in question are commonly supplied;

(b) appearance and finish;

(c) freedom from minor defects;

(d) safety; and

(e) durability.

It should be remembered that these 'aspects of quality' will only be relevant in appropriate cases. They must not be considered to be absolute requirements of quality. For example, goods sold as scrap might not satisfy any of the five aspects yet a reasonable person would nevertheless consider them to be satisfactory.

It should also be noted that goods only need to be of satisfactory quality and not necessarily perfect. However, 'in some cases, such as a high-priced quality product, the customer may be entitled to expect that it is free from even minor defects, in other words perfect or nearly so' (per Hale LJ in *Clegg v Olle Andersson t/a Nordic Marine* (2003)).

Is the buyer dealing as a consumer?

If the buyer is dealing as a consumer then the relevant circumstances mentioned in s 14(2A) above include any public statements on the specific characteristics of the goods made about them by the seller, the producer, or his representative, particularly in advertising or on labelling (s 14(2D)). However, this will not be the case if the seller is able to show that:

s 14(2E)(a)	at the time the contract was made, he was not, and could not reasonably have been, aware of the statement; or
s 14(2E)(b)	before the contract was made, the statement had been withdrawn in public or, to the extent that it contained anything which was incorrect or misleading, it had been corrected in public; or
s 14(2E)(c)	the decision to buy the goods could not have been influenced by the statement.

Section 61(5A) SGA tells us (in a rather roundabout way) when a buyer is dealing as a consumer by referring to s 12(1) of the Unfair Contract Terms Act 1977 (UCTA). It also provides that it is for a seller claiming that the buyer does not deal as consumer to show that he does not.

Section 12(1) UCTA provides that a party to a contract deals as a consumer in relation to another party if:

(a) he neither makes the contract in the course of a business nor holds himself out as doing so; and

(b) the seller does make the contract in the course of a business.

Furthermore, the goods must be of a type ordinarily supplied for private use or consumption (s 12(1)(c) UCTA).

'In the course of a business' for the purpose of **s 12(1) UCTA** has a more complex meaning than that given to the same phrase in **s 14 SGA** (see 'In the course of a business', p 16) and can be summarised by Table 2.1.

✅ Looking for extra marks?

When discussing the phrase 'in the course of a business' you should explain that a different meaning is given to it depending on whether it is used in the **SGA** or the **UCTA**. This so-called 'dual meaning' of the same phrase was confirmed as correct by the Court of Appeal in **Feldarol Foundry Plc v Hermes Leasing (London) Ltd (2004)**.

Revision tip

Note that **s 12 UCTA** defines consumer status by reference to the transaction itself rather than by reference to the individual. This means that it is perfectly possible for a business to be a consumer when buying goods of a type ordinarily supplied for private use or consumption and not of a type they would usually buy for their own business.

Table 2.1 Meaning of 'in the course of a business'

Section	Meaning	Case
s 12(1) UCTA	The purchase must be an integral part of the business, or if the goods are bought as a 'one-off' purchase they must have been bought with the intention of selling them on for a profit, or if the goods purchased are of a kind which the business has bought with some degree of regularity	**R & B Customs Brokers Ltd v United Dominions Trust Ltd (1988)**
s 14 SGA	A sale by a business is a sale in the course of a business	**Stevenson v Rogers (1999)**

The condition as to satisfactory quality will not be implied in the following situations

In addition to where the seller does not sell the goods in the course of a business, the implied condition as to satisfactory quality does not extend to any matter making the quality of the goods unsatisfactory:

s 14(2C)(a)   which is *specifically* drawn to the buyer's attention before the contract is made. A generalised statement indicating that there may be some defect in the goods will not protect the seller.

s 14(2C)(b)   where the buyer examines the goods before the contract is made, which that examination ought to reveal. There is no obligation on the part of the buyer to examine the goods before the contract is made but if he does so, and fails to notice a defect which his examination ought to have revealed, he cannot later complain that that particular defect renders the goods unsatisfactory.

s 14(2C)(c)   in the case of a contract for sale by sample, which would have been apparent on a reasonable examination of the sample.

✅ *Looking for extra marks?*

It might appear odd that a buyer who does not examine the goods before agreeing to buy them should be in a stronger position than a buyer who does examine them. But that is the effect of **s 14(2C)(b)**. For this reason, a buyer would be well advised either not to examine the goods at all or to ensure that his examination is as thorough as reasonably possible. However, a buyer might not be expected to notice every defect and this rule may depend on the nature of the examination. For example, a buyer who examines the bodywork of a car he is looking to buy is likely to be expected to notice any defects in the bodywork, but unless he examines the car mechanically it might not be reasonable to expect mechanical defects to be revealed.

Summary of s 14(2)

See Figure 2.2. Also see Chapter 10, 'Summary of remedies for breach of s 14(2)', p 140, for the remedies available to the buyer for a breach of **s 14(2)**.

Contracts other than of sale of goods

Revision tip

Don't forget Chapter 1, 'Contracts other than of sale of goods', Table 1.1, p 6, which identifies the corresponding implied terms in other types of contract.

Fitness for purpose—s 14(3) SGA

✱✱✱✱✱✱✱✱✱✱

Figure 2.2 Breach of s 14(2)

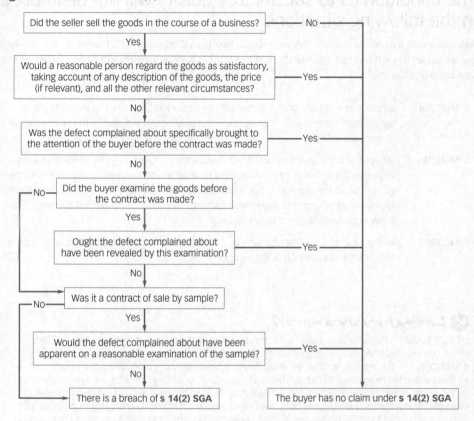

Did the seller sell the goods in the course of a business? — No

Yes ↓

Would a reasonable person regard the goods as satisfactory, taking account of any description of the goods, the price (if relevant), and all the other relevant circumstances? — Yes

No ↓

Was the defect complained about specifically brought to the attention of the buyer before the contract was made? — Yes

No ↓

— No — Did the buyer examine the goods before the contract was made?

Yes ↓

Ought the defect complained about have been revealed by this examination? — Yes

No ↓

— No — Was it a contract of sale by sample?

Yes ↓

Would the defect complained about have been apparent on a reasonable examination of the sample? — Yes

No ↓

There is a breach of **s 14(2) SGA**

The buyer has no claim under **s 14(2) SGA**

Fitness for purpose—s 14(3) SGA

Where the seller sells goods in the course of a business and the buyer, either expressly or by implication, makes known any particular purpose for which the goods are being bought, there is an implied condition that the goods supplied under the contract are reasonably fit for that purpose, whether or not that is a purpose for which such goods are commonly supplied, except where the circumstances show that the buyer does not rely, or that it is unreasonable for him to rely, on the skill or judgement of the seller.

> *Revision Tip*
>
> As we saw with s 14(2) above, the condition implied by s 14(3) applies only where the seller sells the goods in the course of a business. *Stevenson v Rogers* (1999) applies here in the same way as it did in s 14(2).

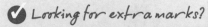

Looking for extra marks?

As with s 14(2) above, liability under s 14(3) is strict. The seller need not be at fault.

Where the buyer buys the goods for their usual (and possibly only) use

In the majority of cases, a buyer will buy the goods for their usual (and possibly only) purpose. For example, a buyer is likely to buy a coat to keep him warm and dry. In this situation, by the mere fact of making the purchase, the buyer will be taken to have made known to the seller the purpose for which he bought the goods and the requirement in s 14(3) about knowledge will be satisfied (*Grant v Australian Knitting Mills Ltd* (1936)).

Revision tip

The words in s 14(3) *'the buyer, either expressly or by implication, makes known any particular purpose for which the goods are being bought'* do not mean that a buyer must communicate to the seller the particular purpose for which he requires the goods. When goods are produced for a single purpose (such as the coat in the above example) it will be easy for the court to infer that the goods have been bought for that purpose and therefore must be reasonably fit for that purpose. Nothing needs communicating unless the buyer requires the goods for a particular or unusual purpose or has a particular idiosyncrasy.

Where the buyer requires the goods for a particular or unusual use or has a particular idiosyncrasy

In these kinds of situations, it is essential for the buyer to make known to the seller the specific use or idiosyncrasy (*Griffiths v Peter Conway Ltd* (1939); *Jewson Ltd v Kelly* (2003); *Slater v Finning Ltd* (1997)).

As noted above, s 14(3) will not apply in cases where the buyer does not rely, or where it is unreasonable for him to rely, on the skill or judgement of the seller. Such reliance, however, may be partial. In *Ashington Piggeries Ltd v Christopher Hill Ltd* (1972) the House of Lords held that there may be cases where the buyer relies on his own skill or judgement for some purposes and on that of the seller for others.

'Reasonably fit'

The words 'reasonably fit' in s 14(3) tell us that the standard of the goods does not need to be of an exceptionally high quality. The quality that a buyer can expect will depend on all the circumstances of the sale. For example, second-hand goods may not need to be of the same quality as new ones. But it will be for the claimant to prove on the balance of probabilities that the goods sold were not fit for their purpose (*Leicester Circuits Ltd v Coates Brothers plc* (2003)).

Not only do the goods need to be reasonably fit for purpose at the time of delivery, but they must continue to be so for a reasonable time after delivery. The condition in **s 14(3)** is a continuing obligation (*Lambert v Lewis* (1982)).

Relationship between ss 14(2) and 14(3) SGA

Notwithstanding the overlap between the implied conditions in **ss 14(2)** and **14(3) SGA**, they do serve different purposes. The relationship between these sections was considered by the Court of Appeal in *Jewson Ltd v Kelly* (2003). As Sedley LJ explained:

> Section 14(2) is directed principally to the sale of substandard goods. This means that the court's principal concern is to look at their intrinsic quality, using the tests indicated in subsection (2A), (2B) and (2C). Of these, it can be seen that the tests postulated in paragraphs (a) and (d) of subsection (2B), and perhaps others too, may well require regard to be had to extrinsic factors. These will typically have to do with the predictable use of the goods. But the issue is still their quality: neither these provisions nor the residual category of 'all the other relevant circumstances' at the end of subsection (2A), make it legitimate, as a general rule, to introduce factors peculiar to the purposes of the particular buyer. It is section 14(3) which is concerned with these.

Summary of s 14(3)

See Figure 2.3. Also see Chapter 10, 'Summary of remedies for breach of **s 14(3) SGA**', p 140, for the remedies available to the buyer for a breach of **s 14(3)**.

Contracts other than of sale of goods

Revision tip

Don't forget Chapter 1, 'Contracts other than of sale of goods', Table 1.1, p 6, which identifies the corresponding implied terms in other types of contract.

Sales by sample—s 15 SGA

Rather unhelpfully, **s 15(1)** tells us that 'a contract of sale is a contract for sale by sample where there is an express or implied term to that effect in the contract'.

It can be seen from **s 15(1)** that a sale by sample is one where there is a term to that effect in the contract. With written contracts, it will be easy to determine whether or not the sale is by sample because there will be a written term to that effect. The House of Lords explained the function of a sample in *Drummond & Sons v Van Ingen & Co* (1887) in terms that a

Figure 2.3 Breach of s 14(3)

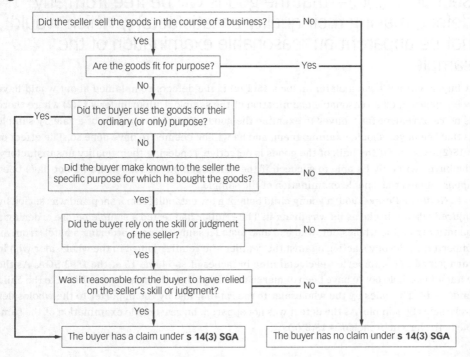

sample presents to the eye the real meaning and intention of the parties with regard to the subject matter of the contract which, owing to the imperfection of language, it may be difficult or impossible to express in words.

In the case of a contract for sale by sample there are two implied conditions:

Section 15(2)(a)—that the bulk will correspond with the sample in quality

A seller will not have a defence just because the bulk can easily be made to correspond with the sample. So, in *E & S Ruben Ltd v Faire Bros & Co Ltd* (1949), it was no defence that the crinkly material supplied could have been made soft as per the sample by a simple process of warming.

Section 15(2)(c)—that the goods will be free from any defect, making their quality unsatisfactory, which would not be apparent on reasonable examination of the sample

A buyer will not have a claim under s 15(2)(c) if the defects complained about would have been apparent on a reasonable examination of the sample. Unlike under s 14(2) where there is no requirement for a buyer to examine the goods, the whole purpose of a sale *by* sample is that the buyer should examine them, and he will be deemed to have done so. The effect of s 15(2)(c) is that if the bulk of the goods is defective, rendering their quality unsatisfactory, the buyer will only be able to succeed if the defect complained about would not have been apparent on a reasonable examination of the sample.

In *Godley v Perry* (1960) a young child bought a toy catapult from a shop and was seriously injured when it broke as he was firing it. The retailer had tested a sample before ordering a quantity from the wholesaler, who had also tested a sample before ordering a batch from an importer. In the boy's action against the retailer, the retailer joined in the wholesaler who in turn joined in the importer, each claiming breaches of ss 14 and 15 of the 1893 SGA. As the catapult was held not to have been of merchantable quality, the retailer was liable to the child under s 14. The sales by the wholesaler to the retailer and by the importer to the wholesaler were sales by sample. As the defect was not apparent on reasonable examination of the sample both were in breach of s 15(2)(c).

Revision Tip

Many sales are concluded by the seller showing the buyer a sample of the goods. This will not, by itself, amount to a sale by sample (because there is no 'bulk') unless the parties agree that it is to be such a sale. However, it is likely that the court will imply a term into such contracts that the goods supplied should be identical to the ones shown.

Summary of s 15

See Figure 2.4. Also see Chapter 10, 'Summary of remedies for breach of s 15', p 141, for the remedies available to the buyer for a breach of s 15.

Contracts other than of sale of goods

Revision Tip

Don't forget Chapter 1, 'Contracts other than of sale of goods', Table 1.1, p 6, which identifies the corresponding implied terms in other types of contract.

Figure 2.4 Breach of s 15

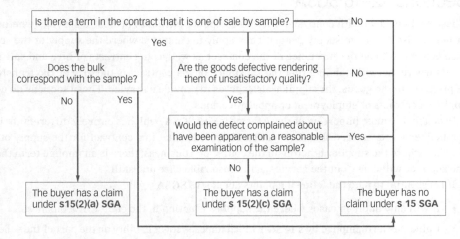

Supply of Goods and Services Act 1982 (SGSA)

In the main, we have so far considered the terms implied by the SGA into contracts of sale of goods. Many of the terms implied by the SGSA are modelled on the SGA. The SGSA contains three different groups of implied terms:

Sections 2–5 SGSA

These sections deal mainly with contracts of exchange or barter as well as contracts where the main substance is the provision of a service. As noted in Chapter 1, 'Contracts other than of sale of goods', Table 1.1, p 6, contracts of exchange or barter are not contracts of sale of goods because there is no money consideration as required by s 2(1) SGA. Similarly, in a contract for the provision of a service, even though some goods might be supplied, the substance of the contract is the provision of the overall service rather than the transfer of property in the goods as required by s 2(1) SGA. However, terms are implied into these contracts by the SGSA that are almost identical to those implied into contracts of sale by the SGA.

Sections 6–11 SGSA

These sections deal with contracts of hire. Although under a contract of hire (also known as a contract of bailment) the hirer (or **bailee**) obtains possession of the goods, he does not obtain property (ownership) in them. Since s 2(1) SGA demands a transfer or agreement to transfer property in the goods, contracts of hire are not contracts of sale of goods and therefore the terms implied by the SGA do not apply. However, terms are implied into hire contracts by the SGSA that are similar to those implied into contracts of sale by the SGA.

Supply of Goods and Services Act 1982 (SGSA)

✳✳✳✳✳✳✳✳✳✳✳✳

Sections 12–16 SGSA

These sections deal with contracts where the supplier agrees to provide a service (whether or not he also agrees to supply goods). They apply to contracts where the supply of the service is deemed to be the substance of the contract as well as to contracts of hire and sale of goods where, notwithstanding that the substance of the contract is the hire or the transfer of property in the goods, the supplier also agrees to provide a service. These sections do not apply to contracts of employment or apprenticeships.

Probably the most important of these terms is s 13 SGSA, which is entirely different to the implied terms considered thus far. Section 13 provides that in a contract for the supply of a service, where the supplier is acting in the course of a business, there is an implied term that the supplier will carry out the service with reasonable care and skill.

It is essential to note the following points about s 13 SGSA:

- It will only apply in cases where the supplier is acting in the course of a business.

- Unlike the term implied by s 14 SGA which imposes strict liability on the part of the seller, the term implied by s 13 SGSA will require the supplier to be at fault. It is tort-based and requires the supplier to exercise reasonable care and skill. This means that unlike s 14 SGA where the seller can be liable without being at fault, a supplier who is not at fault will not be in breach of the term implied by s 13 SGSA. This can be seen in *Thake v Maurice* (1986) where the Court of Appeal held that a surgeon could not be said to have guaranteed that surgery would achieve a particular result and although the contract between him and his patient required him to exercise all proper skill and care, the fact that the desired result was not achieved did not, of itself, mean that the surgeon was in breach of the contract.

- Unlike the terms implied by the SGA which pre-classify them either as **conditions** or **warranties**, the term implied by s 13 SGSA is neither classified as a condition or a warranty. It is, therefore, an **innominate term**. You will recall from 'Classification of terms', pp 9–10, that an innominate term is one where the consequences or seriousness of the breach determine whether or not it takes effect as a condition or a warranty. In this way, if the consequences of the breach are so fundamental that the innocent party has been deprived of substantially the entire benefit of the contract, he will be entitled to treat the contract as **repudiated** and sue for damages. If the effects of the breach are only minor, it will only be treated as a breach of warranty (see *Hong Kong Fir Shipping Co Ltd v Kawasaki Kisen Kaisha Ltd* (1962)).

Section 14 SGSA

Section 14 provides that where, under a contract for the supply of a service by a supplier acting in the course of a business, the time for the service to be carried out is not fixed by the contract; left to be fixed in a manner agreed by the contract; or determined by the course of dealing between the parties, there is an implied term that the supplier will carry out the service within a reasonable time. What is a reasonable time is a question of fact.

Section 15 SGSA

Section 15 provides that where, under a contract for the supply of a service, the consideration for the service is not determined by the contract; left to be determined in a manner agreed by the contract; or determined by the course of dealing between the parties, there is an implied term that the party contracting with the supplier will pay a reasonable charge. What is a reasonable charge is a question of fact. It should be noted that this implied term applies whether or not the supplier was acting in the course of a business.

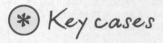
(✱) **Key cases**

Case	Facts	Held/Principle
Bramhill v Edwards [2004] EWCA Civ 403	The buyers purchased a motor-home from D. It was 102 inches wide, which was two inches wider than that permitted under the relevant road regulations. They had inspected, but not measured, the vehicle before purchase. It was only after they had used the vehicle for about six or seven months that they measured it and found it to be 102 inches wide. It was then some months later that they formally complained about its width. The main issues for the court were whether, because it was too wide to be driven legally on the roads in the UK, it was of satisfactory quality (**s 14(2)**) and, if not, whether **s 14(2C)(b)** disentitled them from relying on any such breach that might be found on the ground that they examined it before purchase and that their examination should have revealed its unlawfully excessive width. The sellers accepted that the vehicle was in excess of the maximum permitted width and therefore could not be driven lawfully on the roads in the UK. However, they said that the relevant authorities turned a blind eye to such minor infringements of the Regulations.	The Court of Appeal held that the vehicle was of satisfactory quality. Although the test is objective, the reasonable person referred to in **s 14(2A)** must be one who is in the position of the buyer with knowledge of all relevant background facts. The buyer was knowledgeable about motor-homes and was aware that the authorities turned a blind eye to the illegality. This was a common occurrence. The court also considered (*obiter*, because of the finding that the vehicle was of satisfactory quality) that **s 14(2C)(b)** would have disentitled the buyers from relying on any breach that might have been found because they had examined the vehicle before purchase and their examination, had they gone on to measure it, should have revealed its unlawfully excessive width.

Key cases

✳✳✳✳✳✳✳✳✳✳

Case	Facts	Held/Principle
Egan v Motor Services (Bath) Ltd [2007] EWCA Civ 1002	E purchased an expensive car. He found that it had a tendency to veer to the left and tried to reject it on the ground it was not of satisfactory quality. The judge found that although E perceived that the car was pulling to the left, it handled normally for this kind of vehicle although the wheel alignment was outside of the manufacturer's specification. As a result, he found that a reasonable person would not have regarded it as unsatisfactory. The vehicle was therefore of satisfactory quality and there was no breach of **s 14(2) SGA**.	The fact that the vehicle was unsatisfactory to the purchaser is not enough: it is only unsatisfactory for the purposes of **s 14(2) SGA** if it does not meet the standard that a reasonable person would regard as satisfactory. This is a wholly objective test. As to the defect in the wheel alignment, Smith LJ stated that it was unlikely that a buyer would be entitled to reject goods because of such a minor defect unless he was able to show that a reasonable person would think that the minor defect was of sufficient consequence to render the goods unsatisfactory.
Geddling v Marsh [1920] 1 KB 668	A bottle containing a drink burst, causing injury. It was held that the drink as well as the bottle were 'supplied' under a contract of sale and both had to comply with the requirements of **s 14 SGA**.	The conditions implied by **s 14(2)** apply not only to the goods bought but also to the 'goods supplied' under the contract.
Grant v Australian Knitting Mills Ltd [1936] AC 85 (PC)	The buyer contracted dermatitis as a result of wearing new woollen underpants which, when purchased from the retailer, were in a defective condition owing to the presence of excess sulphites which had been negligently left in during the process of manufacture. One aspect of the claim was that the garment was not fit for purpose. A question for the court was whether the buyer, either expressly or by implication, had made known any particular purpose for which the goods were bought as was required under **s 14(3) SGA**.	The reason the purpose needs to be made known to the seller is so as to show that the buyer relies on the seller's skill or judgment. This reliance must be brought home to the mind of the seller, expressly or by implication. The reliance will seldom be express: it will usually arise by implication from the circumstances. With a purchase made from a retailer, the reliance will in general be inferred from the fact that a buyer goes to the shop in the confidence that the retailer has selected his stock with skill and judgement. There is no need to specify in terms the particular purpose for which the buyer requires the goods if it is the only purpose for which anyone would ordinarily want the goods.

Case	Facts	Held/Principle
Rogers v Parish (Scarborough) Ltd [1987] QB 933	R bought a new Range Rover which had a number of serious defects on delivery. During a six-month period, he drove the car about 5,500 miles while a number of (generally unsuccessful) attempts were made to rectify the defects. He then brought a claim arguing the vehicle was neither of satisfactory quality nor fit for purpose.	Where a vehicle is sold as new, but is seriously defective, it is not to be taken as being of satisfactory quality or fit for its purpose just because it is capable of being driven and the defects repaired. The court held that where goods as delivered are defective, they are not of satisfactory quality and do not become so simply because they are capable of being used in some way. The car was not fit for its purpose as R expected and he was entitled to reject it. The Court of Appeal added that when a new car is bought the purchaser is entitled to get it to give the pleasure, pride, and performance he expected. Defects which might be acceptable in a second-hand vehicle would not be acceptable in a new car.
Wilson v Rickett Cockerell & Co Ltd [1954] 1 QB 598	C ordered a ton of Coalite from D. When it was delivered she made up a fire. The delivery inadvertently contained an explosive which exploded causing damage. C claimed that the fuel was not fit for purpose or alternatively that it was not of merchantable quality. It was held that the entire consignment was defective because it was all potentially dangerous.	The words 'goods supplied' mean the goods delivered in purported pursuance of the contract. **Section 14** applies to all goods supplied whether or not they conform to the contract. It did not matter that the explosive was not what C had ordered nor (in the literal sense) 'sold' by D.

💬 Key debates

Topic	Examination prior to purchase: a cautionary note
Author/ Academic	Christian Twigg-Flesner
Viewpoint	Discusses the Court of Appeal's decision in *Bramhill v Edwards* (2004) and its views on s 14(2C)(b) of SGA.
Source	(2005) 121 *Law Quarterly Review* 205

Exam questions

✱✱✱✱✱✱✱✱✱

Topic	The relationship between satisfactory quality and fitness for purpose
Author/ Academic	Christian Twigg-Flesner
Viewpoint	Discusses the Court of Appeal's decision in *Jewson Ltd v Kelly* (2003) where it sought to clarify the relationship between the terms implied by **ss 14(2)** and **(3) SGA**. Discusses the distinction between satisfactory quality and fitness for purpose.
Source	(2004) 63(1) *Cambridge Law Journal* 22

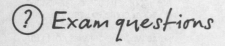

Questions on the statutory implied terms and the remedies available will frequently be asked together. For this reason, please see Chapter 10, 'Exam questions', p 143.

#3

Passing of property and risk

Key facts

- It is essential to determine precisely when property (ownership) and risk in the goods passes to the buyer.
- The rules on the passing of property are different for specific goods and unascertained goods.
- Risk often passes to the buyer with property, but this is not always the case.
- There is a different rule concerning the passage of risk for consumer buyers.
- The parties are generally free to agree when property and risk passes to the buyer.
- In the absence of such agreement, the **SGA** has certain 'Rules' that will apply.
- Which party bears the legal risk in cases where the goods are destroyed or in the event of insolvency will determine who suffers the loss.

Introduction

The main purpose of a **contract of sale** of goods is to transfer property (ownership) in the goods from the seller to the buyer. The parties to a contract of sale of goods are, subject to certain rules, free to agree terms as to the transfer of property and of risk.

It is important to remember that ownership and possession are two different things. The SGA is concerned with ownership. We are not, therefore, discussing the physical delivery and possession of the goods. Sometimes the transfer of ownership in the goods will occur at the same time as their physical delivery but this is not necessary. A seller might therefore:

- still have physical possession of the goods even though property in them has passed to the buyer; or
- deliver the goods to the buyer yet still retain property in them.

✅ *Looking for extra marks?*

You should explain the reason why it is important to know precisely when the property in the goods passes from the seller to the buyer under a sale of goods contract. Unless the parties have agreed otherwise, as soon as the buyer has paid the price, he is entitled to take *delivery* of the goods whether or not *property* in them has passed to him. This means, of course, that the buyer can take possession of the goods even if he is not the owner. You should emphasise, where appropriate, that ownership and possession are different concepts.

Why is it important to know when the property in the goods passes?

The following examples explain why it is important to know when the property in the goods has passed to the buyer:

Payment

Unless otherwise agreed, the seller may only sue the buyer for the price once property in the goods has passed (s 49 SGA).

Insolvency

If either the seller or the buyer becomes insolvent, then the rights of the other (non-insolvent) party may depend on whether or not property in the goods has passed to the buyer.

Subsequent transfer of ownership

Unless the buyer has acquired ownership in the goods he cannot transfer that ownership to another party. (This rule is subject to a number of exceptions which are dealt with in Chapter 7, 'Transfer of ownership by a non-owner', p 84.)

Risk

Unless the parties have agreed otherwise, risk is borne by the owner of the goods (s 20 SGA). Risk in this context means the risk of theft, loss, or damage to the goods, but not the risk of non-payment. Different rules apply depending on whether or not the buyer deals as a consumer.

The SGA sets out a number of rules explaining the precise time when property in the goods passes to the buyer. It is crucial to know whether the goods in question are specific or unascertained (see Chapter 1, 'Specific goods and unascertained goods', p 5) because the point at which property in them passes will depend on this distinction.

Revision tip

You must first decide whether or not the goods in question are specific or unascertained because different rules will apply to each. It is equally important to remember that in the case of a contract for the sale of **unascertained goods**, no property in them can be transferred to the buyer unless and until the goods are ascertained (s 16 SGA).

The transfer of property in specific goods

You should *first* apply s 17(1) SGA which provides that property in **specific** or **ascertained goods** will transfer to the buyer when the parties to the contract intend it to pass. For the purpose of ascertaining the intention of the parties, regard shall be had to the terms of the contract, the conduct of the parties, and the circumstances of the case (s 17(2)).

Where the parties fail to make clear their intentions as to when property in the goods will be transferred to the buyer (which in consumer cases is quite likely to be the norm, as these parties are unlikely even to direct their thoughts to this question) you will need to consider the four Rules contained in s 18. These provide the rules for ascertaining the intention of the parties and are summarised in Table 3.1.

See Figure 3.1 for a diagram of when property in goods passes to the buyer.

The transfer of property in unascertained goods

You should recall from the above that s 16 SGA provides that in the case of a contract for the sale of **unascertained goods**, no property in them can be transferred to the buyer unless and until the goods are ascertained. This is the case even if the parties agree otherwise.

Revision tip

Section 16 SGA is subject to s 20A SGA which was added by the Sale of Goods (Amendment) Act 1995 and is concerned with undivided shares in goods forming part of a bulk. This will be considered below, 'Undivided shares in goods forming part of a bulk', p 38.

The transfer of property in unascertained goods
****

Table 3.1 The Rules for ascertaining the intention of the parties

Rule	Circumstances when Rule applies	Property in the goods passes to the buyer when . . .
1	where there is an unconditional contract for the sale of specific goods in a deliverable state	the contract is made. This is irrespective of whether the time of payment or the time of delivery, or both, are postponed
2	where there is a contract for the sale of specific goods and the seller is bound to do something to the goods for the purpose of putting them into a deliverable state	the thing is done and the buyer has notice that it has been done
3	where there is a contract for the sale of specific goods in a deliverable state but the seller is bound to weigh, measure, test, or do some other act or thing with reference to the goods for the purpose of ascertaining the price	the act or thing is done and the buyer has notice that it has been done
4	when goods are delivered to the buyer on approval or on sale or return or other similar terms	(a) the buyer signifies his approval or acceptance to the seller or does any other act adopting the transaction; (b) if he does not signify his approval or acceptance to the seller but retains the goods without giving notice of rejection, then, if a time has been fixed for the return of the goods, on the expiration of that time, and, if no time has been fixed, on the expiration of a reasonable time

Since property in the goods cannot be transferred to a buyer until the goods are ascertained, it is important to understand when goods will become ascertained. This was simply stated by the Court of Appeal in *Re Wait* (1927) as when the goods are identified as *the* goods to be used in the performance of the contract.

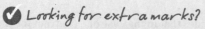 Looking for extra marks?

You should explain that although **unascertained goods** will never become **specific goods**, once the goods have become ascertained they are, in effect, not that dissimilar to specific goods.

In the case of unascertained goods, you should apply the statutory sections in the following order:

- s 16 SGA which explains that no property in the goods can be transferred to a buyer unless and until the goods are ascertained;

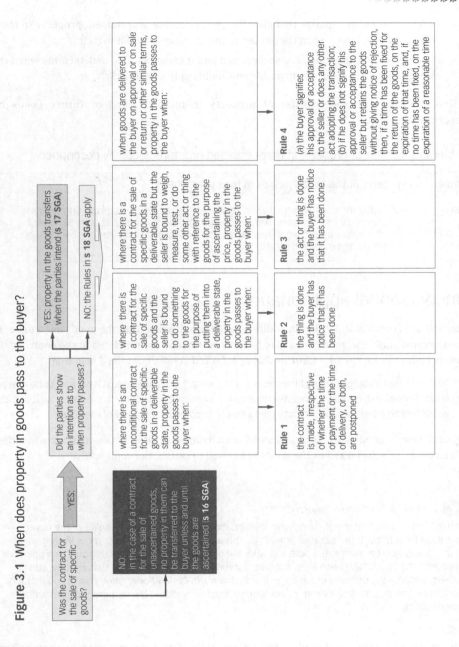

Figure 3.1 When does property in goods pass to the buyer?

Was the contract for the sale of specific goods?

YES:

NO:
in the case of a contract for the sale of unascertained goods, no property in them can be transferred to the buyer unless and until the goods are ascertained (**s 16 SGA**)

Did the parties show an intention as to when property passes?

YES: property in the goods transfers when the parties intend (**s 17 SGA**)

NO: the Rules in **s 18 SGA** apply

where there is an unconditional contract for the sale of specific goods in a deliverable state, property in the goods passes to the buyer when:

Rule 1
the contract is made, irrespective of whether the time of payment or the time of delivery, or both, are postponed

where there is a contract for the sale of specific goods and the seller is bound to do something to the goods for the purpose of putting them into a deliverable state, property in the goods passes to the buyer when:

Rule 2
the thing is done and the buyer has notice that it has been done

where there is a contract for the sale of specific goods in a deliverable state but the seller is bound to weigh, measure, test, or do some other act or thing with reference to the goods for the purpose of ascertaining the price, property in the goods passes to the buyer when:

Rule 3
the act or thing is done and the buyer has notice that it has been done

when goods are delivered to the buyer on approval or on sale or return or other similar terms, property in the goods passes to the buyer when:

Rule 4
(a) the buyer signifies his approval or acceptance to the seller or does any other act adopting the transaction;
(b) if he does not signify his approval or acceptance to the seller but retains the goods without giving notice of rejection, then, if a time has been fixed for the return of the goods, on the expiration of that time, and, if no time has been fixed, on the expiration of a reasonable time

The transfer of property in unascertained goods

✳✳✳✳✳✳✳✳✳✳

- s 17(1) SGA which explains that once the goods become ascertained, property in them will pass to the buyer when the parties to the contract intend it to pass;
- then (and only if the goods are ascertained *and* it is not possible to determine when the parties intended ownership to pass) you should apply **s 18 Rule 5.**

Rule 5 deals with the transfer of property in unascertained or **future goods** by description.

Table 3.2 Transfer of property in unascertained or future goods by description

Rule	Property in the goods passes to the buyer when . . .
5(1)	goods that match the contract description and in a deliverable state are unconditionally appropriated to the contract. This can be by either the seller or the buyer, but must be with the other's assent which may be express or implied and may be given either before or after the appropriation is made

Unconditional appropriation

You will see from Table 3.2 that in addition to the requirement that the goods need to be 'in a deliverable state' the goods must also be 'unconditionally appropriated to the contract'. In *Carlos Federspiel & Co SA v Charles Twigg & Co Ltd* (1957), Pearson J held that:

> To constitute an appropriation of the goods to the contract, the parties must have had, or be reasonably supposed to have had, an intention to attach the contract irrevocably to the goods, so that those goods and no others are the subject of the sale and become the property of the buyer.

In other words, goods will become unconditionally appropriated to the contract when they are irrevocably earmarked as *the* goods to be used to satisfy the contract.

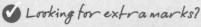

Looking for extra marks?

You should explain that the unconditional appropriation may be by either the seller or the buyer, but must be with the other's assent (Rule 5(1)). This assent may be express, or more likely it will be implied, and may be given either before or after the appropriation is made. You should also point out that once the goods have been irrevocably appropriated to the contract then those goods, and no others, become the property of the buyer (per Pearson J, in *Carlos Federspiel*, above) and that it is for this reason that the seller cannot then supply substitute goods in the purported performance of the contract.

In practical terms, goods will often be ascertained and unconditionally appropriated simultaneously.

✅ **Looking for extra marks?**

You will impress the examiner by providing an example, taken from the criminal law, of the requirement for unconditional appropriation of the goods as required by **Rule 5** (under the **SGA 1893**). In *Edwards v Ddin* (**1976**), D drove into a garage and requested the attendant to fill up the tank with petrol and put oil in the engine. After the attendant had done so, D drove off without paying. He was charged with theft, contrary to **s 1 of the Theft Act 1968**, which requires a dishonest appropriation of property *belonging to another* with the intention of permanently depriving the other of it. P contended that the property in the goods had not passed to D because the garage had reserved its rights of disposal over the goods under **s 19(1) SGA** until the condition of payment had been met and that therefore the goods still belonged to the garage and were capable of being stolen. It was held that once the petrol and oil had mixed with the petrol and oil in D's car, the garage could not be said to have reserved, as a term in the contract, the right of disposal under **s 19** and that the delivery of the petrol and oil was an unconditional appropriation of the goods to the contract with the assent of both parties. This meant that under **Rules 5 (1) and (2) of s 18 of the 1893 SGA**, the property passed to D the moment it was placed in his car and, as it was then his property, he did not appropriate the goods of *another* (the owner of the garage) as was required to satisfy the offence of theft. Of course, in civil law, the garage could have sued D for the price of the fuel.

Appropriation by delivery to a carrier

See Table 3.3.

Table 3.3 Appropriation by delivery to carrier

Rule	Property in the goods passes to the buyer when . . .
5(2)	the seller delivers the goods to the buyer or carrier for the purpose of transmission to the buyer, and does not reserve the right of disposal, he is to be taken to have unconditionally appropriated the goods to the contract

Revision tip

This Rule will not apply in cases where the seller reserves the right of disposal. This simply means where he has reserved title in the goods. Reservation of title is dealt with in Chapter 4, 'Retention of title clauses', p 45.

Ascertainment and appropriation 'by exhaustion'

Rules 5(3) and 5(4) were added to s 18 SGA by the Sale of Goods (Amendment) Act 1995 and placed on a statutory footing by the decision in *Karlshamns Oljefabriker A/B v Eastport Navigation Corp (The Elafi)* (1981). They apply to cases where the buyer agrees to buy goods out of a specified bulk as the following example shows:

Undivided shares in goods forming part of a bulk
****

Table 3.4 Ascertainment and appropriation by exhaustion

Rule	Property in the goods passes to the buyer when . . .
5(3)	where there is a contract for the sale of a specified quantity of unascertained goods in a deliverable state forming part of a bulk which is identified either in the contract or by subsequent agreement between the parties and the bulk is reduced to (or to less than) that quantity, then, if the buyer under that contract is the only buyer to whom goods are then due out of the bulk:
	(a) the remaining goods are to be taken as appropriated to that contract at the time when the bulk is so reduced, and
	(b) the property in those goods then passes to that buyer
5(4)	rule 5(3) applies also (with the necessary modifications) where a bulk is reduced to (or to less than) the aggregate of the quantities due to a single buyer under separate contracts relating to that bulk and he is the only buyer to whom goods are then due out of that bulk

Example

Bob owns a fuel distribution business and has 10,000 litres of fuel in stock which is stored in his tank. Bill and Mike both agree to buy 4,000 litres each. Eric agrees to buy the remaining 2,000 litres. Bob delivers Bill's and Mike's fuel leaving 2,000 litres in the tank. As soon as the bulk has reduced to 2,000 litres (or less), the property in it passes to Eric under Rule 5(3).

Provided all of the following conditions (taken from **Rule 5(3)**) are satisfied, the goods will be unconditionally appropriated *by exhaustion*, which will mean that the property in them will be transferred to the buyer:

- the goods must be in a deliverable state;
- the sale must be of a specified quantity of **unascertained goods** that form part of a bulk;
- the bulk referred to must have been identified by the contract or alternatively by subsequent agreement between the parties;
- the bulk must have been reduced to the amount of, or less than, the goods due to the buyer; and
- the buyer is the only buyer remaining who is entitled to the goods from the bulk.

Undivided shares in goods forming part of a bulk

This is dealt with by **s 20A SGA (inserted by s 1 of the Sale of Goods (Amendment) Act 1995)**.

Undivided shares in goods forming part of a bulk

****

It might be useful first to consider the judgment of the Court of Appeal in *Re Wait* (1927) so as to understand the kind of injustice that s 20A sought to remedy.

Re Wait [1927] 1 Ch 606

W purchased 1,000 tons of wheat that was then loaded on a ship for delivery. The following day, he sold 500 tons of the bulk to a sub-purchaser (X) who paid W for the goods. By the date the ship docked, W had been declared bankrupt and his trustee in bankruptcy claimed the entire consignment of 1,000 tons. The Court of Appeal held that W's trustee in bankruptcy was entitled to succeed and that X was entitled to nothing even though he had already paid W for his 500 tons of wheat. As X's 500 tons had not been ascertained (i.e. separated from the 1,000 tons bulk and identified as *the* goods to be used in the performance of the contract), property did not pass to him.

Section 20A SGA permits a buyer who has purchased a specified quantity of **unascertained goods** from an identified bulk to become co-owner of the bulk (together with other co-owners) provided that he has paid for some or all of the goods. In other words, such a buyer may obtain a share in the ownership of the bulk.

Revision tip

The section does not alter the rule that property must be ascertained before it can pass to a buyer, but it provides some protection to a buyer who has paid for a specified quantity of otherwise **unascertained goods** from an identified bulk from the consequences of a seller becoming insolvent before the property is ascertained.

The following conditions must be met for s 20A to apply:

- the contract must be for the sale of a specified quantity of **unascertained goods**. This must be expressed in units of quantity (e.g. 50 or 1,000) and not fractions or percentages (such as a quarter or 25%);
- the goods (or some of them) must form part of a bulk which is identified either in the contract or by subsequent agreement between the parties; and
- the buyer must have paid the price for some or all of the goods which are the subject of the contract and which form part of the bulk.

Provided the above conditions have been satisfied then, unless the parties agree otherwise, s 20A(2) explains that:

- property in an undivided share in the bulk is transferred to the buyer; and
- the buyer becomes an owner in common of the bulk.

The undivided share of a buyer in a bulk at any time shall be 'such share as the quantity of goods paid for and due to the buyer out of the bulk bears to the quantity of goods in the bulk at that time' (s 20A(3)).

Passing of risk
✳✳✳✳✳✳✳✳✳✳

> *Revision tip*
>
> To calculate the extent of a buyer's co-ownership at any time, you should divide the quantity of the goods paid for by the buyer and due to him by the quantity of goods in the bulk. Applying this to the facts in *Re Wait*, the sub-purchaser would have become a 50% co-owner of the goods, with the remaining 50% belonging to Wait's trustee in bankruptcy.

You should also note that where the aggregate of the undivided shares of buyers in a bulk determined under s 20A(3) would at any time exceed the whole of the bulk at that time, then the undivided share in the bulk of each buyer shall be reduced proportionately so that the aggregate of the undivided shares is equal to the whole bulk (s 20A(4)).

Deemed consent by co-owner to dealings in bulk goods

As we have just seen, the effect of s 20A is to create undivided shares in an identified bulk. This would create a problem because it would require *all* of the co-owners to be joined in order to transfer any part of the bulk. In some cases, this would also require the tracing of title to each part share.

To overcome this problem, s 20B(1) states that 'a person who has become an owner in common of a bulk by virtue of s 20A shall be deemed to have consented to any delivery of goods out of the bulk to any other owner in common of the bulk, being goods which are due to him under his contract'. In other words, a co-owner will not need the consent of the other co-owners in order to deal with his own share of the goods.

Passing of risk

Risk in this context means the risk of theft, loss, or damage to the goods, but not the risk of non-payment.

Who has the risk?

This will depend on whether or not the buyer deals as a consumer:

- *When the buyer deals as a consumer*, the goods remain at the seller's risk until they are delivered to the consumer (s 20(4) SGA). See also s 32(4) regarding risk when the delivery of the goods is to a carrier.

- *When the buyer does not deal as a consumer*, then unless otherwise agreed, the goods remain at the seller's risk until the property in them is transferred to the buyer. When the property in them is transferred to the buyer the goods are at the buyer's risk whether delivery has been made or not (s 20(1) SGA). See also s 32(1)–(3) regarding risk when the delivery of the goods is to a carrier.

Delivery to a third party carrier is prima facie delivery to the non-consumer buyer and risk will pass then.

> ## Revision tip
>
> Understanding the difference between property and possession is essential to the understanding of (sale of goods law generally, including) s 20(1). You will see from the above that, unless otherwise agreed, the goods remain at the seller's risk until the property (ownership) in them is transferred to the buyer and that once the property in them has been transferred to the buyer they are then at the buyer's risk whether or not the buyer has possession of them. In other words, property in the goods and the risk are transferred together. This means that a buyer might have to bear the risk of loss even if the seller has possession of the goods. Thus:
>
> - when a buyer deals as a consumer, risk only passes to him on delivery of the goods;
> - when a buyer does not deal as a consumer, risk ordinarily passes to him as soon as the property in the goods passes to him *even if the seller retains possession of them*.
>
> The distinction between property and possession cannot be over-emphasised. By understanding this distinction, you will appreciate that if goods are destroyed whilst at the buyer's risk, he will not be able to claim for non-delivery and must still pay the price. The sensible, well-advised buyer will therefore consider the question of insurance to cover this problem.

There are two other things to note about risk where the buyer does not deal as a consumer:

- where delivery has been delayed through the fault of either buyer or seller, the goods are at the risk of the party at fault as regards any loss which might not have occurred but for such fault (s 20(2));
- nothing in s 20 will affect the duties or liabilities of either seller or buyer who acts as a **bailee** or custodier of the goods of the other party (s 20(3)). Neither a bailee nor a custodier actually owns the goods they possess. Parties are frequently bailees of goods. For example, a buyer who buys goods on a sale or return basis is merely a bailee of the goods until such a time as he either returns the goods or otherwise causes the property in them to pass to himself under s 18 **Rule 4** (discussed under 'The transfer of property in specific goods', p 33).

Example

Ownership and risk

Irene sees a sofa on sale in Sue's furniture store. She needs it the following week for her new home and agrees to buy the one on display. She pays Sue in full. Sue uses an independent carrier to make her deliveries. The delivery van catches fire with this sofa in it and the sofa is destroyed. The following consequences arise:

- the property (ownership) in the sofa passed to Irene when the contract was made (s 18, **Rule 1**). This is because there was an unconditional contract for the sale of specific goods in a deliverable state;

- the risk in the sofa remained with Sue because it had not been delivered to Irene who dealt as a consumer (**ss 20(4) and 32(4)**).

Irene will be able to recover from Sue the price paid for the sofa and, if she has suffered a loss as a result of Sue's breach of contract, also claim damages for non-delivery of the goods (**s 51(1) SGA**) which is discussed in Chapter 10, 'Damages for non-delivery', p 131.

Had Irene been a trade buyer (and therefore not dealt as a consumer), then, as above, the property in the sofa will have passed to her under **s 18, Rule 1** when the contract was made and the risk would also have passed to her at the same time even though delivery did not occur (**ss 20(1) and 32(1)–(3) SGA**). Had Irene not paid Sue in advance for the sofa, then Sue would be entitled to full payment from Irene even though she has received nothing.

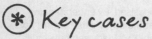

(✱) Key cases

Case	Facts	Held/Principle
***Carlos Federspiel & Co SA v Charles Twigg & Co Ltd* [1957] 1 Lloyd's Rep 240**	Carlos ordered goods from Charles Twigg, paying for them in advance. The goods were to be shipped to Costa Rica. Charles Twigg packed the goods into cases, marked them with the buyer's name, registered them for consignment, and ordered shipping space in a named ship. However, before shipment took place, Charles Twigg became insolvent and the appointed receiver refused to deliver the goods. Carlos contended that the property in the goods had passed to them.	Pearson J held that the intention of the parties was that the property in the goods should pass on *shipment* and that there was no such prior appropriation of the goods and assent thereto as would pass ownership by virtue of **s 18 SGA, Rule 5**. He stated that: 'To constitute an appropriation of the goods to the contract, the parties must have had, or be reasonably supposed to have had, an intention to attach the contract irrevocably to the goods, so that those goods and no others are the subject of the sale and become the property of the buyer'.
***Dennant v Skinner and Collom* [1948] 2 KB 164**	A bidder, falsely calling himself Mr King, bought several vehicles at auction. The auctioneer allowed him to take the vehicles upon receipt of his cheque which later turned out to be worthless. 'King' also agreed that the property in the vehicles would not pass to him until his cheque had been honoured. He then sold one of the vehicles to the third party who in turn sold it to D. The auctioneer sought to recover from D the vehicle or its value.	The court considered whether property in the vehicle had passed to the purchaser. Hallet J quoted **s 18, Rule 1** and stated that 'upon the fall of the hammer the property of this car passed to King unless that prima facie rule is excluded from applying because of a different intention appearing or because there was some condition in the contract which prevented the rule from applying. In my view, this was clearly an unconditional contract of sale, and I can see nothing whatever to make a different intention appear'. Accordingly, the property in the vehicles had passed to King when the hammer fell.

Case	Facts	Held/Principle
Re London Wine Co (Shippers) Ltd [1986] PCC 121	LWC was a company dealing in wines. They ran a scheme whereby customers could purchase quantities of wine for investment. Customers bought wine which remained in LWC's warehouse in bulk. The purchases would be entered in LWC's stock book and allocated an identification number. LWC provided the customers with documents of title confirming them to be the sole owners of the wine purchased. One customer bought LWC's entire stock of a particular wine. In other instances, a number of contracts were made with different buyers exhausting LWC's stock of a particular wine. In each case, LWC issued the customers with a document confirming that they were the sole owners of the wine they had purchased. LWC subsequently went into receivership.	As there were several purchasers of the same kind of wine it was impossible to determine who owned which wine held by LWC. Even had there been just one customer, it was still impossible to attach *specific* bottles of wine to that customer's contract. LWC could have, had it wished, purchased further stock for the customers. Oliver J held that in these cases there was no appropriation of the wines and therefore no property in the wine passed to the customers. This case illustrates that no appropriation can take place unless there is an intention to attach specific goods irrevocably to the contract.
Re Wait [1927] 1 Ch 606	W purchased 1,000 tons of wheat that was then loaded on a ship for delivery. The following day, he sold 500 tons of the bulk to a sub-purchaser (X) who paid W for the goods. By the date the ship docked, W had been declared bankrupt and his trustee in bankruptcy claimed the entire consignment of 1,000 tons.	The Court of Appeal held that W's trustee in bankruptcy was entitled to succeed and that X was entitled to nothing even though he had already paid W for his 500 tons. As 'sx 500 tons had not been ascertained (i.e. separated from the 1,000 tons bulk and identified as *the* goods to be used in the performance of the contract) property did not pass to him. Such facts will now be decided differently because of **s 20A SGA**.

⟫ Key debates

Topic	The passing of risk and s 20A Sale of Goods Act 1979
Author/Academic	Nikki McKay
Viewpoint	Considers the impact of **s 20A SGA** on the passing of risk.
Source	(2010) 15(1) *Coventry Law Journal* 17

Exam questions
✱✱✱✱✱✱✱✱✱

Topic	Some reflections on 'property' and 'title' in the Sale of Goods Act
Author/Academic	Hock Lai Ho
Viewpoint	Discusses the uses and meanings of distinct but related concepts of ownership, property, and title.
Source	(1997) 56 *Cambridge Law Journal* 571

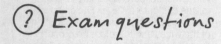 Exam questions

Problem question

Brian is closing down his electrical wholesale business. Amongst the stock remaining in his warehouse are 400 television sets. He agrees to sell 300 of these televisions to Ian, who pays for them in full by cheque and agrees to collect them the following week. Ian is busy the following week and doesn't get round to collecting them until the end of the following month. Unfortunately, the day before Ian went to collect the televisions, Brian's warehouse was broken into and 200 of the televisions were stolen. Brian cannot obtain any more stock but offers Ian delivery of the remaining 200 televisions.

Advise Ian.

Essay question

The **Sale of Goods Act 1979** lays down certain rules relating to the passing of risk.

Critically evaluate these rules and consider whether risk always rests with the party who ought reasonably to bear it.

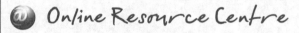 Online Resource Centre

To see an outline answer to this question visit www.oup.com/lawrevision/

#4
Retention of title clauses

Key facts

- Retention of title clauses are also known as reservation of title clauses.

- They are also often referred to as *Romalpa* clauses after the leading case of ***Aluminium Industrie Vaassen BV v Romalpa Aluminium Ltd*** (1976).

- They can enable a seller to deliver goods to a buyer on terms that the seller retains ownership of the goods until the buyer has paid the price.

- These clauses are especially useful in cases where the buyer becomes insolvent.

- As with any contractual provision, a retention of title clause must be properly incorporated into the contract. If it has not been properly incorporated, then it will have no contractual force and will be invalid.

Introduction

Businesses frequently sell their goods by offering credit terms to their trade customers. Often, these customers will wish to pay for these goods only after they have sold them to their own customers. The problem for the seller is what happens to their goods in the event that their customer is unable to pay, possibly because of insolvency. The seller will want to know whether he has any rights over these goods entitling him to recover them, or their value, and in the event of the buyer's insolvency, whether they have any priority over any of the other **creditors**.

As we saw in Chapter 3, 'Passing of property and risk', p 31, property in the goods will pass to the buyer under **ss 16–18 SGA 1979**, that is, *unless the parties have agreed otherwise*. One way sellers might be able to protect themselves is by inserting a clause into their contracts to the effect that no property in the goods will be transferred to the buyer until the goods have been paid for. However, this might not be what a seller wants. After all, unless their customers are permitted to sell the goods, they may not be in a position to pay the price. Therefore, sellers need a way of permitting their customers to sell their goods whilst protecting their own position in the event their customer becomes insolvent. This can be achieved by inserting into their contracts of sale a **retention of title** clause.

Retention of title clauses

As we saw in Chapter 3, 'Passing of property and risk', p 31, where there is a contract for the sale of **specific** or **ascertained goods** the property in them is transferred to the buyer at such time as the parties to the contract intend it to be transferred (**s 17(1) SGA**).

Section 19(1) goes even further than this and provides that where there is a contract for the sale of **specific goods**, or where goods are subsequently appropriated to the contract, the seller may, by the terms of the contract or appropriation, reserve the right of disposal of the goods until certain conditions are fulfilled, and in such a case, notwithstanding the delivery of the goods to the buyer, the property in the goods does not pass to the buyer until the conditions imposed by the seller are fulfilled. In this context, the most obvious condition a seller would want to impose would be a condition that reserves to themselves property in the goods until payment has been made.

The combination of **ss 17(1)** and **19(1)** therefore opens the doors to sellers to insert into their contracts **retention of title** clauses.

A **retention of title** clause will typically be invoked in the event of the buyer's insolvency where the buyer has yet to make full payment to the seller for goods bought. It is not, of course, necessary for the buyer to become insolvent before such a clause can be invoked: it can be invoked whenever the buyer owes money to the seller beyond the terms that were agreed in the contract.

Responsibility for identifying and proving title to goods under a **retention of title** clause falls solely on the seller of the goods and not the administrators dealing with any insolvency (*Blue Monkey Gaming Ltd v Hudson & Others* (2014)).

It is important to appreciate that although there are clear benefits to sellers incorporating **retention of title** clauses into their contracts of sale there are also dangers. *FG Wilson (Engineering) Ltd v John Holt & Co (Liverpool) Ltd* (2014) illustrates how sellers can be denied a claim for the price under the contract by virtue of a **retention of title** clause. This is because although the goods may be in the physical possession of the buyer, since the seller has retained ownership of them until payment he cannot bring an action for the price under **s 49(1) SGA** because that remedy is only available where property in the goods has passed to the buyer. Furthermore, the court held that **s 49(1)** provided an exclusive (rather than a permissive) remedy for the price and, whilst acknowledging the existence of conflicting earlier Court of Appeal authorities on the point, held that no claim for the price could be brought unless **s 49** applied which it did not in this case. This left the seller without any effective remedy against the buyer which is quite ironic given that the entire purpose of the **retention of title** clause was to provide seller protection. Sellers should, therefore, consider the effect of **s 49(2)** and make the price payable on a day certain, irrespective of delivery, so as to ensure they do not fall foul of the protection they thought they had secured when incorporating a **retention of title** clause into their contract of sale. This will be discussed further in Chapter 9 ('Action for the price', p 120).

Revision tip

A simple **retention of title** clause will provide that no property in the goods sold will pass to the buyer until paid for. Or, to put this the other way round, property in the goods sold will remain with the seller until paid for.

In the simplest of cases, provided the **retention of title** clause has been properly incorporated into the sale contract, an unpaid seller will be able to recover the goods sold. This is because the property in the goods will not have passed to the buyer. This type of retention of title clause is often referred to as a 'simple retention' clause and permits the seller to recover unaltered goods sold but not paid for. It does not attempt to create any other kind of security.

Revision tip

A simple **retention of title** clause ought to cause little difficulty for the unpaid seller. Difficulties usually arise with these clauses when the seller attempts to secure more extensive remedies against the buyer, especially where these greater remedies create a charge. We will consider these circumstances below.

Retention of title clauses

****

The *Romalpa* case *(Aluminium Industrie Vaassen BV v Romalpa Aluminium Ltd)* (1976)

This case requires careful consideration because of its influence in **retention of title** cases.

A sold aluminium foil to R. The **contract of sale** contained an extensive retention of title clause which provided that:

- ownership of the foil will only be transferred to the buyers when they have met all that is owing to the sellers;
- goods manufactured by the buyers from the seller's foil will become the property of the sellers as surety for full payment;
- until full payment has been made, the sellers will keep such articles in their capacity of **fiduciary** owners for the sellers, and they have the power to sell such articles to third parties in the normal course of their business.

The sheer breadth of this clause is remarkable. A regularly sold foil to R on credit terms. For this reason, R will likely have owed A money at any given time. The first of the bulleted terms noted above indicates that in this situation property in the foil will never pass to R. The retention of title clause also meant that A was entitled to the proceeds of sale of goods sold by R to their own customers. It is this latter point that has proven to be the most controversial.

When R became insolvent, they owed A more than £120,000. They also had foil worth around £50,000 in stock and around £35,000 held in a separate bank account representing the goods sold using A's foil. The Court of Appeal held that the sellers were entitled to recover the £35,000 proceeds of sale and also the remaining stock of foil.

> ✅ *Looking for extra marks?*
>
> The proposition in **Romalpa** that the seller may be entitled to the proceeds of sale has been criticised in subsequent cases (see, for example, *Re Weldtech Equipment Ltd* (1991); *Compaq Computer Ltd v Abercorn Group Ltd* (1991); and *Pfeiffer Weinkellerei-Weineinkauf GmbH & Co v Arbuthnot Factors Ltd* (1988)). In these cases, the seller's claims to the proceeds of resale were held to be void as an unregistered charge. Phillips J went further in *Tatung (UK) Ltd v Galex Telesure Ltd* (1989), suggesting that **Romalpa** was wrongly decided as the seller's interest should have been held to be a charge.
>
> The decision in **Romalpa** has been said to have turned on its own facts. One important point to note is that R's counsel conceded that they owed **fiduciary** obligations to A.

It is important to emphasise that although the proceeds of sale claim succeeded in *Romalpa*, such claims are unlikely to succeed again in the future, for reasons including:

1. As noted above in *Romalpa*, the buyer's counsel conceded that there was a **fiduciary relationship** between the buyer and the seller. This was followed by a further concession that the buyer held the goods manufactured from the foil as **bailee** for the seller

and that the seller was a **fiduciary** owner of the goods. These concessions are unlikely to be made in future cases and it is in any event doubtful that the relationship involved a bailment or even that a fiduciary relationship existed on the facts.

2. If all proceeds of sale are paid into a separate bank account (which should be the case if there is a **fiduciary relationship** between buyer and seller) then it would appear to frustrate the commercial reality of business. Any buyer is likely to need the money from the proceeds of their sales for their own business, and therefore paying such monies into a separate bank account would not likely be the intention of the parties. Furthermore, if the buyer did hold the foil in a **fiduciary** capacity he ought to have kept it entirely separate from his own goods.

3. The basis of a **fiduciary relationship** would mean that the seller would have been entitled to all the proceeds of sale which might be more than he was in fact owed. On the other hand, if the seller was only entitled to recover the amount he was actually owed by the buyer from the proceeds of sale, then this would have required registering as a charge. But is it really likely that either of the parties would have intended that the seller should receive a sum greater than he was actually owed?

All-liabilities clauses

An 'all-liabilities' (or 'all-monies') clause goes further than a simple **retention of title** provision and provides that a buyer will not get ownership in the goods bought until all monies or liabilities owed to the seller have been satisfied. As noted above in the *Romalpa* case, where buyers make regular purchases from sellers, the buyers are likely to owe money to the sellers at any given time. A seller who has an all-liabilities clause would argue that this means that even where buyers have paid in full for a particular delivery of goods, they would not own them if they still owed money in respect of another consignment of goods. The question is, do such clauses create a charge and are therefore void if not registered? The House of Lords in *Armour v Thyssen Edelstahlwerke AG* (1991) held that an all-monies clause did not create a charge. Lord Keith explained:

> I am . . . unable to regard a provision reserving title to the seller until payment of all debts due to him by the buyer as amounting to the creation by the buyer of a right of security in favour of the seller. Such a provision does in a sense give the seller security for the unpaid debts of the buyer. But it does so by way of a legitimate retention of title, not by virtue of any right over his own property conferred by the buyer.

✅ Looking for extra marks?

You should explain that the House of Lords in *Armour v Thyssen* only considered the position of goods that remain unpaid and missed the opportunity to consider whether a seller could recover goods that had earlier been paid for.

Attacks against retention of title clauses

Clearly the unpaid seller will be pleased that he incorporated a **retention of title** clause into his contract, but this comes at the expense of other unsecured **creditors**. The ways in which these clauses have been attacked are as follows:

The goods sold have been incorporated into manufactured goods

This situation would occur where the buyer has used the goods in the manufacture of finished products, such as where the seller sells leather and the buyer uses this to manufacture handbags. The handbags are not the same goods as sold and therefore cannot be said to be the property of the seller. The question is: can the seller reclaim the finished goods?

Re Peachdart Ltd [1984] Ch 131

The sellers (S) sold leather to P who used it in the manufacture of handbags. S's sale contract stated that ownership of the leather and of any mixed goods using this leather would remain with S until full payment had been received. P went into receivership owing S money for the leather bought. It was held that although S could reserve title over the leather they sold, they could not do so over the finished goods as the leather sold had changed its identity once it had been made into handbags.

In the following cases, the courts have held that, as in *Re Peachdart*, the goods sold lost their identity when made into finished products:

- *Re Bond Worth Ltd* (1980)—man-made fibre used in the manufacture of carpet.

- *Borden (UK) Ltd v Scottish Timber Products Ltd* (1981)—resin used in the manufacture of chipboard.

- *Modelboard Ltd v Outer Box Ltd* (1993)—sheets of cardboard used in the manufacture of cardboard boxes.

Whether or not goods sold have changed their identity and therefore can no longer be said to be the property of the seller will be a matter of fact in each case. These cases can be contrasted with *Hendy Lennox (Industrial Engines) Ltd v Grahame Puttick Ltd* (1984).

Hendy Lennox (Industrial Engines) Ltd v Grahame Puttick Ltd [1984] 1 WLR 485

Staughton J held that a diesel engine, sold by the sellers who had reserved title until it had been paid for, and which had been incorporated by the buyers into a generating set, could be reclaimed by the sellers upon the buyers going into receivership. This was because it had remained an engine throughout and could be easily identified by its serial number as belonging to the sellers and dismantled with relative ease from the finished generating set.

The retention of title clause was void because it created a registrable charge

Some cases have argued that certain **retention of title** clauses might create a charge which, if unregistered, will be void. It is clearly impracticable to register all sales where a retention of title clause exists and, even if registered, it would still rank behind other (pre-)registered charges. *However, in the main, retention of title clauses are not security interests and do not need registering.* They do not give the seller the kind of security usually demanded by commercial lenders such as banks (which need registering). The intention behind a **retention of title** clause is merely to prevent *title* passing to the buyers before they have paid the price and not to assert continuing property rights in the goods.

> **Re Bond Worth Ltd [1980] 1 Ch 228**
>
> A retention of title clause, where property passes to the buyer only on payment and which refers to 'equitable and beneficial ownership' creates a floating equitable charge granted by the buyers in favour of the sellers which as such was registrable and was void for non-registration.

In *Re Peachdart*, the sellers could also have had a charge over the handbags including any proceeds of sale, but because the charge had not been registered pursuant to (the then) **s 95 of the Companies Act 1948** it was void. Accordingly, the sellers had no priority over the debenture holder and other **creditors** in respect of the proceeds of sale.

A situation might arise where a retention of title clause seeks to protect not only the goods sold but, where the buyer uses these goods to manufacture finished goods which he then sells on, also an interest in the property of those finished goods. This situation was considered by the Court of Appeal in *Clough Mill Ltd v Martin* (1985), where it held that no registrable charge arises in the case of a simple **retention of title** clause where the seller merely seeks to reserve title in goods sold until he is paid, but that it was possible that a registrable charge would be created in relation to the interests a seller might claim in the finished manufactured goods that his buyer then sold on. This latter point did not arise in the *Clough Mill* case as the claim was not formulated on these grounds.

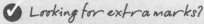 ✅ *Looking for extra marks?*

You should note the potential hidden danger of creating a charge and explain that, as a result, these clauses should be drafted so as not to create a charge registrable under **s 859A of the Companies Act 2006**. In cases where the seller needs to assert a continuing property interest in his goods, then those rights will need to be registered under **s 859A**, failing which they will be invalid as against a liquidator or other **creditors**.

As pointed out in *Clough Mill*, **retention of title** clauses would not ordinarily require registering. This is simply because such clauses merely act to prevent property in the goods sold passing to the buyer until payment has been made. This means that the buyer in such circumstances does not own the goods and therefore is quite unable to grant a charge or mortgage over them.

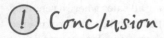 **Conclusion**

It is fair to conclude that although **retention of title** clauses can be very effective in protecting the unpaid seller, especially where the goods sold can be identified and recovered, clauses that seek to claim the proceeds of sale must now be considered to be extremely speculative. The problem with proceeds of sale clauses is that they are likely to be construed as charges that will be void unless registered. Even then, they face others (for example, factoring companies) taking priority over them.

As Andrew Hicks notes in his article '*Romalpa* is dead' (1992) 13(11) *Comp Law* 217, 'in the absence of any unexpected intervention by the Court of Appeal this aspect of the process of drafting terms of sale will be more in the realms of alchemy than science and the resulting small print may not be worth the paper that it is written on'.

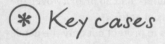 **Key cases**

Case	Facts	Held/Principle
Aluminium Industrie Vaassen BV v Romalpa Aluminium Ltd [1976] 1 WLR 676)	The sellers sold quantities of aluminium foil to the buyers. Amongst the terms of the retention of title clause was that property in the goods would not pass to the buyers until all monies owing had been paid. When the buyers later went into receivership they still had in their possession about £50,000 worth of foil and the receiver recovered from sub-buyers about £35,000 representing the price of finished goods made from the foil and resold to them.	The £50,000 worth of foil still belonged to the sellers by virtue of the retention of title clause. That part of the claim was uncontroversial. However, the Court of Appeal also held that the sellers could claim the £35,000 proceeds of sale on the ground that the buyers were mere bailees of the seller's foil and which they had sold with the seller's implied authority and therefore had to account to them in equity. Mocatta J held (at first instance) that no registrable charge arose in these circumstances. Unfortunately, this was not further argued on appeal.
Armour v Thyssen Edelstahlwerke AG [1991] 2 AC 339	The sellers sold steel to the buyer for use in its manufacturing process. The contract of sale contained a condition that the steel remained the property of the sellers after delivery.	The House of Lords held that a condition in a contract reserving title in the seller after delivery until all debts whatsoever are paid is valid, enforceable, and does not create a charge.

Case	Facts	Held/Principle
	until all debts were paid. Receivers were appointed to the buyer's business and a dispute arose as to the ownership of the steel.	
Borden (UK) Ltd v Scottish Timber Products Ltd [1981] 1 Ch 25	The sellers supplied resin to the buyers to be used in the manufacture of chipboard. The sale contract stated that property in the resin was to pass when all goods supplied to the buyers had been paid for. The manufacturing process was such that the resin could no longer be recovered. After manufacturing the chipboard, the buyers became insolvent without having paid for the resin. The sellers claimed against the buyers' receiver a sum in respect of the unpaid resin.	The Court of Appeal held that where a product, such as resin, is used in a manufacturing process pursuant to the intention of the parties, and on such use becomes irreversibly part of a new product, it ceases to exist as such and so does the owner's title to it. As a consequence, the initial product is no longer identifiable and an interest in it cannot be traced into the new product. Further, if a charge had arisen, then it would have been void as against the liquidator and the buyer's creditors.
FG Wilson (Engineering) Ltd v John Holt & Co (Liverpool) Ltd [2014] 1 WLR 2365	Wilson was a manufacturer and seller of generators and parts. Wilson's standard terms included a **retention of title** clause providing that title to the purchased goods did not pass until Holt had paid in full. When Holt failed to pay a number of invoices, Wilson brought proceedings for the price.	The Court of Appeal held that a claim for the price under the contract meant a claim falling within **s 49 SGA**. Wilson could not have a claim for the price independently of that section. Wilson's claim had to comply with the condition in **s 49(1)** that property in the goods had to have passed to Holt. The court observed that if an action for the price could be maintained whenever the obligation to pay had arisen, **s 49** would be largely otiose, which indicated that the section was intended to specify the only circumstances in which a seller could maintain an action for the price. Thus, unless Wilson could establish that property in the goods had passed to Holt, it would have no claim for the price. That was an inherent result of a **retention of title** clause, and it showed the dangers, as well as the benefits, of such clauses. As title in the goods had not passed to Holt, Wilson did not have a valid action for the price. This could have been avoided by the seller stipulating that the price is payable on a day certain irrespective of delivery, thereby bringing it within the scope of **s 49(2)** and giving it an entitlement to bring an action for the price. Section **49(2)** applies irrespective of whether or not delivery has been made or title has passed.

Key cases

✳✳✳✳✳✳✳✳✳✳✳✳

Case	Facts	Held/Principle
***Hendy Lennox (Industrial Engines) Ltd v Grahame Puttick Ltd* [1984] 1 WLR 485**	The sellers sold a diesel engine to the buyers who used it in the manufacture of a generating set. The sellers had reserved title in the engine until it had been paid for. When the buyers went into receivership, the sellers sought to recover the engine. The receiver argued that property in the engine had passed to the buyers when they incorporated it into the generating set.	Staughton J held that the engine could be reclaimed by the sellers. This was because it had remained an engine throughout and could be easily identified by its serial number as belonging to the sellers and could be dismantled with relative ease from the finished generating set. If the goods sold have merely been incorporated by the buyers into other goods, then a seller with an appropriate retention of title clause will be entitled to recover the goods sold provided they can still be identified and dismantled from the finished goods without damaging those goods.
***Re Bond Worth Ltd* [1980] 1 Ch 228**	The buyers, a carpet manufacturing company, purchased man-made fibre from the sellers which they used in the manufacture of carpets. The conditions of sale included a retention of title clause. The buyers went into receivership when a large sum of money was owing to the sellers under various contracts containing the retention of title clause.	A retention of title clause, where property passes to the buyer only on payment and which refers to 'equitable and beneficial ownership', creates a floating equitable charge granted by the buyers in favour of the sellers which, as such, was registrable and was void for non-registration.
***Re Peachdart Ltd* [1984] Ch 131**	The sellers (S) sold leather to P who used it in the manufacture of handbags. S's sale contract stated that ownership of the leather and of any mixed goods using this leather would remain with S until full payment had been received. P went into receivership owing S money for the leather bought.	Vinelott J held that although S could reserve title over the leather they sold, they could not do so over the finished goods as by then the leather sold had changed its identity once it had been made into handbags. The judge also held that the parties must be presumed to have intended that once P had appropriated the leather so that it became unrecognisable, a charge over the finished goods or their proceeds should arise. In this case such a charge arose in relation to the manufactured handbags and the proceeds of the handbags which had been sold. However, as the charge had not been registered, it was void under s 95 of the Companies Act 1948.

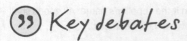
Key debates

Topic	Title and transformation: who owns manufactured goods?
Author/Academic	Duncan Webb
Viewpoint	Discusses the historical doctrines on the **retention of title** to manufactured goods when the manufacturer and owner of raw materials are different people. Discusses cases for transfer of ownership when raw materials have been transformed into finished goods.
Source	[2000] *Journal of Business Law* 513

Topic	*Romalpa* is dead
Author/Academic	Andrew Hicks
Viewpoint	Discusses the entitlement of sellers to claim the proceeds of sale and asks whether the effects of *Romalpa* are dead in this regard.
Source	(1992) 13(11) *Company Lawyer* 217

Topic	Retention of title clauses and claims for the price
Author/Academic	Ewan McKendrick
Viewpoint	Discusses the Court of Appeal decision in *FG Wilson (Engineering) Ltd v John Holt & Co (Liverpool) Ltd* (2014) on whether a seller could bring an action for the price under **s 49 SGA** relating to goods sold under a contract containing a retention of title clause. Discusses why the seller could not satisfy **s 49** as property in the goods had not passed to the buyer owing to the retention of title clause, thus demonstrating that retention of title clauses can prove disadvantageous for sellers.
Source	(2014) Aug/Sep *Building Law Monthly* 1–5

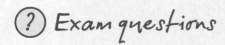
Exam questions

Problem question

George sells 100,000 litres of milk each month to Dave's Bakeries Limited which it uses in the manufacture of bread and cakes that it sells through a number of retail shops. Dave's Bakeries Limited also buys milk from several other suppliers. A clause in the contract between George and Dave's Bakeries Limited provides:

> Goods are supplied on the condition that the supplier shall retain legal and equitable ownership of them until full payment has been received by them for all sums owing. Any money from the sale of

the goods shall be paid into a separate bank account noting on it the supplier's name. All goods shall be clearly labelled as belonging to the supplier until all sums owing have been paid.

Dave's Bakeries Limited has now gone into administration owing £20,000 to George. In total, it owes in excess of £1 million to other suppliers. It has 50,000 litres of milk stored in their cold stores and £10,000 worth of bread and cakes in their freezers. £5,000 is left in the company's general bank account and £1,000 in the specially designated account in accordance with the contract.

Advise George.

Essay question

Eleanor Timber Supplies Ltd (ETS) sells timber to its customers, some of whom are regular customers while others just make a single purchase. ETS's terms require payment within 30 days of the date of delivery. Some of ETS's customers resell the timber but others use it to manufacture various goods which they then store for subsequent sale.

Although ETS has written terms of sale they do not include a retention of title clause.

Advise ETS why they ought to incorporate a retention of title clause into their standard terms of sale and what protection such a clause might provide.

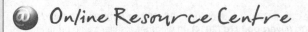

Online Resource Centre

To see an outline answer to this question visit www.oup.com/lawrevision/

#5

Exclusion and limitation clauses

Key facts

- One party to a contract may seek to reduce or avoid their liability for certain breaches of the contract by referring to exclusion or limitation clauses in the contract. These are subject to legal control both by the common law and by statute, namely, the **Unfair Contract Terms Act 1977**.

- The **Unfair Terms in Consumer Contracts Regulations 1999** might also be relevant as they render ineffective certain unfair terms in consumer contracts.

- Exemption clauses is the term used to describe both exclusion and limitation clauses.

- Exemption clauses are frequently found in 'standard form' contracts.

- Some exemption clauses will be allowed if they are reasonable. Others are void.

- Some statutes imply certain terms into different kinds of contracts. It is important to understand whether it is possible for parties to exclude or limit the effects of these statutorily implied terms.

Introduction

One party to a contract may seek to exclude or limit liability for certain breaches of the contract. They do this by inserting **exclusion** or **limitation clauses** into the contract. Whether such clauses are effective in excluding or limiting liability is another matter. Exclusion or limitation clauses are strictly controlled by:

- common law rules;
- the **Unfair Contract Terms Act 1977**; and
- the **Unfair Terms in Consumer Contracts Regulations 1999**.

Exclusion and limitation clauses distinguished

The difference between an **exclusion clause** and a **limitation clause** can be simply stated:

- Exclusion—where the party to the contract seeks to *exclude* all liability for certain breaches of the contract.
- Limitation—where the party to the contract seeks to *limit* his liability for certain breaches of the contract.

An **exemption clause** is the term often used to describe both exclusion and limitation clauses.

A clause which *limits* liability will not be construed as strictly as one which *excludes* liability altogether and may be valid notwithstanding a complete failure by the party seeking to rely upon it to perform the contract (*Ailsa Craig Fishing Co Ltd v Malvern Fishing Co Ltd & Securicor (Scotland) Ltd* (1983)).

Common law controls of exemption clauses

The courts adopt two main methods of controlling **exemption clauses**:

1. Has the exemption clause been incorporated into the contract?
2. Does the exemption clause cover the alleged breach of the contract?

Incorporation

An **exemption clause** may be incorporated into a contract in a number of ways:

By signature

The general rule is that if a party to a contract signs it then he will be bound by its terms whether or not he has read them or understood them (*L'Estrange v Graucob Ltd* (1934)).

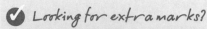 Looking for extra marks?

The 'incorporation by signature' rule does not apply in cases where the seller has misrepresented the nature of the document that the buyer has signed (*Curtis v Chemical Cleaning and Dyeing Co* (1951)).

By reasonable notice

Cases where **exemption clauses** were said to be incorporated by reasonable notice are often ticket cases or those where the exemption clause was displayed on a notice or sign. Whether these clauses are incorporated into the contract will depend on whether or not the recipient had reasonable notice of them (*Parker v The South Eastern Railway Company* (1876–77)).

The courts will consider the following matters when determining whether reasonable steps have been taken to bring the exemption clause to the notice of the buyer or user of the service:

When the notice was given

Generally, any term (which of course includes **exemption clauses**) will only be incorporated into a contract if was brought to the other party's attention before the contract was made (*Olley v Marlborough Court Ltd* (1949) and *Thornton v Shoe Lane Parking Ltd* (1971)).

What form the notice took

A court will not be likely to uphold an **exemption clause** unless it is in a form or document that a reasonable person would consider likely to contain contractual terms (*Chapelton v Barry Urban District Council* (1940)).

Unusual or onerous clauses

Exemption clauses that are unusual or particularly onerous will require a greater degree of notice to be given. Unless such specific notice has been given they will not be incorporated and therefore will not have contractual effect (*Interfoto Picture Library Ltd v Stiletto Visual Programmes Ltd* (1989)).

Just because the document in question refers to another document for the terms does not in itself prevent those terms from being incorporated into the contract by reasonable notice (*O'Brien v MGN Ltd* (2001)).

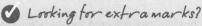 Looking for extra marks?

When considering unusual or particularly onerous clauses, you should mention the so-called 'red hand' test from *Spurling Ltd v Bradshaw* (1956), where Denning LJ stated that:

the more unreasonable a clause is, the greater the notice which must be given of it. Some clauses which I have seen would need to be printed in red ink on the face of the document with a red hand pointing to it before the notice could be held to be sufficient.

Common law controls of exemption clauses
✱✱✱✱✱✱✱✱✱✱

By a previous course of dealing

Where the parties have previously dealt together and their previous dealings have contained **exemption clauses**, then those clauses may apply to subsequent dealings between them even where the clauses have not been expressly incorporated into those subsequent dealings (*Spurling Ltd v Bradshaw* (1956)).

Does the exemption clause cover the alleged breach of the contract?

Even where the **exemption clause** has been incorporated into the contract, in order for it to be effective, it must cover the specific breach of the contract. Any ambiguity in the wording of the clause will be construed *contra proferentem*, that is, construed against the party seeking to rely on it.

Andrews Bros (Bournemouth) Ltd v Singer & Co Ltd [1934] 1 KB 17

Singer appointed Andrews Bros as sole dealers within a named area for the sale of 'new Singer cars'. The contract contained a clause which excluded 'all conditions, warranties and liabilities implied by statute, common law or otherwise'. One of the cars delivered had already covered more than 550 miles and was therefore not new within the meaning of the contract. Resisting a claim for breach of contract in supplying a car which was not new, D sought to rely on the **exclusion clause** as exempting them from liability. The Court of Appeal held that the words 'new Singer car' constituted an **express** and not an **implied term** of the contract, and that as a new Singer car had not been delivered, D was liable for breach of contract and could not claim exemption from liability by its contract which only covered implied terms.

Fundamental breach

At one time, the courts held that some breaches of contract were so serious that no **exclusion clauses** could ever excuse them (*Karsales (Harrow) Ltd v Wallis* (1956)). So, if a seller was contracted to sell 100 chairs but instead supplied 100 tables, it would not appear sensible to allow him to rely on a term in his contract that permitted him to substitute the goods ordered for the same quantity of other goods. The courts considered the promise to supply 100 chairs as a fundamental term of the contract and such a significant breach of it as noted above would provide the buyer with a remedy irrespective of any exclusion clause in the seller's contract.

However, the so-called doctrine of fundamental breach was rejected by the House of Lords in *Suisse Atlantique Societe d'Armement SA v NV Rotterdamsche Kolen Centrale* (1967), where their Lordships stated (*obiter*) that there was no rule of substantive law that a fundamental breach of a contract nullifies an **exemption clause** and that it is a matter of construction whether the clause was intended to apply to such a breach as has occurred. If a breach by one party entitles the other to **repudiate** the contract, but he affirms it, the exemption clause continues in force unless on its construction it was not intended to operate in those circumstances.

Any doubts remaining from the decision in *Suisse Atlantique* were finally put to bed by the House of Lords in *Photo Production Ltd v Securicor Transport Ltd* (1980).

Photo Production Ltd v Securicor Transport Ltd [1980] AC 827

Securicor contracted with Photo Production to provide a night-patrol service at its factory. The contract excluded Securicor's liability for any injurious act or default of any of its employees unless such act or default could have been foreseen and avoided by the exercise of due diligence on the part of the employer. The contract further provided that Securicor shall not be responsible for any loss suffered through fire or any other cause except in so far as is solely attributable to the negligence of the company's employees acting within the cause of their employment. One of Securicor's employees deliberately started a fire in the factory that destroyed it. The House of Lords held that whether an **exclusion clause** was able to exclude or limit liability was a matter of construction of the contract and that, generally, parties to a contract, when they bargained on equal terms, should be free to apportion liability in the contract as they see fit. Their Lordships confirmed that there was no rule of law that a fundamental breach of the contract prevented an exclusion clause from being effective. As a result, it was held that the wording of the exclusion clause was adequate to exclude liability for what occurred.

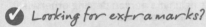 **Looking for extra marks?**

As well as explaining the ruling in **Photo Production** you should explain that it serves as a strong affirmation of the freedom to contract approach to commercial contracting as opposed to the interventionist approach seen in some of the earlier cases (*Karsales (Harrow) Ltd v Wallis*). Furthermore, since these earlier cases, we now have UCTA 1977 which prevents **exemption clauses** from being used freely in consumer contracts. The problem is not as serious in commercial transactions because many parties are likely to be of similar bargaining power and more able to negotiate their own contracts. They are also more able to protect their own risks by insurance.

Exclusion or restriction of the statutory implied terms

We saw in Chapter 2, 'Statutory implied terms', p 8, that some statutes imply certain terms into different kinds of contracts. We will now consider whether it is possible to exclude or limit the effects of these statutorily implied terms.

The SGA and the Supply of Goods (Implied Terms) Act 1973 (SGITA)

As we saw in Chapter 2, 'Statutory implied terms', p 8, the SGA and the SGITA statutorily imply certain terms into **contracts of sale** of goods (the SGA) and **hire purchase**

Exclusion or restriction of the statutory implied terms

✱✱✱✱✱✱✱✱✱✱

(the **SGITA**). This means that the parties need not agree such terms expressly. But can a party effectively exclude or restrict their liability under these statutory implied terms?

Unfair Contract Terms Act 1977 (UCTA)

A seller may wish to exclude or restrict his liability in respect of the terms implied under the **SGA** or the **SGITA** (or the **Supply of Goods and Services Act 1982** in respect of the other kinds of transaction noted in Chapter 1, 'Contracts other than of sale of goods', Table 1.1, p 6). Whether he may do this depends on the term in question and the status of the parties. In relation to non-consumer sales, **s 55(1) SGA** provides that 'where a right, duty or liability would arise under a contract of sale of goods by implication of law, it may (subject to the **Unfair Contract Terms Act 1977**) be negatived or varied by express agreement, or by the course of dealing between the parties, or by such usage as binds both parties to the contract'.

Table 5.1 explains whether or not a seller may exclude or restrict his liability under the **SGA** or the **SGITA** (**ss 6 and 20 UCTA**):

Table 5.1 Can a seller exclude or restrict his liability under the SGA or the SGITA?

Implied term as to	As against a person dealing as a consumer	As against a person dealing otherwise than as a consumer
title S 12 SGA S 8 SGITA	Cannot exclude or restrict	Cannot exclude or restrict
description s 13 SGA S 9 SGITA	Cannot exclude or restrict	Can exclude or restrict but only if reasonable
quality/fitness for purpose ss 14(2) and 14(3) SGA ss 10(2) and 10(3) SGITA	Cannot exclude or restrict	Can exclude or restrict but only if reasonable
sample s 15 SGA s 11 SGITA	Cannot exclude or restrict	Can exclude or restrict but only if reasonable

See 'The Supply of Goods and Services Act 1982 (SGSA)', p 65, for the rules on excluding the terms implied by the **Supply of Goods and Services Act 1982**.

Exclusion or restriction of the statutory implied terms

When does a buyer deal as a consumer?

You can see from Table 5.1 that the status of the parties is important in determining whether or not a seller may exclude or restrict his liability under the **SGA** or the **SGITA**.

Section **61(5A) SGA** tells us (in a rather roundabout way) when a buyer is dealing as a consumer by referring to s **12(1)** of UCTA. It also provides that it is for a seller claiming that the buyer does not deal as consumer to show that he does not.

Section **12(1) UCTA** provides that a party to a contract deals as a consumer if:

(a) he neither makes the contract in the course of a business nor holds himself out as doing so; and

(b) the seller does make the contract in the course of a business.

Furthermore, the goods must be of a type ordinarily supplied for private use or consumption (s **12(1)(c) UCTA**).

You should note that 'in the course of a business' for the purpose of s **12(1) UCTA** has a more complex meaning than that given to the same phrase in s **14 SGA** (see Chapter 2, 'Satisfactory quality—s 14(2) SGA', p 16) and can be summarised by Table 5.2:

Table 5.2 Meaning of 'in the course of a business'

Section	Meaning	Case
s 12(1) UCTA	The purchase must be an integral part of the business, or if the goods are bought as a 'one-off' purchase they must have been bought with the intention of selling them on for a profit, or if the goods purchased are of a kind which the business has bought with some degree of regularity	*R&B Customs Brokers Ltd v United Dominions Trust Ltd* (1988)
s 14 SGA	A sale by a business is a sale in the course of a business	*Stevenson v Rogers* (1999)

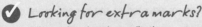

Exclusion or restriction of the statutory implied terms

✳✳✳✳✳✳✳✳✳✳

Reasonableness

You can see from Table 5.1, p 62, that certain terms may be excluded but only if reasonable. Terms which may be excluded or restricted only if reasonable are subject to s 11(1) UCTA which lays down guidance as to the meaning of reasonableness for these purposes. It is for the party claiming that the term satisfies the requirement of reasonableness to show that it does (s 11(5) UCTA).

Under s 11(1) UCTA the court should ask itself whether the term is 'a fair and reasonable one to be included having regard to the circumstances which were, or ought reasonably to have been, known to or in the contemplation of the parties when the contract was made'.

The guidelines for the application of reasonableness can be found in **Schedule 2 of UCTA**. These are:

Schedule 2 of UCTA:

   (a) the strength of the bargaining positions of the parties relative to each other, taking into account (among other things) alternative means by which the customer's requirements could have been met;

   (b) whether the customer received an inducement to agree to the term, or in accepting it had an opportunity of entering into a similar contract with other persons, but without having a similar term;

   (c) whether the customer knew or ought reasonably to have known of the existence and the extent of the term (having regard, among other things, to any custom of the trade and any previous course of dealing between the parties);

   (d) where the term excludes or restricts any relevant liability if some condition was not complied with, whether it was reasonable at the time of the contract to expect that compliance with that condition would be practicable;

   (e) whether the goods were manufactured, processed, or adapted to the special order of the customer.

The Supply of Goods and Services Act 1982 (SGSA)

Section 7 UCTA sets out the rules on excluding or restricting the statutory implied terms for other types of contract where goods pass from one party to another, for example, where goods are supplied with a service:

---

s 7 UCTA:

s 7(2)   As against a person dealing as consumer, liability in respect of the goods' correspondence with description or sample, or their quality or fitness for any particular purpose, cannot be excluded or restricted by reference to any such term.

s 7(3)   As against a person dealing otherwise than as consumer, that liability can be excluded or restricted by reference to such a term, but only in so far as the term satisfies the requirement of reasonableness.

s 7(3A)   Liability for breach of the obligations arising under section 2 of the Supply of Goods and Services Act 1982 (implied terms about title etc in certain contracts for the transfer of the property in goods) cannot be excluded or restricted by reference to any such term.

s 7(4)   Liability in respect of:
    (a)   the right to transfer ownership of the goods, or give possession; or
    (b)   the assurance of quiet possession to a person taking goods in pursuance of the contract,

cannot be excluded or restricted by reference to any such term except in so far as the term satisfies the requirement of reasonableness.

Section 13 SGSA

The rules in relation to excluding the implied terms contained in s 13 SGSA are necessarily different.

It was noted (above, at p 26) that in order for liability to be established against the supplier, s 13 SGSA requires him to be at fault. It is tort-based and requires the supplier to exercise reasonable care and skill. The required fault amounts to negligence: s 1(1)(a) UCTA explains that 'negligence means the breach ... of any obligation, arising from the express or implied terms of a contract, to take reasonable care or exercise reasonable skill in the performance of the contract'. As a result, any exclusions of s 13 SGSA will be subject to ss 2(1) and 2(2) UCTA which provide that:

ss 2(1) and 2(2) UCTA:

s 2(1)	A person cannot by reference to any contract term or to a notice given to persons generally or to particular persons exclude or restrict his liability for death or personal injury resulting from negligence
s 2(2)	In the case of other loss or damage, a person cannot so exclude or restrict his liability for negligence except in so far as the term or notice satisfies the requirement of reasonableness.

We have already considered the meaning of reasonableness under 'Reasonableness', p 64.

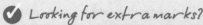

✔ Looking for extra marks?

The provisions of the **UCTA** were strengthened originally by the **Consumer Transactions (Restrictions on Statements) Order 1976 (as amended)** which made it an offence for a business to purport to introduce into a consumer transaction any term that is void because of **ss 6 and 20 of UCTA**. This might be a term in a contract, a notice in a shop or in an advertisement, or in any other form such as on an order form, invoice, or delivery note. This is now contained in the **Consumer Protection from Unfair Trading Regulations 2008, reg 5(4)(k)**.

The Unfair Terms in Consumer Contracts Regulations 1999

These Regulations revoke and replace the Unfair Terms in Consumer Contracts Regulations 1994 and came into force on 1 October 1999.

Although these Regulations do not deal specifically with exclusion clauses, they can render ineffective any terms that purport to exclude liability for breaching the statutory implied terms.

The Regulations apply equally to contracts for the sale of goods as well as for the supply of services.

The Regulations deal with unfair terms in contracts where the buyer is a consumer (reg 4(1)). However, the definition of 'consumer' is different from that in the UCTA.

Definition of 'consumer' for the purpose of the Regulations

Regulation 3(1) defines a consumer as:

any natural person who, in contracts covered by these Regulations, is acting for purposes which are outside his trade, business or profession.

Revision tip

You can see from this definition that 'any natural person' precludes a company from being a consumer for the purpose of the Regulations.

What is an unfair term?

Unlike the **UCTA** which, despite its rather misleading title, was passed to control the use of clauses or notices that purport to exclude or limit a party's liability, these Regulations really do deal with 'unfair terms'.

Regulation 5(1) tells us when a contractual term will be unfair:

A contractual term which has not been individually negotiated shall be regarded as unfair if, contrary to the requirement of good faith, it causes a significant imbalance in the parties' rights and obligations arising under the contract, to the detriment of the consumer.

Revision tip

The words in italics reflect the key aspects of an unfair term. A term will always be regarded as not having been individually negotiated where it has been drafted in advance and the consumer has therefore not been able to influence the substance of the term (**reg 5(2)**). It will be for any seller or supplier who claims that a term was individually negotiated to show that it was (**reg 5(4)**).

Core terms are excluded from the Regulations

'**Core terms**' of the contract are not covered by the Regulations (**reg 6(2)**). A contractual term will be 'core' if it is in plain intelligible language and relates:

- to the main subject matter of the contract (**reg 6(2)(a)**); or
- to the adequacy of the price or remuneration, as against the goods or services supplied in exchange (**reg 6(2)(b)**).

Regulation 6(2)(b) means that the courts are not able to consider whether or not the parties had made a good bargain or paid a fair price.

Two cases, both involving banks and the fairness of certain terms, had to consider whether the terms in question were 'core', which meant that if they were the Regulations did not apply to them and the question of considering their fairness would not arise. Although these cases are hard to distinguish, the courts (one the House of Lords and the other the Supreme Court) came to different conclusions as to how a **core term** should be defined.

In *Director General of Fair Trading v First National Bank Plc* (2002) the House of Lords stated that **reg 6** should be interpreted restrictively. Their Lordships distinguished terms that were 'ancillary' to those that were 'core' and held that terms 'ancillary to the core' of the contract should be subject to assessment for fairness.

In *Office of Fair Trading v Abbey National Plc & others* (2010) the Supreme Court focused on reg 6(2)(b). In reaching a contrary view to the decisions of the lower courts, the Justices concluded that if a term concerned only a *part* of the price or remuneration, it should still fall within the scope of reg 6(2)(b). Therefore, since the charges in question were a part of the price the bank received in exchange for providing its customers with a current account, the relevant terms fell within reg 6(2)(b) and could not be assessed for fairness.

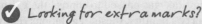 Looking for extra marks?

As well as explaining the different approaches taken to the meaning of '**core terms**' in these two cases, you should explain that the Supreme Court's decision in ***Abbey National*** significantly expands the scope of **reg 6** and as a consequence reduces the protection given to consumers. Furthermore, the Supreme Court adopted a less restrictive interpretation of **reg 6** because it said that the purpose of the Regulations was consumer choice rather than consumer protection.

Examples of terms which may be regarded as unfair

Schedule 2 of the Regulations provides an *indicative and non-exhaustive list* of terms which may be regarded as unfair.

Revision tip

Don't forget that the list in **Schedule 2** is only indicative and is non-exhaustive. Therefore, just because a term does not resemble a term on the list will not automatically mean it will be regarded as fair.

The list of terms contained in Schedule 2 are terms which have the object or effect of:

(a) excluding or limiting the legal liability of a seller or supplier in the event of the death of a consumer or personal injury to the latter resulting from an act or omission of that seller or supplier;

(b) inappropriately excluding or limiting the legal rights of the consumer vis-à-vis the seller or supplier or another party in the event of total or partial non-performance or inadequate performance by the seller or supplier of any of the contractual obligations, including the option of offsetting a debt owed to the seller or supplier against any claim which the consumer may have against him;

(c) making an agreement binding on the consumer whereas provision of services by the seller or supplier is subject to a condition whose realisation depends on his own will alone;

(d) permitting the seller or supplier to retain sums paid by the consumer where the latter decides not to conclude or perform the contract, without providing for the consumer to receive compensation of an equivalent amount from the seller or supplier where the latter is the party cancelling the contract;

(e) requiring any consumer who fails to fulfil his obligation to pay a disproportionately high sum in compensation;

(f) authorising the seller or supplier to dissolve the contract on a discretionary basis where the same facility is not granted to the consumer, or permitting the seller or supplier to retain the sums paid for services not yet supplied by him where it is the seller or supplier himself who dissolves the contract;

(g) enabling the seller or supplier to terminate a contract of indeterminate duration without reasonable notice except where there are serious grounds for doing so;

(h) automatically extending a contract of fixed duration where the consumer does not indicate otherwise, when the deadline fixed for the consumer to express his desire not to extend the contract is unreasonably early;

(i) irrevocably binding the consumer to terms with which he had no real opportunity of becoming acquainted before the conclusion of the contract;

(j) enabling the seller or supplier to alter the terms of the contract unilaterally without a valid reason which is specified in the contract;

(k) enabling the seller or supplier to alter unilaterally without a valid reason any characteristics of the product or service to be provided;

(l) providing for the price of goods to be determined at the time of delivery or allowing a seller of goods or supplier of services to increase their price without in both cases giving the consumer the corresponding right to cancel the contract if the final price is too high in relation to the price agreed when the contract was concluded;

(m) giving the seller or supplier the right to determine whether the goods or services supplied are in conformity with the contract, or giving him the exclusive right to interpret any term of the contract;

(n) limiting the seller's or supplier's obligation to respect commitments undertaken by his agents or making his commitments subject to compliance with a particular formality;

(o) obliging the consumer to fulfil all his obligations where the seller or supplier does not perform his;

(p) giving the seller or supplier the possibility of transferring his rights and obligations under the contract, where this may serve to reduce the guarantees for the consumer, without the latter's agreement;

(q) excluding or hindering the consumer's right to take legal action or exercise any other legal remedy, particularly by requiring the consumer to take disputes exclusively to arbitration not covered by legal provisions, unduly restricting the evidence available to him, or imposing on him a burden of proof which, according to the applicable law, should lie with another party to the contract.

The effect of an unfair term

A term that is regarded by the Regulations as being unfair will not be binding on the consumer (reg 8(1)).

However, the remainder of the contract will continue to bind the parties if it is capable of continuing in existence without the existence of the term that has been rendered unfair (reg 8(2)).

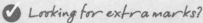

✅ **Looking for extra marks?**

Regulation 8(2) is very similar to the 'blue-pencil' rule used in the doctrine of severance in contractual terms, a good example of which can be found in *Goldsoll v Goldman* (1915). C purchased D's imitation jewellery business. D agreed not to deal in real or imitation jewellery for a period of two years in a large number of countries, including the UK. The Court of Appeal held that the geographical area of the restraint was too extensive and, by applying the blue-pencil rule, struck out all countries apart from the UK.

① Conclusion

The co-existence of the **UCTA** and the **Unfair Terms in Consumer Contracts Regulations** is often inconsistent and overlapping, and is unnecessarily complex. The Law Commission has recommended that both pieces of legislation are merged into a new single statute (Law Commission Report on Unfair Terms in Contracts, Law Com No 292 (2005)). It also produced a draft bill that unifies the law on unfair contract terms and exemption clauses. Legislative reform is long overdue. The **Consumer Rights Bill** is currently passing through Parliament.

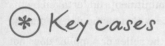

✳ Key cases

Case	Facts	Held/Principle
Director General of Fair Trading v First National Bank Plc [2002] 1 AC 481	The Bank entered into consumer credit agreements on its standard form terms. The term that gave rise to the case provided that if the bank obtained judgment against its customer for default then it would be entitled to charge interest at the same contract rate until the full amount had been paid.	The House of Lords stated that reg 6 should be interpreted restrictively. Their Lordships distinguished terms that were 'ancillary' from those that were 'core' and held that terms 'ancillary' to the 'core' of the contract should be subject to an assessment for fairness.

Case	Facts	Held/Principle
Karsales (Harrow) Ltd v Wallis [1956] 1 WLR 936	The supplier contracted to supply a Buick car which had been inspected and found to be in good working order. However, when it was delivered late at night it had been towed to its destination as it was incapable of being driven. The cylinder head had been removed, some of the pistons were broken, and the valves were burned out. The supplier sought to rely on a term of his contract that provided that 'no condition or warranty that the vehicle is roadworthy, or as to its age, condition or fitness for any purpose is given by the owner or implied herein'.	The Court of Appeal held that as there had been such a fundamental breach of the contract, the supplier was not entitled to rely on the exclusion clause in the agreement. There was a substantial deviation between what had been contracted for and what was eventually delivered.
O'Brien v MGN Ltd [2001] EWCA Civ 1279)	C purchased a Sunday newspaper containing a scratchcard game relating to a competition being held the following week in the *Daily Mirror*. The scratchcard told readers to refer to the *Daily Mirror* for the full rules and how to claim. Rule 5 provided that in the event of more prizes being claimed than were available a simple draw would take place to determine the winner. C had a winning scratchcard and called the claims line where he was told that he had won a £50,000 prize. However, due to an error, 1,472 other people had also claimed this prize. The newspaper then held a draw in accordance with Rule 5 and added a further £50,000 to be shared amongst the other winners. C won only a £34 share. In C's claim against the newspaper for the full £50,000 prize money, the issue was whether the contract incorporated the rules, and in particular, Rule 5.	The test was whether the newspaper had reasonably brought the rules to the attention of its readers and further whether Rule 5, which in effect turned an apparent winning card into a losing one, was unusual or particularly onerous. The Court of Appeal held that the rules were incorporated into the parties' contract as they had been referred to on the face of C's scratchcard and could also be ascertained from back issues of the newspaper or by means of an enquiry to the newspaper offices. Hale LJ said that Rule 5 could not by any normal use of language be called 'onerous' or 'outlandish', since 'it merely deprives the claimant of a windfall for which he has done very little in return'. She went on to say that the rules were not unusual or uncommon in the field of such games and competitions and 'indeed it would have been surprising if there had been no protection on the lines of Rule 5'.
Office of Fair Trading v Abbey National Plc & others [2010] 1 AC 696	The OFT began an investigation, under the Unfair Terms in Consumer Contracts Regulations 1999, into the fairness of certain personal current account charges levied by banks on transactions for	The Supreme Court focused on **reg 6(2)(b)**. In reaching a contrary view to the decision of the Court of Appeal, the Justices concluded that if a term concerned only a *part* of the price, it should fall within the ambit of **6(2)(b)**.

Case	Facts	Held/Principle
	which their customers did not have sufficient funds in their accounts to meet the payments. It then issued proceedings against the defendants, seeking a declaration that the standard terms and charges in question were not excluded by **reg 6(2)(b)** of the 1999 Regulations and could therefore be assessed for fairness.	Therefore, since the charges in question were a part of the price the bank received in exchange for providing its customers with a current account, the relevant terms fell within **6(2)(b)** as 'core terms' which are excluded from the Regulations and therefore could not be assessed for fairness.

⑨⑨ Key debates

Topic	**Bank charges in the Supreme Court**
Author/Academic	Paul Davies
Viewpoint	Discusses *Office of Fair Trading v Abbey National Plc* on whether bank charges for the unauthorised use of overdraft facilities were part of the bank's price for offering current account services and so fell within the scope of the **Unfair Terms in Consumer Contracts Regulations 1999, reg 6(2)(b)** and could not be assessed for fairness. Calls for a reappraisal of the law on unfair consumer contract terms in the light of the ruling.
Source	(2010) 69(1) *Cambridge Law Journal* 24

Topic	**Companies 'dealing as consumers'—a missed opportunity?**
Author/Academic	Christian Twigg-Flesner
Viewpoint	Comments on the Court of Appeal decision in *Feldarol Foundry Plc v Hermes Leasing (London) Ltd* on whether the rejection of a sports car which was unsatisfactory was valid in the light of an exclusion clause which sought to exclude all liability. Considers whether the company had been dealing as a consumer within the meaning of **s 12 of UCTA** and the effect of the ruling in *R&B Customs Brokers Co Ltd v United Dominions Trust Ltd.*
Source	(2005) 121 *Law Quarterly Review* 41

⑦ Exam questions

Problem question

Peter is a musician and makes copies of his own music which he sells via the internet. He needs a new machine to speed up the copying of his music. He contacts Music Copy Machines Ltd who recommend a machine which they claim is more than 10 times quicker than his old machine. Peter buys this machine for cash and takes it with him. When he tries it he finds it to be no quicker than his old one. He also finds that it starts making loud grinding noises when it is being used.

Peter returns the machine to the store and asks for his money back. The store manager, Mr Grumpy, reminds him that the contract he signed contained a clause stating: 'Music Copy Machines Ltd excludes all conditions relating to the quality or description of equipment purchased'. Peter tells him that when he signed it he wasn't wearing his glasses and therefore didn't read the clause. Mr Grumpy then points out that it is his company's policy to post a copy of contracts to customers immediately following purchase and therefore Peter should have been aware of the clause from this. Peter says that he did receive a copy of the contract containing this clause and that although he read it he didn't appreciate its significance until now.

Advise Peter.

Essay question

The co-existence of the Unfair Contract Terms Act 1977 and the Unfair Terms in Consumer Contracts Regulations 1999 is often inconsistent and overlapping, and is unnecessarily complex.

Critically evaluate this statement.

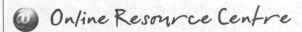

Online Resource Centre

To see an outline answer to this question visit www.oup.com/lawrevision/

#6
Non-existent and perishing of goods

- A contract for the sale of specific goods which, without the knowledge of the seller, have perished at the time when the contract is made, is void.

- An agreement to sell specific goods which, without any fault on the part of either of the parties, subsequently perish before the risk passes to the buyer, is avoided.

- The above two points are dealt with by **ss 6 and 7**, respectively, of the **SGA**.

- A contract for the sale of unascertained goods from an identified source which, without the knowledge of the seller, have perished at the time when the contract is made, is void at common law.

- A contract for the sale of unascertained goods from an identified source which, without any fault on the part of either of the parties, subsequently perish, is frustrated at common law.

- Where the contract is frustrated at common law the question of monies owing or to be repaid is governed by the **Law Reform (Frustrated Contracts) Act 1943**. The 1943 Act has no application where the contract is avoided by **s 7 of the SGA**.

Introduction

In Chapter 3, 'Passing of property and risk', p 31, we looked at the rules for the passing of property and risk. In this chapter, we consider the effect of the contract in the event that the goods never existed or, if they did at one time exist, are no longer in existence. It is important to distinguish the events that caused the goods not to exist from the position before the contract is made to those that arose after the contract is made.

Principally, these problems are dealt with by ss 6 and 7 SGA. You will see from these sections that they only apply to contracts of **specific goods**. However, **future goods** that are already in existence are likely to be considered specific goods for the purpose of **ss 6 and 7**.

Revision Lip

Section 6 deals with events *before* the contract is made and s 7 deals with events *after* the contract has been made. Another way of looking at this is to consider s 6 under the category of 'impossibility' or 'mistake' and s 7 under the category of '**frustration**'. The key difference between these sections is that where a contract is impossible to perform *at the time it was made*, it might be void for mistake, whereas if the contract *subsequently* becomes impossible to perform, illegal, or radically different from that which was intended, then it might be deemed frustrated.

Events before the contract is made—s 6 SGA

In *Couturier v Hastie* (1856), the House of Lords held that as the contract had contemplated the existence of the goods which unbeknown to the parties had ceased to exist, the buyer was not liable to pay because they were not in existence at the time the contract was made.

The effect of the decision in *Couturier v Hastie* can now be seen in s 6 SGA.

Section 6: Goods which have perished

---

s 6 SGA:

Where there is a contract for the sale of specific goods, and the goods without the knowledge of the seller have perished at the time when the contract is made, the contract is void.

Revision Lip

You should note from the wording in s 6 that the section only applies to goods that have perished. It will not apply in cases where the goods never existed. However, if X agrees to sell to Y **specific goods** which both of them believe to exist but which in fact did not exist, then the contract would be void at common law.

When will the goods be deemed to have perished?

If the goods have been destroyed then there can be little doubt that they have perished. Beyond total destruction, the courts have also held that goods will be deemed to have perished if they become significantly altered so that, for commercial purposes, they can no longer be said to be the same goods that were the subject of the contract (*Asfar & Co v Blundell* (1896)). However, a different decision was reached by Morris J in *Horn v Minister of Food* (1948), where he held that provided the goods were still in existence and remained in a form that could be identified as the goods relating to the contract, then the goods will not have perished even if they are worthless. This view appears to be wrong and is out of line with the other authorities on the matter.

But what if there has only been a partial loss of the goods sold? Will they still be deemed to have perished?

Barrow, Lane & Ballard Ltd v Phillip Phillips & Co Ltd [1929] 1 KB 574

The buyer bought a specific 'lot' of 700 bags of ground nuts. Unknown to either party, before the contract had been made, a thief had made off with 109 of these bags and before collection a total of 400 bags had been stolen. Wright J found that there was no prospect of the goods being recovered and held that **s 6** (of the **1893 SGA**) applied where even part of the goods have perished at the time the contract is made, and that the contract was therefore void. This case turned on its facts. The sale was for a specific indivisible 'lot' of 700 bags of nuts. Had the contract been severable (i.e. for the sale of separate lots with each lot being invoiced and paid for separately) then it would seem that only the contract(s) representing the missing goods would have been held to be void.

It has been suggested that in a case where only part of the goods have perished the seller might be required to make the remaining (unperished) goods available to the buyer, although the buyer will not be under any obligation to accept them (*Sainsbury Ltd v Street* (1972)).

Events after the contract is made—s 7 SGA

At common law, after a contract has been made and through the fault of neither party something happens to make its performance impossible, the contract is said to be frustrated and the parties are released from future obligations.

Section 7 of the SGA mirrors this common law position.

Section 7: Goods perishing before sale but after agreement to sell

s 7 SGA:

Where there is an agreement to sell specific goods and subsequently the goods, without any fault on the part of the seller or buyer, perish before the risk passes to the buyer, the agreement is avoided.

In this instance, the word 'avoided' in s 7 is synonymous with 'frustrated'.

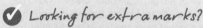

✅ Looking for extra marks?

You should explain your understanding of the application of s 7 by pointing out that although it is similar to the common law rules on **frustration**, the **Law Reform (Frustrated Contracts) Act 1943** (which applies to common law frustration by setting out the legal consequences of a contract that has been held to have been frustrated) has no application to contracts avoided by **s 7 of the SGA** (s 2(5)(c) of the 1943 Act).

Frustration, for the purpose of s 7, can arise (as the section says) when the goods subsequently perish before the risk passes to the buyer. It can also arise in cases where, after the contract has been made, its performance becomes illegal (*Avery v Bowden* (1855)).

Revision tip

Don't forget that s 7 (as with s 6) only applies in the case of **specific goods**. In all other cases where the contract becomes impossible or illegal to perform, you should consider whether it has been frustrated at common law. Just as goods that have never existed cannot perish, a contract for the sale of **future goods** that do not materialise will not be avoided by s 7 (as this section only covers specific goods). However, such a contract may be frustrated at common law (*Howell v Coupland* (1875–76)).

The decision in *Howell v Coupland* should be contrasted with *Sainsbury Ltd v Street* (1972) where MacKenna J held that where a buyer contracts with a seller to purchase a specific portion of a crop, and performance becomes impossible owing to a failure of the crop without any default on the part of the seller, then the seller is not liable to the buyer in damages although he is obliged to deliver the actual amount that has been harvested.

In the event the contract is held to be avoided (or frustrated) the parties are relieved from further performance. This means that, subject to what was said in *Sainsbury Ltd v Street* about partial delivery, the seller is relieved from having to deliver the goods and the buyer from paying for them. This reflects the presumed intention of the parties to the contract had they put their minds to the events that later occurred. Of course, had they put their minds to the problem and reflected this in the contract, then neither s 6 nor s 7 will apply, as these only apply in the absence of agreement to the contrary.

The difference between s 7 and common law frustration
****

It is likely that, had the parties to the contract put their minds to the problem, they would have agreed that in the event the contract becomes impossible to perform, future performance will be excused. But, the courts are unlikely to excuse all further performance of the contract if it appears to be an unreasonable presumption of what the parties will have intended. This can be seen from the decision of MacKenna J in *Sainsbury Ltd v Street*, where he held that the seller was not liable to the buyer in damages although he was obliged to deliver the actual amount that had been harvested.

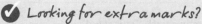 **Looking for extra marks?**

You should explain the difference in the decisions in *Howell v Coupland* and *Sainsbury Ltd v Street* by pointing out that the courts will try to ascertain what the parties would have intended had they put their minds to the problem. It seems reasonable to assume that in the *Sainsbury* case the parties are likely to have agreed that, on the facts that arose in that case, the buyer should have had the option of accepting the reduced quantity of barley that was, in fact, harvested.

Key points on ss 6 and 7 SGA

- Both **ss 6 and 7** relate only to **specific goods** and in the absence of any agreement by the parties to the contrary.

- Neither section applies to **unascertained goods** nor to goods that were **ascertained** after the contract was made.

- s 6 deals with *sales* (of **specific goods**).

- s 6 applies only where, without the knowledge of the seller, **specific goods** perish before the contract is made. It does not apply where the goods never existed in the first place.

- s 7 does not cover immediate sales but only *agreements to sell* **specific goods** where property in the goods will pass to the buyer at a future date.

- With s 7, the perishing of the goods must arise after the contract was made but before risk in the goods passes to the buyer.

- If the risk in the goods has already passed to the buyer then s 7 will not apply and the buyer will bear the loss and have to pay the contract price.

- Neither party can be at fault for s 7 to apply.

The difference between the contract being avoided by s 7 and frustrated at common law

Section 7 SGA

Where the contract is avoided under s 7, and the buyer has suffered a total failure of **consideration**, then he can claim the return of monies paid under the contract. He will have suffered a total failure of consideration if he received nothing for what he had bargained for. The failure of consideration must be total and the goods must have perished before any of them were delivered to the buyer. If the failure of consideration was only partial, for example, in the unlikely event that the buyer had some use of the goods before they perished, then he will not be entitled to recover any of the money paid under the contract.

Note that this possibility is unlikely to arise because, once the goods have been delivered to the buyer, risk will usually also have passed to him and s 7 only applies in cases where the goods 'perish before the risk passes to the buyer'.

Frustration at common law

Where the contract is frustrated at common law, the effects of **frustration** and the question of monies is governed by the **Law Reform (Frustrated Contracts) Act 1943**. (You should already have noted that the 1943 Act has no application where the contract is avoided by s 7 of the SGA.)

Although the contract is discharged and automatically terminates upon a court holding it to be frustrated, it is important to appreciate that the contract is not treated as void or as if it never existed. The legal consequences of acts that were performed before the frustrating event will need to be considered.

At one time, the courts adopted the harsh position that the parties' obligations were not discharged by a frustrating event and that a party would be in breach of contract if it failed to carry out its obligations as if the frustrating event had not arisen (*Paradine v Jane* (1647)).

Following a number of cases where justice remained both harsh and unpredictable, and where the arbitrary principle of the 'loss lies where it falls' (*Chandler v Webster* (1904)) produced results that were in many cases largely a matter of luck, the House of Lords attempted to improve matters in *Fibrosa Spolka Akcyjna v Fairbairn Lawson Combe Barbour Ltd* (1943).

Fibrosa Spolka Akcyjna v Fairbairn Lawson Combe Barbour Ltd [1943] AC 32

An English company contracted with its Polish customer to supply machinery for which they paid £1,000 in advance towards the cost of the equipment. When Germany invaded Poland in 1939, followed two days later by Britain declaring war on Germany, the contract became frustrated. The buyers sought to recover the £1,000 paid. The House of Lords held that as the buyers had received no benefit under the contract there was a total failure of **consideration** and they could recover the monies paid.

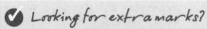 **Looking for extra marks?**

The decision in **Fibrosa**, whilst almost certainly an improvement on cases such as **Chandler v Webster**, still left problems unanswered. First, it only applies to cases of total failure of **consideration**. This means that where one party has received some benefit (no matter ➜

➡ how small) under the contract the failure of consideration will not be total and the recovery of monies already paid will not be possible. Second, and arguably more serious, the party who has received some money under the contract as a part-payment is likely to have expended some money in relation to the performance of the contract and will therefore suffer a loss if the entire sum received has to be repaid. **The Law Reform (Frustrated Contracts) Act 1943** addresses both of these concerns. Don't forget that the Act applies to contracts frustrated at common law but does not apply to contracts avoided by **s 7 SGA**.

The Law Reform (Frustrated Contracts) Act 1943

The allocation of loss is decided by the Act which provides:

* all sums payable under the contract cease to be payable and any money already paid may be recovered. If the party to whom the sums were paid or payable incurred expenses before the time of discharge, the court may, if it considers it just to do so having regard to all the circumstances of the case, allow him to retain or recover the whole or part of the sums paid or payable but not an amount in excess of the expenses that have been incurred (s 1(2));

* where, before the time of discharge, a party to the contract has obtained a valuable benefit as a result of something done by another party (other than a payment of money referred to in s 1(2)), the other party will be entitled to recover from him such sum (if any), not exceeding the value of the benefit, as the court considers just, having regard to all the circumstances of the case (s 1(3));

* where the parties make their own provisions for the effects of a frustrating event then those provisions will apply to the contract rather than those contained in the Act (s 2(3)).

The effect of s 1(3) on the recovery of a valuable benefit can be seen in *BP Exploration Co (Libya) Ltd v Hunt (No 2)* (1983).

BP Exploration Co (Libya) Ltd v Hunt (No 2) [1983] 2 AC 352

H was granted a concession by the Libyan government to explore for and extract oil in a specified part of the desert. H subsequently entered into an agreement with BP for them to drill and extract the oil. In this agreement, H agreed to split the benefit of his concession with BP who, in return, also agreed to assume all risks associated with the extraction of the oil. The Libyan government later nationalised the oil industry and expropriated first BP's interest and then, nearly two years later, H's interest. After BP's interest had been expropriated, but before H's interest had been, H obtained 74 million barrels of oil. BP brought a claim in damages under the 1943 Act in respect of its lost benefit. The House of Lords held that the contract had become frustrated and that by virtue of **s 1(3)** of the Act, BP was entitled to recover a share of H's profits as a valuable benefit received.

✓ Looking for extra marks?

Notwithstanding the provisions in the **Law Reform (Frustrated Contracts) Act 1943**, the parties would be well advised to agree their own contractual provisions for the allocation of risk because there are gaps in the Act that will not always provide a satisfactory solution to the division of losses. An example of this can be seen in *Appleby and Another v Myers* (1866–67). C contracted to build machinery in D's premises and to keep it in good working order for two years with the price to be paid upon the completion of the whole works. After part of the work had been finished, and others were in the course of completion, the premises with all the machinery and materials in it were destroyed by fire. It was held that both parties were excused from the further performance of the contract and that C was not entitled to sue in respect of those portions of the works which had been completed, whether or not the materials used had become the property of D. Even under the 1943 Act, C would not be entitled to payment because there was no valuable benefit to which **s 1(3)** could apply.

✱ Key cases

Case	Facts	Held/Principle
Asfar & Co v Blundell [1896] 1 QB 123	A vessel carrying a shipment of dates sank during the course of the voyage, and was subsequently salvaged. On arrival at the port, it was found that although the dates still retained the appearance of dates, and although they were of value for the purpose of distillation into spirit, they were so impregnated with sewage and in such a condition of fermentation as to be no longer merchantable as dates in accordance with the contract of sale.	The Court of Appeal held that the dates had perished because, for commercial purposes, they were so altered that they were no longer the same goods that were the subject of the contract.
Avery v Bowden (1855) 26 LJ QB 3	The parties entered into an agreement to bring goods from Russia. Before the ship had been loaded, war broke out and it became illegal to trade with the enemy.	It was held that the subsequent illegality of the contract had frustrated the contract and that no claim could succeed against D for failing to load the ship.
Couturier v Hastie (1856) 5 HL Cas 673	A contract was entered into for the sale of a cargo of corn. At the time of making the contract, both seller and buyer believed that the cargo existed. However, the previous month the ship's captain had sold	The House of Lords held that as the contract had contemplated the existence of the corn, which unbeknown to the parties had ceased to exist because of the earlier sale, the buyer was not liable to pay for the goods because they were

Case	Facts	Held/Principle
	the cargo to a third party as a result of its deterioration during the early part of the voyage so as to render impossible its intended transmission to England. When the English buyer discovered the facts he repudiated the contract. The seller brought an action against the buyer for the price.	not in existence at the time the contract was made. The effect of the decision in *Couturier v Hastie* can now be seen in s 6 SGA.
***Horn v Minister of Food* [1948] 2 All ER 1036**	H entered into a contract with the Minister of Food, under which the Minister purchased 33 tons of Majestic ware potatoes in a certain clamp. When the clamp was opened the potatoes were found to be rotten. The delivery was cancelled.	Morris J held that as the potatoes had not ceased to exist and were still in a form that would permit their being called potatoes, the potatoes had not 'perished' within the meaning of **s 7** (of the 1893 Act). This view was *obiter* because the judge held that as the risk in the goods had already passed to the buyer, the section had no application.
***Howell v Coupland* (1875–76) LR 1 QBD 258**	Coupland agreed to sell to Howell 200 tons of Regent potatoes to be grown on a specific piece of land. The land in question ought not to have had any problems in producing this quantity, although, due to the fault of neither party, the crop failed and only 80 tons were harvested, which Howell accepted and then sued Coupland for non-delivery of the remaining 120 tons.	The Court of Appeal held that Coupland was not liable to Howell for non-delivery because the unforeseen potato blight made further delivery impossible, the effect of which frustrated the contract and released Coupland from his obligation to deliver any more than could reasonably have been harvested. The court implied a term into the contract to the effect that each party should be free of further performance if the crop perished. The position would, of course, have been otherwise had the contract not specified a particular crop because the seller could then have supplied Regent potatoes from another source.
***Sainsbury Ltd v Street* [1972] 1 WLR 834**	A farmer entered into a contract with a corn merchant to sell 275 tons of barley which was to be grown on the farmer's farm. Due to a poor harvest and without any fault of the farmer, the crop only came to 140 tons. As a result, the farmer acted on the basis that the contract was frustrated and he sold the available crop to a third party.	MacKenna J held that where a buyer contracts with a seller to purchase a specific portion of a crop, and performance becomes impossible owing to a failure of the crop without any default on the part of the seller, then the seller is not liable to the buyer in damages although he is obliged to deliver the actual amount that has been harvested. The judge confirmed the rule in ***Howell v Coupland*** but held that that did not affect the farmer's obligation to deliver the quantity of barley actually produced.

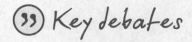 **Key debates**

Topic	On the perishing of goods
Viewpoint	Discusses the meaning of 'perished' and **'specific goods'** in the provisions of the 1979 Act making contracts void where specific goods have perished.
Source	(1997) 19 (10) *Buyer* 7

Topic	Frustration: a limited future
Author/Academic	Celia Battersby
Viewpoint	Discusses the strict limits of the application of the doctrine of **frustration**.
Source	(1990) 134 (13) *Solicitors Journal* 354

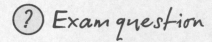 **Exam question**

It is important to distinguish the events that caused the goods subject to the contract of sale not to exist both from the position before the contract was made to those that arose after the contract was made.

Critically evaluate this statement.

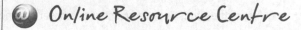 **Online Resource Centre**

To see an outline answer to this question visit www.oup.com/lawrevision/

#7

Transfer of ownership by a non-owner

- *Nemo dat quod non habet* is often abbreviated to *nemo dat*. It means 'no-one can transfer what he has not got'.

- Therefore, a seller can only pass ownership of goods to a buyer if he owns or has the right to sell them at the time of sale.

- The *nemo dat* rule might apply where a buyer purchases stolen property but also arises where a seller has no right to sell the goods but nevertheless sells them.

- The *nemo dat* rule protects the true owner of the goods and the innocent purchaser gets no title whatever.

- There are several exceptions to the *nemo dat* rule. They are contained in the **Sale of Goods Act 1979** (hereafter referred to as the **SGA**), the **Factors Act 1889** (referred to as the **FA**), and the **Hire Purchase Act 1964** (referred to as the **HPA**). When any of these exceptions apply, the original owner of the goods loses his title in favour of the purchaser who would have lost out if the exception did not apply. These exceptions protect the innocent purchaser.

Chapter overview

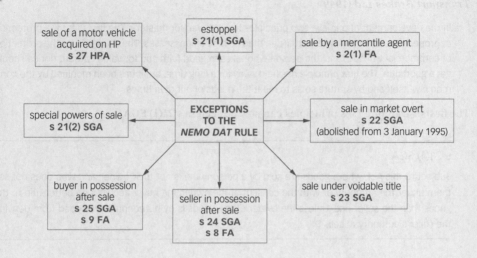

Introduction

This chapter deals with the situation where a seller, who has no right to the goods, is nevertheless able to pass good title to a third party.

Typical situations where this might arise include:

- A steals the goods and sells them to B who buys them in good faith for value.

- A sells the goods to B1 but retains possession of them and then wrongly sells them again to B2.

- A passes his goods to B to seek offers for sale but B sells them without A's authority and keeps the proceeds of sale.

- A buys goods on credit terms and then resells or pledges them to B with no intention of paying for them.

The typical question that arises in such circumstances is: which of two innocent parties should suffer for the fraud of a third? The courts have to choose between upholding the rights of the original owner of the goods and protecting the interests of a purchaser who buys the goods in good faith and for value.

Nemo dat quod non habet

The position was explained by Denning LJ in *Bishopgate Motor Finance Corporation Ltd v Transport Brakes Ltd* (1949):

> In the development of our law, two principles have striven for mastery. The first is for the protection of property: no one can give a better title than he himself possesses. The second is for the protection of commercial transactions: the person who takes in good faith and for value without notice should get a good title. The first principle has held sway for a long time, but it has been modified by the common law itself and by statute so as to meet the needs of our own times.

The first of Denning LJ's principles can now be seen in s 21(1) SGA:

---

s 21(1) SGA:

Subject to this Act, where goods are sold by a person who is not their owner, and who does not sell them under the authority or with the consent of the owner, the buyer acquires no better title to the goods than the seller had, unless the owner of the goods is by his conduct precluded from denying the seller's authority to sell.

✅ *Looking for extra marks?*

The words in the above section 'where goods are sold' do not cover a situation where there is a mere agreement to sell goods (*Shaw v Commissioner of Police of the Metropolis* (1987)).

Revision tip

The *nemo dat* rule is simply stated in that no-one can transfer that which he does not have. There are exceptions to this rule and it is the exceptions that are key to your understanding of this subject.

Before looking at the exceptions to the *nemo dat* rule, let us briefly consider the position of a sale by an agent. It can be seen from s 21(1) that unless the goods are sold with the authority or consent of the owner then a buyer can acquire no title in them. However, the opening words in the subsection ('Subject to this Act') mean that the section is subject to the provisions of the Act, s 62(2) of which preserves the common law rules pertaining to **principal** and **agent**. Therefore, a sale that is within the usual or **ostensible authority** of an agent will bind the owner of the goods even if outside the agent's **actual authority**.

See, further, Chapter 12, 'The creation of agency and the agent's authority', p 171.

The exceptions to the *nemo dat* rule are as follows:

Estoppel—s 21(1) SGA

Estoppel applies in cases where the owner of the goods acts in such a way that it appears that the seller has the right to sell the goods. As a consequence, the owner is then prevented (estopped) from denying the facts as he represented them to be. The third party purchaser then becomes the owner of the goods at the expense of the original owner.

The concluding words of s 21(1) '. . . unless the owner of the goods is by his conduct precluded from denying the seller's authority to sell' set out this exception. This is little more than the common law doctrine of estoppel. Nothing is said in the section as to when the owner is by his conduct precluded from denying the seller's authority to sell, although merely giving the third party possession of the goods will not amount to a representation that the third party is the owner or has the right to sell the goods (*Jerome v Bentley & Co* (1952)).

There are two distinct categories of estoppel to which s 21(1) applies:

1. estoppel by representation; and
2. estoppel by negligence.

Estoppel by representation

Estoppel by representation might arise where the owner of the goods has by his words or conduct represented to the buyer that the seller is the true owner of the goods, or has his authority to sell the goods. This category of estoppel is, therefore, sometimes sub-divided into estoppel by words and estoppel by conduct.

Shaw v Commissioner of Police of the Metropolis [1987] 1 WLR 1332

The owner of a Porsche advertised his car for sale. He was contacted by a swindler, Mr London, who claimed to be interested in purchasing it on behalf of a client. The owner allowed London to take delivery of the car. He also gave London a note stating that he had sold the car to him. This was, in fact, untrue as the owner merely authorised London to sell it on his behalf. C agreed to purchase the car from London (who had not paid the owner for it). London subsequently vanished and the ownership of the car became an issue. Notwithstanding that C had not paid London (or indeed anyone) for the car, he claimed that he had acquired good title under **s 21(1)**. This was rejected by the Court of Appeal, although on the rather unsatisfactory basis that **s 21(1)** only applies to a party who has actually purchased goods and not to one who has merely agreed to do so. This is unsatisfactory because **s 21(1)** appears to be a simple restatement of the common law principle of estoppel and, as such, ought to protect a party which has on the representation made acted to its prejudice. On this basis, the Court of Appeal could easily have rejected C's claim simply because he had not acted to his prejudice as he had not paid the price.

A good example of the operation of the doctrine of estoppel can be seen in *Eastern Distributors Ltd v Goldring* (1957) (overruled on another ground by *Worcester Works Finance v Cooden Engineering Co* (1972)).

Estoppel—s 21(1) SGA

✳✳✳✳✳✳✳✳✳✳✳✳

Eastern Distributors Ltd v Goldring [1957] 2 QB 600

M wanted to raise finance on a van that he owned. He got together with a motor dealer (G) and they devised a scheme to deceive a finance company (E). They completed forms stating that M's van was in fact owned by G and M wished to acquire it on **hire purchase** (HP). E approved the HP agreement believing that the van was owned by G. This sort of transaction operates by the finance company (in this case E) purchasing the vehicle from the dealer (G) and then supplying it on HP terms to the customer (M). M failed to make his HP payments to E and sold the vehicle to an innocent purchaser (X). When the deception was discovered a dispute arose as to the ownership of the van. M was clearly the original owner and as such would be free to pass good ownership to X unless he had lost his ownership because of the deceit. It was held that because of M's representation that the van was not owned by him but by G he was estopped from asserting his ownership of it. Therefore, M had lost his title to the van under the doctrine of estoppel and E obtained good title when it purchased the van from G. E's ownership of the van did not pass (back) to M because under an HP agreement ownership is not transferred until all instalments have been made. Thus, as M did not own the van he could not transfer ownership to X.

See also *Moorgate Mercantile Co Ltd v Twitchings* (1977), under 'Estoppel by negligence'.

Estoppel by negligence

Estoppel by negligence is where the owner of goods, by reason of his negligence or negligent failure to act, allows the seller of the goods to appear to the buyer as the true owner or as having the true owner's authority to sell the goods. For this kind of estoppel to arise it must first be shown that the owner of the goods had a duty to take care so as not to act negligently.

In *Moorgate Mercantile Co Ltd v Twitchings* (1977) both estoppel by representation and estoppel by negligence were pleaded. Both failed. C was a finance company and supplied a car on HP to X. C failed to register the HP transaction with HPI (an organisation set up by finance companies to prevent fraud in connection with the supply of vehicles on HP). Registering such a transaction with HPI was not compulsory, although the majority of HP transactions were registered with it. X then offered to sell the car to D (a motor dealer). As X had not paid all the instalments he did not own the car and therefore did not have the right to sell it. D contacted HPI to see if the car was registered with them (as having outstanding finance) and was told that it was not. D then bought the car from X. When the finance company discovered what had occurred they commenced proceedings against D. D contended that the finance company was estopped from asserting their title to the car, arguing that:

- there existed an estoppel by representation because HPI had represented that the car was not the subject of an outstanding HP agreement and that this representation was given as agent of the finance company; and

- there also existed an estoppel by negligence on the ground that the finance company failed to register the HP agreement with HPI.

By a majority, the House of Lords rejected both limbs of the doctrine and upheld the finance company's claim. They rejected the argument based on estoppel by representation because the statement made by HPI was in fact true. HPI did not say that there was no outstanding finance on the car but only that nothing was registered with them. Furthermore, when responding to the finance company's request for information, HPI were acting in their own capacity and not as agents for them. Estoppel by negligence was rejected (Lords Wilberforce and Salmon dissenting) because the registering of HP agreements with HPI by its members was not compulsory and therefore the finance company was not under a duty to do so.

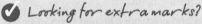 **Looking for extra marks?**

The doctrine of estoppel in relation to the transfer of ownership by a non-owner is almost identical to the apparent or ostensible authority of an agent to transfer title in the goods in excess of his actual authority to do so.

Sale by a mercantile agent—s 2(1) FA

A mercantile agent is defined in s 1(1) FA:

---

s 1(1) FA:

The expression 'mercantile agent' shall mean a mercantile agent having in the customary course of his business as such agent authority either to sell goods, or to consign goods for the purpose of sale, or to buy goods, or to raise money on the security of goods.

This exception to the *nemo dat* rule is intended to deal with a situation in which the owner of goods has given a mercantile agent possession of the goods or of the documents of title to them but not authority to sell them, but the mercantile agent sells them anyway.

It refers *only* to a person who is acting as a *mercantile* agent and is able to satisfy *all* of its requirements. These will not be easy to establish. Whether an agent will be considered in law to be a mercantile agent is not dependent on him being labelled as such in the contract but will be a matter of substance (*Weiner v Harris* (1910)). However, if this person (whether a mercantile agent or not) has **actual** or **apparent authority** to sell the goods then ownership will pass to the buyer under common law agency rules and it will be unnecessary to consider the rules of mercantile agency.

Section 21(2)(a) SGA expressly preserves the FA, s 2(1) of which sets out (together with the various cases) the requirements of mercantile agency, *all* of which must be satisfied:

1. He must be independent from the person for whom he is **agent** (his **principal**).
2. He must act in a business capacity (even if only occasionally).

3. He must be in possession of the actual goods or documents of title to the goods when he sells them on to the third party.

4. Such possession must:

    (i) be with the owner's consent (*National Employers Mutual General Insurance Association Ltd v Jones* (1990)). However, such consent may be established even if the owner was tricked into giving the agent possession (*Pearson v Rose & Young* (1951));

    (ii) be in his capacity as mercantile agent and for a purpose connected with his business as a mercantile agent and the sale (*Pearson v Rose & Young* (1951)). Thus, possession of the goods by a mercantile agent for the purpose of, for example, repairing them would not satisfy this requirement; and

    (iii) amount to current possession of the goods and not where he had been in possession in the past (*Beverley Acceptances Ltd v Oakley* (1982)).

5. He must actually sell or dispose of the goods. A mere agreement to sell them will not be enough.

6. The dealing in the goods by the mercantile agent must be in the ordinary course of business of mercantile agents generally. This means that the sale or disposition:

    (i) must be made during business hours;

    (ii) from business premises; and

    (iii) acting in such a way as the third party would expect a mercantile agent to act (*Oppenheimer v Attenborough* (1908)).

7. The third party must acquire the goods in good faith and without knowing that the mercantile agent lacked the authority to sell them. The burden of proof in this regard rests with the third party (*Heap v Motorists Advisory Agency Ltd* (1923)). The test of good faith is subjective and is satisfied when it is done honestly, irrespective of whether it is done negligently (s 61(3) SGA).

These requirements are lengthy and complex and will be difficult to establish. Unless all have been satisfied a non-owner will not be able to pass good title to a third party under s 2(1).

Finally, it should be noted that a mercantile agent is only able to pass that title which the person who consented to him having the goods or documents of title had in the first place. If that person was not in fact the owner of the goods (for example, because he had stolen the goods) then no title will be passed by the mercantile agent to the buyer.

Example

Jim has bought a new hi-fi system and leaves his old one with his friend Peter who owns an electrical goods shop. Jim asks Peter to sell it for him but for no less than £500. Although Peter's main business is selling general electrical goods, he does occasionally sell hi-fi systems and therefore agrees to sell Jim's old one. Peter is absent-minded and sells Jim's old hi-fi for only £200 to Fred. Had Peter had authority (actual or apparent) to sell the hi-fi for this price then the contract with Fred would have been binding without there having been any need to consider the rules of mercantile agency. However, Peter had no such authority and therefore whether or not Fred is now the owner of the hi-fi turns on whether the requirements of **s 2(1) FA** have been satisfied. In this example, they have been satisfied and Fred has thereby become the owner of the hi-fi system. Jim would, of course, have a claim against Peter for breaching his duty as **agent** to obey Jim's instructions. See Chapter 13, 'The relationships created by agency—the rights and liabilities of the parties', p 185.

Sale under a voidable title—s 23 SGA

It is important first to understand the difference between a **void contract** and one that is merely **voidable**, since s 23 will only operate in the case of the latter.

Section 23 is only relevant in cases where the third party has actually bought the goods: it has no application in cases where there was merely an agreement to buy them. Further, s 23 is distinguishable from the other exceptions in that it is incumbent on the original owner to show that the third party did not act in good faith (*Whitehorn Bros v Davison* (1911)). This can be contrasted with the other exceptions where it is for the third party purchaser to show that he did act in good faith.

Section 23 provides that if a party who has a voidable title to the goods resells them to an innocent third party, then that third party will gain good title to them provided that the original contract has not by then been avoided. If the party with the voidable title resells the goods to an innocent third party after the contract has been avoided, then there will no longer be any title in the goods which would be capable of being passed to the third party.

This calls for consideration of two points:

In what circumstances might a contract be voidable?

Examples of situations where a seller has a title that he may choose to avoid are where he has obtained possession of the goods by fraud (unless the fraud is such that the offer or acceptance is nullified) or where a person induces another to sell goods by means of duress, undue influence, or **misrepresentation**. In such situations the seller can choose, if he so wishes, to avoid the contract.

What needs to be done to avoid a contract that is voidable?

The most obvious way of avoiding a **voidable contract** in this type of situation is for the party defrauded etc to inform the other party that the contract is no longer binding or evincing an intention to do so and taking all possible steps such as notifying the police in cases of fraud (*Car & Universal Finance v Caldwell* (1965)).

Car & Universal Finance v Caldwell [1965] 1 QB 525

A rogue bought a car and fraudulently induced the seller to part with it in return for a cheque which later proved worthless. As soon as the seller was aware of this fraud he informed the police and the Automobile Association. The Court of Appeal held that this was enough to avoid the (voidable) contract. However, before the car or the rogue could be traced the rogue sold the car to an innocent third party. Because by this time the title had already been avoided by the seller the innocent purchaser acquired no title under s 23.

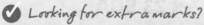

✅ *Looking for extra marks?*

The decision in *Car & Universal Finance* is rather harsh on the innocent third party purchaser. It is also rather arbitrary in application, as the innocent party's claim to the goods bought in good faith will depend on the speed that the original owner takes in avoiding the contract and the speed taken by the rogue to resell the goods. In the almost factually identical Scottish case of *McLeod v Kerr* (1965) the Court of Session held that 'by no stretch of imagination' could the seller's conduct amount to rescission of the contract.

Given the difficulty faced by an innocent purchaser in gaining title under s 23, he should consider a claim under s 25 ('Sale by a buyer in possession after sale—s 25 SGA/s 9 FA', p 93) as he is also likely to be a 'buyer in possession after a sale'.

Sale by a seller in possession after sale—s 24 SGA/s 8 FA

This exception to the *nemo dat* rule allows a seller who, after a sale, remains in possession of the goods or of the documents of title to them to pass a good title to a second buyer. Section 24 SGA is almost identical to s 8 FA, although s 8 is slightly wider in its application than s 24. Provided the requirements are satisfied the effect shall be 'as if the person making the delivery or transfer were expressly authorised by the owner of the goods to make the same'.

This exception operates in the following way:

Example

Suppose a seller (S) sells goods to a buyer (B1). B1 now owns the goods. Therefore, as S no longer has any interest in them he clearly cannot pass title to anyone else. But let's say that S keeps possession of the goods (or the documents of title to them) for a few days until B1 is able to collect them and during this time he sells them again to a second buyer (B2). In this example, even though S no longer has any ownership in the goods and therefore would not ordinarily be in a position to transfer title to anyone, B2 obtains good title to the goods at the expense of B1. B1, of course, could sue S for non-delivery of the goods.

It was once the position that for a third party to succeed under this exception he was required to show that the seller was in possession of the goods as a seller and not in some other capacity (*Staffs Motor Guarantee Ltd v British Wagon Co Ltd* (1934); *Eastern Distributors v Goldring* (1957)). However, the Privy Council in *Pacific Motor Auctions Pty Ltd v Motor Credits Ltd* (1965) said that these decisions had been wrongly decided and held that the words 'continues or is in possession' (under the New South Wales equivalent to our s 24) referred only to the continuity of actual possession rather than the capacity in which the seller had the goods in his possession. Being a decision of the Privy Council, this decision is only of persuasive authority in the English courts, although it has since been followed by the Court of Appeal in *Worcester Works Finance Ltd v Cooden Engineering Co Ltd* (1972), which held that the correct approach is one of continuity of possession rather than examining whether the seller was in possession of the goods 'as seller' or in some other capacity, such as **bailee**. Thus, provided the seller remained, without interruption, in physical possession of the goods, then the innocent second buyer gets good title under this exception to the *nemo dat* rule.

It is important that the seller disposes of the goods to the second buyer under a 'sale, pledge or other disposition'. A 'disposition' will occur whenever a new legal or equitable interest is created, although it will not by merely giving possession of the goods to the second buyer (*Worcester Works Finance Ltd v Cooden Engineering Co Ltd* (1972)).

The second buyer must take delivery of the goods or of the documents of title to them. It was held in *Michael Gerson (Leasing) Ltd v Wilkinson* (2001) that in respect of a sale and leaseback agreement where the original machinery does not actually leave the premises, a constructive delivery of the goods will suffice.

Sale by a buyer in possession after sale—s 25 SGA/s 9 FA

This exception allows a buyer in possession of the goods to pass good title even where such a buyer has not got any such title to pass. This operates in the following way.

Example

A buyer (X) takes possession of goods that he has agreed to buy although he has not yet acquired title to them. The reason why he has not yet acquired title is immaterial but might be because of a **retention of title** clause in the contract or because his cheque in payment of the goods has been dishonoured by his bank and it was a condition of the contract that title will not pass until the goods have been paid for. He then sells the goods to Y. Y obtains good title to the goods even though X did not himself have ownership of them.

The following conditions need to be satisfied for this exception to operate:

1. The protection afforded to a third party is only available if the goods or documents of title were in the possession of the buyer with the consent of the seller. Thus the seller of the goods must have consented to the first buyer obtaining possession of the goods or of the documents of title to the goods.

2. As can be seen from the statute, delivery to the second buyer must be made under a sale, pledge, or other disposition.

3. It will only apply to transactions where the first buyer actually buys or agrees to buy the goods. It will not operate if he merely acquires the goods on **hire purchase** (*Helby v Matthews* (1895)). It will not apply to a contract to provide services or where the first buyer acquired the goods under a 'sale or return' contract.

4. It operates to defeat the title only of an owner who has entrusted to a buyer the possession of his goods or documents of title. Consent only of the owner in respect of such possession is crucial (*National Employers Mutual General Insurance Association Ltd v Jones* (1990)).

5. The goods or the documents of title to the goods must be delivered to the second buyer. As noted under 'Sale by a seller in possession after sale—s 24 SGA/s 8 FA', p 93, constructive delivery will suffice.

6. The second buyer can only succeed under this exception and thereby take good title if he takes the goods in good faith and without notice of the first buyer's defect of title.

7. When selling or otherwise disposing of the goods, the first buyer must act in the way a mercantile agent acting in the ordinary course of business of a mercantile agent would act.

Any title passed under this exception is the same title as the original owner had. It follows, therefore, that if the original owner himself had no title in the goods (for example, if he had stolen them) then s 25/s 9 will not pass any title to the innocent buyer (*National Employers Mutual General Insurance Association Ltd v Jones* (1990)).

Newtons of Wembley Ltd v Williams [1965] 1 QB 560

In this case a rogue bought a car in exchange for a cheque which later proved to be worthless. The seller attempted to trace the rogue and informed the police. Before the rogue could be traced, he sold the car in a market to an innocent purchaser. The Court of Appeal held that the innocent buyer acquired good title. It was significant that the market was one where dealers commonly sold cars because it meant that the rogue had sold it in the way a mercantile agent acting in the ordinary course of business of a mercantile agent would have sold it.

Sale of a vehicle acquired on hire purchase—s 27 HPA

As noted above s 25/s 9 only apply to transactions where the first buyer actually buys or agrees to buy the goods and not to a person who acquires the goods on **hire purchase**.

It follows, therefore, that a person who has acquired goods on hire purchase and sells them before he pays the final instalment will pass no title to a buyer.

Sale of a vehicle acquired on hire purchase—s 27 HPA

Part lll of the HPA makes an exception to the above but only in the case of a sale of a motor vehicle that was acquired by hire purchase. In broad terms, this means that a bona fide purchaser of a motor vehicle from a person in possession under a hire purchase agreement or conditional sale agreement obtains good title to the vehicle. The sale of anything other than a motor vehicle is not covered under this exception. So, if X acquires a car and a piano on hire purchase and sells them both to Y before he has paid the final instalment then (provided the requirements of s 27 are satisfied) Y will obtain good title to the car but not the piano.

A purchaser will acquire good title to a motor vehicle provided the requirements of s 27 are satisfied. (Bicycles, caravans, and the like are not motor vehicles and are therefore not covered.)

1. There needs to be a disposition, the timing of which is important. See *Kulkarni v Manor Credit (Davenham) Ltd* (2010), p 96.

2. The seller must be in possession of the motor vehicle either as a hirer under a hire purchase agreement or purchaser under a conditional sale agreement.

3. Section 27 only applies to pass title to a private purchaser. A few notes about a private purchaser are needed:

   (a) once the private purchaser has acquired title under s 27, he can then pass title on to anyone;

   (b) section 27 protects only the first private purchaser who buys the vehicle in good faith. A private purchaser is a purchaser other than a trade or finance purchaser (s 29(2) HPA). Thus, if X acquires a motor vehicle on hire purchase and before making the last payment wrongly sells it to Y, a motor dealer, who then resells it to Z, a private purchaser, who buys it in good faith and without notice of the hire purchase arrangement and therefore is unaware of the defect in both X's and Y's title, Z acquires good title to the vehicle notwithstanding that he has purchased it from Y rather than from X who was the original hirer and even though Y did not acquire any title himself. Note that in this example, s 27 does not pass ownership to Y, as Y is not a private purchaser. Z is the first private purchaser and, as such, acquires good title to the vehicle. Z can then pass title in the ordinary way to a subsequent purchaser as he now owns the vehicle;

   (c) a person who is a motor dealer, even part-time, is not deemed to be a private purchaser for the purposes of s 27 even if he buys the car for his own personal use (*Stevenson v Beverley Bentinck Ltd* (1976)); and

   (d) neither is a person who buys several cars for the purpose of selling them on for gain (*G E Capital Bank Ltd v Rushton* (2006)).

4. The private purchaser must either purchase the motor vehicle or acquire it on hire purchase.

5. The private purchaser must act in good faith and without notice of the hire purchase or conditional sale agreement.

Sale of a vehicle acquired on hire purchase—s 27 HPA

✱✱✱✱✱✱✱✱✱✱✱

> ### Kulkarni v Manor Credit (Davenham) Ltd [2010] EWCA Civ 69
>
> K ordered a new car from a dealer (G). G then acquired the car from a finance company (M) under a **hire purchase** agreement and, in breach of that agreement, sold and delivered it to K later that same day. Three days earlier G had given K the car's registration number so K could insure it. When M discovered G's fraud they repossessed the car. K brought a claim against M in conversion, asserting title under **s 27**. The key issue was whether there had been a disposition of the car at a time when G was a hirer of it. It was K's case that there could be no transfer of the property in the car until delivery because the car had not been in a deliverable state until its registration plates had been attached. The Court of Appeal held that as there was no evidence that the registration plates had been attached to the car prior to delivery, K would not have been bound to take delivery and therefore the car was not in a deliverable state before delivery. On that basis K was a purchaser under a disposition which first took place upon delivery. The exception under **s 27** therefore applied, meaning K succeeded in his claim against M.

'Disposition' is defined in **s 29(1)** HPA and includes 'any sale or contract of sale (including a conditional sale agreement)'. In *VFS Financial Services Ltd v JF Plant Tyres Ltd* (2013) VFS had let a vehicle on hire purchase terms to a company (X) but had terminated the agreement for the non-payment of instalments and tried to repossess the vehicle. It transpired that X had parted with possession of the vehicle to JF, which refused to return it. JF said that it had accepted the vehicle in settlement of debts owed to it. X had subsequently issued an invoice to JF in respect of the sale of the vehicle. JF argued that it was entitled to rely on the protection afforded by **s 27** HPA because the disposition to it was as a purchaser of a vehicle in good faith without notice of the hire purchase agreement. VFS argued that it was entitled to summary judgment because the taking of the vehicle by JF in settlement of debts was not a 'disposition' within the meaning of **s 29(1)**. HHJ Mackie QC held that both at common law and under **s 2** SGA a 'sale' involved the exchange of goods for money, and that although the words 'sale' and 'contract of sale' in **s 29(1)** were not defined and were not stated to have the same meaning as in the SGA, the concept of the sale of a chattel had at common law and in statute long been associated with a money transaction. Therefore, there was no need to stretch the definitions to cover less conventional transactions and 'disposition' was therefore limited to the specific types of transaction mentioned in **s 29(1)** where a vehicle is transferred in return for money. The taking of property in lieu of a debt could not therefore constitute a 'disposition' under **s 27** HPA.

It was noted above that the seller must be in possession of the motor vehicle either as a hirer under a hire purchase agreement or purchaser under a conditional sale agreement. In *Shogun Finance Ltd v Hudson* (2003) a rogue took possession of a vehicle under a **hire purchase** agreement by using a stolen driving licence as evidence of his name and address. He then resold the vehicle to Mr Hudson and disappeared. When the finance company found out about the fraud they sued Mr Hudson in conversion. The House of Lords held the agreement to be void for mistake as the finance company clearly intended to deal with the person actually named on the agreement rather than the rogue. As the rogue was not a seller in possession of the vehicle under a hire purchase agreement, Mr Hudson could not rely on **s 27** to acquire title.

Finally, it should be noted that any title that passes under s 27 will be the same as the creditor had who let the motor vehicle.

Even in cases where a private buyer acquires title under s 27, it does not exonerate the seller from either civil or criminal liability for making the sale (s 27(6); *Barber v NWS Bank plc* (1996)).

Sale in market overt—s 22 SGA (now repealed)

This was the oldest of the exceptions to the *nemo dat* rule. A sale in market overt occurred when goods were sold in an established market between the hours of sunrise and sunset. The basis of this exception was that a dishonest person would be unlikely to sell stolen goods or goods that he did not own in such a market. The rule seems to reflect the high degree of supervision that was seen in established markets in the Middle Ages.

It was clearly an outdated exception and was abolished by s 1 Sale of Goods (Amendment) Act 1994 for contracts made after 3 January 1995.

Special powers of sale—s 21(2) SGA

Section 21(2) covers miscellaneous situations in which a non-owner of goods may nevertheless pass good title to a purchaser. These situations include:

- common law powers of sale, for example, that of a pawnbroker selling the goods of the pledgor when the loan remains unpaid;
- statutory powers of sale, such as the powers given to law enforcement officers to sell goods seized under a writ of execution. In such a case, it gives a good title to the purchaser of the goods sold by a bailiff which have been taken by the bailiff out of the possession of the execution debtor, irrespective of whether or not the purchaser had notice that the goods in question were not the property of the execution debtor (*Dyal Singh v Kenyan Insurance Ltd* (1954));
- other statutory provisions, such as seen in *Bulbruin Ltd v Romanyszyn* (1994) where the Court of Appeal held that a purchaser who acquired a vehicle from a local authority exercising its power of sale under the Road Traffic Regulation Act 1984 acquired good title to the vehicle even if the vehicle had been stolen before coming into the hands of the local authority;
- sale by order of a court. A court may order the sale of goods 'for any just and sufficient reason . . .' despite any objections or claims by the original owner (*Larner v Fawcett* (1950)).

Exam questions
✳✳✳✳✳✳✳✳✳✳✳✳

Revision tip

Each of the exceptions to the *nemo dat* rule requires that the purchaser who is claiming good title to the goods must have acted in good faith and he has the burden of proving that he has so acted. **Section 23** is different in that the burden of proving lack of good faith rests with the original owner of the goods.

⑨⑨ *Key debates*

Topic	The importance of delivery and possession in the passing of title
Author/Academic	Louise Merrett
Viewpoint	The article evaluates the operation of statutory exceptions to the *nemo dat* rule. It reviews the exceptions in **SGA, ss 24 and 25** governing sales by a seller or buyer in possession of goods and discusses, with reference to case law, the meaning of 'continue in possession', the practical problems caused by the need for continuous physical possession, and the importance of 'delivery' and 'possession' having consistent meanings throughout the Act.
Source	(2008) 67(2) *Cambridge Law Journal* 376–395

Topic	No justice for innocent purchasers of dishonestly obtained goods
Author/Academic	Catherine Elliott
Viewpoint	This article discusses the injustice resulting from the House of Lords' decision in *Shogun Finance Ltd v Hudson* (2003) on an innocent purchaser of a motor vehicle as it removes from the scope of **s 27** a transaction where a rogue impersonates another person in order to acquire a vehicle either on **hire purchase** terms or under a conditional sale agreement.
Source	[2004] *Journal of Business Law* 381–387

⑦ *Exam questions*

Problem question

Roger acquired on hire purchase a car from Dave's Finance Ltd. Immediately on taking delivery of the car Roger sold it to Peter, a car dealer, who wanted it as a gift for his wife's birthday. Before buying the car, Peter carried out an HPI check on the car and was told by HPI that it was not registered with them as being subject to any finance arrangement. It appears that Dave's Finance Ltd frequently forgot to notify HPI of their finance agreements. Peter's wife didn't like the car so Peter sold it on to his friend George, who is another car dealer. George put the car on his forecourt and sold it to James, a retired local butcher.

Roger has not made any payments to Dave's Finance Ltd who have now found out that Roger no longer has the car. They have contacted James requesting the car's return.

Advise the parties as to who now owns the car.

Essay question

In *Bishopgate Motor Finance Corporation Ltd v Transport Brakes Ltd* [1949] 1 KB 322 Denning LJ stated that:

> In the development of our law, two principles have striven for mastery. The first is for the protection of property: no one can give a better title than he himself possesses. The second is for the protection of commercial transactions: the person who takes in good faith and for value without notice should get a good title. The first principle has held sway for a long time, but it has been modified by the common law itself and by statute so as to meet the needs of our own times.

Critically evaluate the principles of transferring ownership in goods by a non-owner in light of this statement.

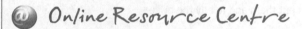 Online Resource Centre

To see an outline answer to this question visit www.oup.com/lawrevision/

#8
Delivery, acceptance, and payment

Key facts

- The seller is under a duty to deliver the goods.

- The buyer is under a duty to accept them and to pay the price.

- Delivery and payment are concurrent conditions.

- 'Delivery' has a specific legal meaning which is different from the colloquial meaning when the grocer delivers your groceries.

- In certain circumstances the buyer will be 'deemed' to have accepted the goods.

- Note the differences that exist between consumer and business buyers.

Introduction

In this chapter, we will consider the duty of the seller to deliver the goods and the duty of the buyer to accept them and to pay the price. We will look at the meanings of 'deliver', 'accept', and 'pay'.

The parties to the contract are free to make whatever agreement they want to make in respect of **delivery** and payment. The provision in the **SGA** in respect of these matters will apply in cases where the parties have not reached agreement themselves.

The duties explained: delivery, acceptance, and payment

Duties of seller and buyer

It is the duty of the seller to deliver the goods, and of the buyer to accept and pay for them, in accordance with the terms of the **contract of sale** (s 27 SGA).

Payment and delivery are concurrent conditions

Unless it is otherwise agreed, **delivery** of the goods and payment of the price are concurrent conditions. This means that the seller must be ready and willing to give possession of the goods to the buyer in exchange for the price and the buyer must be ready and willing to pay the price in exchange for possession of the goods (s 28 SGA).

> ✅ *Looking for extra marks?*
>
> Section 28 only requires the seller to be ready and willing to give possession of the goods to the buyer and the buyer to be ready and willing to pay the price in exchange for possession. There is no requirement for the seller actually to tender **delivery** before he becomes entitled to sue the buyer for the price or for damages provided he can show that the buyer would have refused to accept the goods if delivery had been tendered. All the seller needs to do in such circumstances is to show that he was ready and willing to give possession (*Levey & Co v Goldberg* (1922)).

Delivery

Delivery has a special meaning. It is defined in s 61(1) of the SGA and means the 'voluntary transfer of possession from one person to another'. It must not be confused with its colloquial meaning when the grocer delivers your groceries.

The definition of 'delivery' is rather misleading as it does not require the seller to hand over the goods to the buyer, although in many cases this is what happens. In the case of **hire purchase**, for example, the buyer will already have possession of the goods at the time he

Delivery

✳✳✳✳✳✳✳✳✳✳✳✳

exercises his option to purchase them at the end of the term of hire. 'Delivery' is satisfied because of the different capacity in which the buyer now possesses the goods. Initially, he possessed the goods in the capacity of hirer, but when he exercises his option to purchase, he possesses them as owner. Conversely, goods may be 'delivered' even though the seller retains possession, provided, as above, the capacity in which he is in possession changes. This would occur, for example, in a typical hire purchase 'triangle' where the seller sells the goods to the finance company but delivers them directly to the customer. The goods in this example are never physically delivered to the finance company yet are deemed to have been delivered for the purpose of s 27. A further example of delivery is where the seller hands over control of the goods, for example, by handing over the keys to the premises where they are held. In this example, although actual delivery does not occur, control of the goods is transferred to the buyer which satisfies the legal definition of delivery.

In any event, as we will see, s 29 makes clear that, unless otherwise agreed, it is not the seller's responsibility to convey the goods to the buyer but it is for the buyer to collect them. 'Delivery' has a very specific meaning!

Place and time of delivery

As noted above, unless the parties have otherwise agreed, it is not the seller's responsibility to convey the goods to the buyer but it is for the buyer to collect them. This can be seen from ss 29 (1) and (2):

---

ss 29(1) and (2) SGA:

29(1)   Whether it is for the buyer to take possession of the goods or for the seller to send them to the buyer is a question depending in each case on the contract, express or implied, between the parties.

29(2)   Apart from any such contract, express or implied, the place of delivery is the seller's place of business if he has one, and if not, his residence; except that, if the contract is for the sale of specific goods, which to the knowledge of the parties when the contract is made are in some other place, then that place is the place of delivery.

Within a reasonable time

In cases where the seller is bound to send the goods to the buyer, but no time for sending them has been agreed, the seller is bound to send them within a reasonable time (s 29(3) SGA).

Where the goods are in the possession of a third party

Where the goods at the time of sale are in the possession of a third party, there is no **delivery** by the seller to the buyer unless the third party acknowledges to the buyer that he holds the goods on his behalf (s 29(4) SGA).

Cost of putting the goods into a deliverable state

Unless otherwise agreed, the expenses of and incidental to putting the goods into a deliverable state must be borne by the seller (s 29(6) SGA).

Delivery to a rogue?

The seller's duty on physically delivering the goods to the buyer's premises is limited to handing them over to someone who appears to have the authority to receive them, taking care to see that no-one unauthorised receives them. Therefore once the seller has delivered the goods to such a person, he will not be liable if that person has gained access to the buyer's premises and later misappropriates the goods (*Galbraith and Grant Ltd v Block* (1922)).

Galbraith was followed in *Computer 2000 Distribution Ltd v ICM Computer Solutions Plc* (2004) where a rogue managed to convince the parties to make a **delivery** of equipment to an address where they were signed for by a security guard and then handed over to the rogue, who disappeared. The Court of Appeal held that as the goods had been delivered in accordance with the contract, the buyers were liable to pay for them.

Time of delivery

In ordinary commercial contracts for the sale of goods the rule is that time is prima facie 'of the essence' with respect to **delivery** (*Hartley v Hymans* (1920)).

✔ Looking for extra marks?

As well as stating when time for **delivery** shall be of the essence, you should explain what this means. A seller who has failed to deliver the goods within the stipulated period cannot then require the buyer to accept delivery after that period has expired. This is because he has himself failed to fulfil the bargain (per McCardie J in *Hartley v Hymans*).

Where the time of **delivery** is not met, the buyer is entitled to sue for non-delivery and, if he wishes, treat the contract as **repudiated**. The buyer may be content to accept late delivery of the goods. If he does so, then it must follow that he waives his right to treat the contract as repudiated and reject the goods but will still have the right to sue for damages (s 11(4) SGA). See Chapter 10, 'Remedies of the buyer', p 115.

If the buyer chooses not to repudiate the contract but instead allows an additional specified time for delivery and the goods are still not ready when this additional time has elapsed, he may then treat the contract as repudiated. In effect, by allowing the further specified time for delivery by the giving of reasonable notice he has attached a condition to his waiver which revives his right to treat the contract as repudiated if the goods are still not ready (*Charles Rickards Ltd v Oppenheim* (1950)).

Where the buyer is to collect the goods and the contract does not stipulate a time for delivery, then the seller must be ready to hand them over in return for payment on demand by the buyer at any time after the contract is made. However, the seller may treat any such demand as ineffectual unless it is made at a reasonable hour; and what is a reasonable hour is a question of fact (s 29(5) SGA). If, following such a reasonable demand, the seller fails to hand over the goods, he is in breach of condition, which the buyer may treat as a repudiation of the contract and thus sue for non-delivery. See Chapter 10, 'Remedies of the buyer', p 115.

Delivery of the wrong quantity

Section 30 of the SGA deals with the situation where the seller delivers the wrong quantity of goods to the buyer. This refers to both a quantity less than he contracted to sell (s 30(1)) as well as a quantity larger than he contracted to sell (s 30(2)).

Where the seller delivers less than he contracted to sell

Where the seller delivers to the buyer a quantity of goods less than he contracted to sell, the buyer may reject them, but if the buyer accepts the goods so delivered he must pay for them at the contract rate (s 30(1)).

In so far as the goods that were not delivered, the buyer is entitled to sue for non-delivery.

Where the seller delivers more than he contracted to sell

Where the seller delivers to the buyer a quantity of goods larger than he contracted to sell, the buyer may accept the goods included in the contract and reject the rest, or he may reject the whole (s 30(2)).

Where the seller delivers to the buyer a quantity of goods larger than he contracted to sell and the buyer accepts the whole of the goods so delivered he must pay for them at the contract rate (s 30(3)).

Where the buyer rejects any of the goods under this section, then he is entitled to sue for non-delivery in respect of those goods.

Where the buyer does not deal as a consumer

Where the buyer does not deal as a consumer, s 30(2A) provides that the right of rejection set out in ss 30(1) and (2) cannot be exercised by the buyer if the excess or shortfall is so slight that it would be unreasonable for him to reject them.

Revision tip

Section 30(2A) is expressed only in terms of when the buyer does *not* deal as a consumer. There is no corresponding provision explaining what happens in the case of a buyer who *does* deal as a consumer, although it seems reasonable to conclude that s 30(2A) implies that a buyer who does deal as a consumer will be entitled to reject the goods in the circumstances set out in s 30(2A).

An example of a case where the buyers attempted to reject an entire consignment of goods for a slight breach is *Shipton, Anderson & Co v Weil Bros & Co* (1912) where the sellers were entitled to deliver to the buyers 4,950 tons of wheat. They in fact delivered 55 lbs more than this maximum quantity which, at the contract price, would have added about four shillings to the overall price. The sellers did not charge any additional money. The buyers sought to reject the entire consignment on the ground that the quantity tendered for **delivery** was 55 lbs greater than the contract quantity. Lush J held that as the excess quantity was so trifling and the sellers had not even claimed the price of the excess wheat, the sellers had substantially performed the contract and the buyers were not entitled to reject the whole consignment under s 30(2) of the 1893 SGA.

Delivery by instalments

Unless otherwise agreed, the buyer is not bound to accept **delivery** by instalments (s 31(1)).

> *Revision tip*
> Watch out for a problem where the seller delivers short and argues that he will make up the shortfall at a later stage. Unless the buyer agrees to this, s 31(1) will not excuse such short delivery.

Where only part of the goods that were ordered have been delivered and accepted, the buyers will be entitled to refuse to accept later deliveries of the balance of the goods and will only be liable to pay pro rata for the goods accepted (*Behrend & Co Ltd v Produce Brokers Co Ltd* (1920)).

Where there is a contract for the sale of goods to be delivered by stated instalments, which are to be separately paid for, and the seller makes defective deliveries in respect of one or more instalments, or the buyer neglects or refuses to take delivery of or pay for one or more instalments, it is a question in each case depending on the terms of the contract and the circumstances of the case whether the breach of contract is a repudiation of the whole contract or whether it is a severable breach giving rise to a claim for compensation but not to a right to treat the whole contract as repudiated (s 31(2)).

In the case of a severable contract, just because the buyer has accepted one or more of the instalments it does not prevent him from rejecting later instalments for breach of condition (*Jackson v Rotax Motor and Cycle Company* (1910)).

But, in the case of a sale of goods under a severable contract and where only *some* of the instalments are defective, whether the buyer will be entitled to reject the *entirety* of the goods and regard the entire contract as repudiated will depend largely on the quantitative ratio of the breach to the contract as a whole and the likelihood of the breach manifesting itself in subsequent instalments (*Maple Flock Co Ltd v Universal Furniture Products (Wembley) Ltd* (1934)).

Delivery

✳✳✳✳✳✳✳✳✳✳✳✳

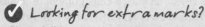 **Looking for extra marks?**

Where **delivery** is to be made by instalments, parties will often contract on the basis that 'each instalment is to be considered as a separate contract'. In this type of case, the courts are likely to hold that there is only one contract, although severable. This means that if there is a breach that is sufficiently serious the entire contract might be repudiated (*Smyth & Co Ltd v TD Bailey Son & Co* (1940)).

Delivery to a carrier

Where the seller is authorised or required to send the goods to the buyer, **delivery** of the goods to a carrier (whether named by the buyer or not) for the purpose of transmission to the buyer is prima facie deemed to be a delivery of the goods to the buyer (s 32(1)).

However, where the buyer deals as a consumer, s 32(1) will not apply, and delivery of the goods to a carrier will not be delivery to the buyer (s 32(4)).

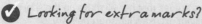 **Looking for extra marks?**

Rule 5(2) in s 18 of the SGA (see Chapter 3, 'Passing of property and risk', p 31) has similar effect to the provision in **s 32(1)**. You will recall from p 37, that **Rule 5(2)** explains that, subject to contrary intention, where the seller delivers the goods to a carrier for the purpose of transmission to the buyer and does not reserve the right of disposal, he is to be taken to have unconditionally appropriated the goods to the contract.

Unless otherwise authorised by the buyer, the seller must make such contract with the carrier on behalf of the buyer as may be reasonable having regard to the nature of the goods and the other circumstances of the case. If the seller fails to do so, and the goods are lost or damaged in course of transit, the buyer may decline to treat the **delivery** to the carrier as a delivery to himself or may hold the seller responsible in damages (s 32(2)). Whether or not the seller has made the contract with the carrier on reasonable terms for the buyer's benefit will be a matter of fact but the seller will not have satisfied this requirement where he contracts with the carrier 'at the owner's risk' where the same carrier would have contracted to deliver the goods at his own risk for the same price (*Thomas Young & Sons v Hobson & Partner* (1949)).

The buyer is not bound to return rejected goods

Unless otherwise agreed, where goods are delivered to the buyer and he refuses to accept them, having the right to do so, he is not bound to return them to the seller, but it is sufficient if he intimates to the seller that he refuses to accept them (s 36).

Acceptance

It was explained above that s 27 SGA provides that it is the duty of the seller to deliver the goods, and of the buyer *to accept* and pay for them, in accordance with the terms of the **contract of sale**.

Revision tip

Don't confuse the buyer's duty to accept the goods with him taking **delivery** of them. **Acceptance** in law is far more complex than that!

Acceptance is explained in s 35. A buyer will be deemed to have accepted the goods when he does one of three things:

1. intimates to the seller that he has accepted them (s 35(1)(a)); or

2. when the goods have been delivered to him, he does any act in relation to them which is inconsistent with the ownership of the seller (s 35(1)(b)); or

3. when after the lapse of a reasonable time he retains the goods without intimating to the seller that he has rejected them (s 35(4)).

However, where goods are delivered to the buyer, and he has not previously examined them, he is *not* deemed to have accepted them until he has had a reasonable opportunity of examining them for the purpose of either ascertaining whether they are in conformity with the contract, or, in the case of a contract for sale by sample, of comparing the bulk with the sample (s 35(2)). In the case of a *consumer* buyer, s 35(3) makes clear that he cannot lose his right to rely on s 35(2) by agreement, waiver, or otherwise.

✅ *Looking for extra marks?*

You should explain the practical significance of **s 35(3)**. It is common for sellers to require a buyer to sign a delivery or acceptance note confirming that the goods are in satisfactory condition and are accepted by the buyer. **Section 35(3)** protects a *consumer buyer* in such a case and a *consumer buyer* will not be deemed to have accepted the goods by express intimation. Business buyers, on the other hand, can exclude **s 35** by agreement, although this will be subject to the test of reasonableness under **UCTA 1977**; see Chapter 5, 'Exclusion and limitation clauses', p 57.

Section 34 extends to the buyer, on request to the seller, a right to examine the goods for the purpose of ascertaining whether they are in conformity with the contract and, in the case of a contract for sale by sample, of comparing the bulk with the sample.

Repairs

A buyer will not be deemed to have accepted the goods merely because he asks for, or agrees to, their repair (s 35(6)(a)). You should not assume that s 35(6)(a) has the effect of 'stopping the clock' for the purpose of determining what is a reasonable time, although the courts are more likely to treat it that way where the buyer has acted reasonably and especially where he is awaiting information from the seller as to the problem and the likelihood of remedying the same.

J&H Ritchie Ltd v Lloyd Ltd [2007] UKHL 9

A farmer bought some equipment which, on its first use, was found to be faulty. He returned it to the seller for inspection and possible repair. After a few weeks, the seller informed the farmer that the equipment had been repaired and was ready for collection. The seller would not tell the farmer what had been done but insisted that the equipment was now to 'factory-gate specification'. The farmer wanted to know what had been done to the equipment and was concerned because he would have been unable to test it properly until the following season. As a result of his concern, the farmer sought to reject the equipment.

The House of Lords noted that prior to the introduction of s 35(6)(a), it was questionable whether asking the seller to repair defective goods might amount to an implied intimation of **acceptance** by the buyer or to an inconsistent act that would prevent him from rejecting the goods. Parties will often attempt to have defective goods remedied but the very informality of these kinds of arrangement gives rise to a problem in identifying the legal situation with regard to the right of rejection. When the buyer took the goods to the seller for inspection and repair, the parties entered into a separate 'inspection and repair' agreement.

Their Lordships, therefore, felt it appropriate to imply a term into that agreement that, so long as the seller was performing his obligations under this agreement, the buyer was not entitled to exercise his right to rescind the **contract of sale**. Although the right to reject is lost when a buyer decides to accept the goods or is deemed to have accepted them, such election could not reasonably be expected to be made until the buyer had received the necessary information to enable him to make an informed decision and the seller could not refuse to provide this information. The seller was under an implied obligation to provide the buyer with the necessary information requested and in the absence of this information, the buyer was entitled to reject the goods even though they had, in fact, been repaired to a satisfactory standard. The seller's refusal to supply the information amounted to a material breach of the inspection and repair agreement which entitled the buyer to rescind it and to refuse to collect the repaired equipment. Once the buyer had rescinded the inspection and repair agreement, there was nothing to prevent him from exercising his right to rescind the sale contract and reclaim the purchase price of the goods bought.

Revision tip

It is important to appreciate that, in respect of a contract of sale of goods, a buyer will lose the right to reject the goods if he is deemed to have accepted them within the meaning of s 35.

Lapse of reasonable time

We saw under 'Acceptance', p 107, that a buyer will be deemed to have accepted the goods when, after the lapse of a reasonable time, he retains the goods without intimating to the seller that he has rejected them (s 35(4)).

But what is a reasonable time? Section 59 tells us that what is a reasonable time is a question of fact. Unfortunately, the cases are not much more helpful and it is very difficult to predict from them the outcome as most cases turn on their own specific facts. Some examples might assist (see Table 8.1):

Table 8.1 A reasonable time to reject goods?

Case	Time before rejecting goods
Bernstein v Pamson Motors (Golders Green) Ltd (1987)	3 weeks was held to be too long before rejecting a new car that had been driven just 140 miles
Clegg v Andersson (2003)	A delay of 7 months was not too long to wait before rejecting a yacht
Jones v Callagher (2004)	17 months was held to be too long before rejecting kitchen units
Fiat Auto Financial Services v Connelly (2007)	9 months and 40,000 miles was not too long to wait before rejecting a taxicab

Goods purchased for the purpose of resale

Goods will often be purchased for the purpose of resale. Where the goods have been purchased for resale, it will often be the case that a particular defect will only be discovered when the goods have been resold. Therefore, a reasonable time in which to intimate rejection for the purpose of s 35(4) would usually be the time taken to resell the goods together with a further period of time during which the ultimate purchaser would have the opportunity to test the goods and determine their fitness for purpose (*Truk (UK) Ltd v Tokmakidis GmbH* (2000)).

Partial acceptance/rejection

Finally, you should note that s 35A (which was added to the SGA by the Sale and Supply of Goods Act 1994) gives a buyer a right of 'partial rejection'. This might be of assistance to a buyer where the seller delivers a consignment of goods where only some of them are defective or where some of the goods delivered were not contracted for. Section 35A applies, unless there is a contrary intention, to cases where a buyer has the right to reject the goods by reason of a breach on the part of the seller that affects some or all of the goods. In such a case, where he accepts some of the goods, he does not by accepting them lose his right to reject the remainder.

Payment

We have seen ('Payment and delivery are concurrent conditions', p 101) that s 28 provides that in the absence of agreement to the contrary, **delivery** of the goods and payment of the price are concurrent conditions. This means that the buyer does not need to make payment until delivery is made. It also means that a buyer is not entitled to credit terms (unless, of course, the seller agrees).

Where the buyer has paid the price and the seller has not delivered the goods, then the buyer will be entitled to recover the price paid plus interest. This is because the consideration for his payment will have failed (s 54 SGA).

However, where the goods have been destroyed at a time they were at the buyer's risk, then the buyer remains under a duty to pay the price and he will not be able to escape payment by arguing that delivery in these circumstances will be impossible. Risk was discussed in Chapter 3, 'Risk', p 33.

How is the price ascertained?

Section 8(1) of the SGA sets out how the price is ascertained:

- it may be fixed by the contract; or
- it may be left to be fixed in a manner agreed by the contract; or
- it may be determined by the course of dealing between the parties.

Where the price is not determined under s 8(1) the buyer must pay a reasonable price (s 8(2)). What is a reasonable price is a question of fact dependent on the circumstances of each particular case (s 8(3)).

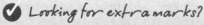 **Looking for extra marks?**

If the contract says nothing about the price and there have been no previous dealings between the parties, you should consider whether there is any binding contract at all or whether it is void for failure to agree an essential term (*May and Butcher Limited v The King* (1934)).

Unless a different intention appears from the terms of the contract, stipulations as to time of payment are not 'of the essence' of a **contract of sale** (s 10(1) SGA). Therefore, late payment of the price will be a breach of **warranty** only and will not entitle the seller to treat the contract as repudiated. However, it is open to the parties to agree that payment of the price is 'of the essence' of the contract denoting that timely payment is a condition. In such a case, late payment will amount to a repudiatory breach of the contract (*Lombard North Central Plc v Butterworth* (1987)). However, the requirement to pay a deposit, including the time for payment, will ordinarily be a **condition** of a contract for sale of land and time will be 'of the essence' in relation to the date for payment. Failure to make timely payment of a deposit will, in this context, amount to a repudiatory breach of contract (*Samarenko v Dawn Hill House Ltd* (2013)).

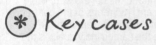 **Key cases**

Case	Facts	Held/Principle
***Behrend & Co Ltd v Produce Brokers Co Ltd* [1920] 3 KB 530**	The parties entered into two similar contracts for the supply of cotton seed to be shipped in Alexandria and delivered in London. Payment was made in exchange for shipping documents. On the arrival of the ship in London, and after payment for the goods by the buyers, only a portion of the seed was delivered. The ship then left with the remainder of the seed on board in order to discharge other cargo. The ship returned to London two weeks later and the balance of the seed was tendered to the buyers, but they refused to accept it. The buyers retained the portion which had been delivered and claimed repayment of the price paid for the rejected portion.	The court held that when the delivery had begun the buyers were entitled to receive the whole quantity that they had ordered before the ship left the port. In the circumstances, the buyers were entitled to keep the part actually delivered and to reject the balance and to be repaid the price of the balance that had been prepaid. Unless the parties agree that delivery could be made by instalments then the buyer is not bound to accept delivery by instalments.
***Charles Rickards Ltd v Oppenheim* [1950] 1 KB 616**	In August 1947, O placed an order with CR to build a body onto the chassis of a car. It was understood that CR could obtain it within six or seven months at the latest. From the following March, O pressed for delivery. In June, O wrote to CR telling them that he would not accept delivery after 25 July. When O was informed by CR that the body of the car would not be ready by that date, he cancelled his order. CR completed the car in the October, but O refused to accept delivery. CR sued for the price.	The Court of Appeal held that although the initial stipulation making time of the essence was waived by O's requests for delivery after March 1948, this did not disentitle him from giving at a later time a reasonable notice making time for delivery of the essence. O's June letter constituted a reasonable notice and was, therefore, valid so as to make time of the essence of the contract. The result was that CR's claim against O failed. If the buyer chooses not to repudiate the contract but instead allows an additional specified time for delivery and the goods are still not ready when this additional time has elapsed he may then treat the contract as repudiated. In effect, by allowing the further specified

Key cases

****

Case	Facts	Held/Principle
		time for delivery by the giving of reasonable notice he has attached a condition to his waiver which revives his right to treat the contract as repudiated if the goods are still not ready.
Computer 2000 Distribution Ltd v ICM Solutions Computer Plc [2004] EWCA Civ 1634	A rogue, purportedly acting on behalf of a reputable company, placed three substantial orders with ICM for electrical goods. ICM acted on the orders and in turn placed orders with its suppliers for the goods. In accordance with the fraudster's instructions, ICM requested that the suppliers deliver the goods to a named individual at a given business address. A security guard at the business address signed for the goods. The goods were later collected by the named individual.	The Court of Appeal held that as the goods had been delivered in accordance with the contract, the buyers were liable to pay for them. The terms of the contract showed that the goods were to be delivered to the named individual. As the goods had been collected by that named individual it followed that the suppliers had delivered the goods in accordance with the terms of ICM's contract. The fact that they had been signed for by the security guard did not matter. It was found that the security guard had authority to receive goods on behalf of persons carrying on business at the business address and there was no reason for the carrier to suspect that the named individual and the reputable company were not carrying on business at the business address.
Galbraith and Grant Ltd v Block [1922] 2 KB 155	The sellers, who were wine merchants, sued a licensed victualler for the cost of a case of champagne which they had sold to them on terms that it should be delivered at the buyer's premises. The buyer argued that the champagne was never delivered to him. The sellers engaged a carrier to deliver the champagne to the buyer's premises. The delivery driver said that he delivered the goods to a man at a side entrance at the buyer's premises, and that someone on the premises signed the delivery note in the name of the buyer. The buyer argued that his premises were closed at the time this delivery was meant to have occurred, that he had never received the goods, and that the signature was not his nor had he authorised anyone to sign it.	The court held that a seller who is told to deliver goods at the buyer's premises discharges his obligations if he delivers them there without negligence to a person apparently having authority to receive them. He cannot know what authority the actual recipient has. His duty is to deliver the goods at the proper place and to take all proper care to see that no unauthorised person receives them. He is under no obligation to do more. If the buyer has been unfortunate enough to have had access to his premises obtained by some apparently respectable person who takes his goods and signs for them in his absence, the loss must fall on him, and not on the innocent carrier or seller.

Case	Facts	Held/Principle
Jackson v Rotax Motor and Cycle Company [1910] 2 KB 937	The buyer purchased a large number of motor horns of different descriptions and prices. The horns were delivered in several instalments. After accepting the first instalment the buyer rejected the later instalments on the ground that they were not of (what was then referred to as) merchantable quality. At first instance, it was found that a large proportion of the horns were dented and badly polished owing to defective packing and careless workmanship, but that they could easily and cheaply have been made merchantable. As a result, the court refused to hold that the consignment as a whole was unmerchantable, but made an allowance to the buyer in respect of the defective goods.	The Court of Appeal held that acceptance of the first instalment of the goods did not preclude the buyer from rejecting the later instalment and that on the facts of this case the buyer was justified in rejecting the later instalments as they were not of merchantable quality. The earlier decision was reversed.
Maple Flock Co Ltd v Universal Furniture Products (Wembley) Ltd [1934] 1 KB 148	There was a severable contract for the sale of 100 tons of flock to be delivered by instalments. The first 15 instalments of the flock were satisfactory but the 16th was defective. This was followed by four more satisfactory instalments. The buyers sought to repudiate the entire contract. The Court of Appeal held that they could not do so.	The Court of Appeal said that where there is a sale of goods under a severable contract and only some of the instalments are defective, whether the buyer will be entitled to reject the entirety of the goods and regard the entire contract as repudiated will turn on the true meaning of s 31(2) with the main tests to be considered being, first, the quantitative ratio which the breach bears to the contract as a whole and, second, the degree of probability that such a breach will be repeated.
Thomas Young & Sons v Hobson & Partner (1949) 65 TLR 365	The seller sold seven electric engines to the buyer. It was a term of the contract that the engines should be delivered by rail. The seller sent the engines at the buyer's risk. The seller loaded the engines onto the rail in box wagons but failed adequately to secure them, which resulted in them arriving in a damaged condition. The buyer refused to accept them from the railway. There was no difference in the freight costs as between 'owners' risk' and 'company's risk'.	The Court of Appeal held that the seller had failed in its duty under s 32(2) of the (1893) SGA to make such contract with the carrier on behalf of the buyer as was reasonable having regard to the nature of the goods and the other circumstances of the case, and that the buyer was accordingly entitled to refuse to treat the delivery to the railway company as delivery to itself and was therefore entitled to reject the goods.

Exam question
****

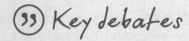 **Key debates**

Topic	Sale of goods—delivery
Author/Academic	Paul Dobson
Viewpoint	Considers the Court of Appeal judgment in *Computer 2000 Distribution Ltd v ICM Computer Solutions Plc* on whether the defendant was liable to pay the cost of goods it had ordered from three suppliers, which had been correctly delivered according to its instructions to an individual who was found to be a fraudster, or whether it was relieved of this liability by the fact that it had never received the goods.
Source	(2005) 45 *Student Law Review* 12

Topic	Repair, rejection & rescission: an uneasy resolution
Author/Academic	Kelvin Low
Viewpoint	Comments on the House of Lords ruling in *J&H Ritchie Ltd v Lloyd Ltd* on whether the buyer of defective agricultural equipment was entitled to reject the goods as materially defective after they had been returned to the vendor for inspection and repair and where the vendor refused to disclose the nature of the problem.
Source	(2007) 123 *Law Quarterly Review* 536

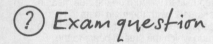 **Exam question**

Essay question

Although the seller is under a duty to deliver the goods, this obligation might not be as straightforward as it might first appear.

Critically evaluate the seller's duty to deliver the goods.

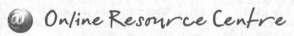 **Online Resource Centre**

To see an outline answer to this question visit www.oup.com/lawrevision/

#9

Remedies of the unpaid seller

Key facts

- This chapter examines the remedies that are available to a seller who is unpaid.

- There are two different types of remedies available to the unpaid seller: real remedies and personal remedies. Both will be discussed in this chapter.

- A real remedy is a remedy against the goods. An example of a real remedy is a lien over the goods.

- A personal remedy is a remedy against the buyer personally. An example of a personal remedy is an action for the price.

Introduction

In this chapter, we will consider the specific remedies available to a seller who has not been paid by the buyer and the position when the buyer refuses delivery of the goods.

The remedies available to an unpaid seller are set out in **Parts V and VI of the SGA 1979**. **Part V** deals with the rights of the unpaid seller *against the goods* and **Part VI** deals with his remedies *against the buyer for breach of contract*.

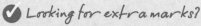 ✅ *Looking for extra marks?*

You should explain that:

- remedies that are sought against the goods in question are known as 'real remedies'; and
- remedies that are sought personally against the buyer are known as 'personal remedies'.

When is a seller unpaid?

Section 38(1) defines an unpaid seller in the following terms:

(a) when the whole of the price has not been paid or tendered;

(b) when a bill of exchange or other negotiable instrument has been received as conditional payment, and the condition on which it was received has not been fulfilled by reason of the dishonour of the instrument or otherwise.

Revision tip

The typical situation envisaged by s 38(1)(b) is where the buyer tenders a cheque or other negotiable instrument to the seller in payment for the goods but that cheque or instrument has not been honoured. In this situation, s 38(1)(b) provides that the tendering of such instrument is to be treated as a 'conditional payment' which, until honoured, means that the seller is an unpaid seller.

Notwithstanding the conditionality of payment attached to payment by cheque, the situation with credit cards is entirely the opposite and is treated as absolute even if the credit card company fails to pay the seller. In such a case, the seller (although unpaid) will have no claim against the buyer (*Re Charge Card Services Ltd (No 2) (1989)*).

Real remedies: the rights of the unpaid seller against the goods

These are set out in **s 39 SGA** and exist notwithstanding that the property in the goods may already have passed to the buyer. These rights exist by implication of law, and are:

- a **lien** on the goods or right to retain them for the price while the seller is in possession of them;
- in case of the insolvency of the buyer, a right of stopping the goods in transit after the seller has parted with the possession of them;

- a limited right of resale (limited by the **SGA**);
- where the property in the goods has not passed to the buyer, the unpaid seller has (in addition to his other remedies) a right of withholding delivery similar to and co-extensive with his rights of lien or retention and stoppage in transit where the property has passed to the buyer.

The unpaid seller's lien

The unpaid seller's **lien** is set out in **s 41 of the SGA**. The unpaid seller of goods who is in possession of them is entitled to retain possession of them until payment or tender of the price in the following circumstances:

- where the goods have been sold without any stipulation as to credit;
- where the goods have been sold on credit but the term of credit has expired; or
- where the buyer becomes insolvent.

✅ Looking for extra marks?

You should explain that the seller may exercise his **lien** or right of retention notwithstanding that he is in possession of the goods as **agent**, **bailee**, or custodier for the buyer (**s 41(2) SGA**). But in order to exercise a lien, he must be in possession of the goods (**s 39(1)(a) SGA**). In a different context, the Court of Appeal has held that it is not possible to exercise a **lien** over intangible property such as an electronic database (*Your Response Ltd v Datateam Business Media Ltd* (2014)).

Revision tip

A problem might arise where the unpaid seller has already made part delivery of the goods. The question then is, does he need to deliver the remainder whilst money is still owing? **Section 42** answers this question by explaining that in this situation he may exercise his **lien** or right of retention on the remainder of the goods, unless the part delivery has been made in circumstances which show an agreement to waive the lien or right of retention (**s 42 SGA**).

Termination of the unpaid seller's lien

The unpaid seller of goods will lose his **lien** or right of retention in respect of the goods in the following circumstances (**s 43**):

- when he delivers the goods to a carrier or other **bailee** or custodier for the purpose of transmission to the buyer without reserving the right of disposal of the goods;
- when the buyer or his **agent** lawfully obtains possession of the goods; or
- by waiver of the lien or right of retention.

✅ Looking for extra marks?

Notwithstanding any **lien** he might have, an unpaid seller still wants his money. He is, therefore, entitled to sue for the price. If he succeeds, he will obtain judgment against the buyer. His right ➡

➡ to sue and his lien over the goods are co-existing rights. In practice, the seller, who must be in possession of the goods (see **s 41**), will simply keep hold of them. Having retained possession of the goods, if he then succeeds in an action for the price and obtains judgment against the buyer he *still* retains his lien or right of retention over the goods (**s 43(2)**). This can be very valuable in cases where, notwithstanding the judgment, the buyer still fails to pay the price, maybe because of insolvency.

Stoppage in transit

If the buyer becomes insolvent, the unpaid seller who has parted with possession of the goods, has the right of stopping them in transit. In other words, provided the goods are in the course of transit to the buyer, he may resume possession of them, and may retain them until payment or tender of the price (s 44).

✓ Looking for extra marks?

You should be able to explain precisely when goods are deemed to be in transit. This is explained in **s 45**. Goods are deemed to be in transit from the time they are delivered to a carrier for the purpose of transmission to the buyer, until the buyer or his **agent** takes delivery of them from the carrier. This is probably stating the obvious but there are a number of additional points to consider and these are worth noting:

- If the buyer or his agent obtains delivery of the goods *before* their arrival at the appointed destination, the transit is at an end there and then (**s 45(2)**).
- If the buyer rejects the goods, and the carrier continues in possession of them, the transit is *not* deemed to be at an end, even if the seller refuses to receive them back (**s 45(4)**).
- If the carrier wrongfully refuses to deliver the goods to the buyer, the transit is deemed to be at an end (**s 45(6)**).
- Where a part delivery of the goods has been made to the buyer, the remainder of the goods may be stopped in transit, unless it was agreed that by making the part delivery the seller was to give up possession of the whole of the goods (**s 45(7)**).

How the unpaid seller stops the goods in transit

The unpaid seller may exercise his right of stoppage in transit in two different ways (s 46(1)):

1. either by taking actual possession of the goods; or
2. by giving notice of his claim to the carrier who has possession of the goods.

Revision tip

As the goods are already in transit to the buyer, the seller needs to act quickly if he is to stop delivery being made. Therefore, the notice referred to in **s 46(1)** may be given either to the ➡

➡ person who is in actual possession of the goods (i.e. the driver) or to his **principal** (s 46(2)). If the notice is given to the principal, it will not be effective unless it was given at a time and in such circumstances that he may communicate it to his servant in time to prevent the delivery being made to the buyer (s 46(3)).

Where the buyer has already resold the goods

Some buyers will purchase goods for the purpose of resale. In such circumstances, the unpaid seller's right of **lien** or retention or stoppage in transit is not affected by any sale or other disposition of the goods which the buyer may have made, unless the seller has agreed to it (s 47(1)).

Where the seller rescinds the contract and resells the goods

The first thing to note is that a **contract of sale** is not rescinded by the mere exercise by an unpaid seller of his right of **lien** or retention or stoppage in transit (s 48(1)).

However, s 48(2) provides that where an unpaid seller who has exercised his right of lien or retention in transit then resells the goods, the (new) buyer acquires a good title to them as against the original buyer.

If the goods sold, but not paid for, are of a perishable nature, or where the unpaid seller gives notice to the buyer of his intention to resell the unpaid goods, and the buyer does not within a reasonable time pay or tender the price, then the unpaid seller will be entitled to resell the goods and recover from the original buyer damages for any loss occasioned by his breach of contract (s 48(3)).

Revision Tip

You should note that where the seller expressly reserves the right of resale to protect his position in case the buyer fails to pay for the goods, then if the buyer does fail to pay for the goods and the seller goes on to resell the goods, the original **contract of sale** is rescinded and this is without prejudice to any claim the seller may have against the defaulting buyer for damages (s 48(4)).

Personal remedies: the unpaid seller's remedies against the buyer for breach of contract

Perhaps the most important remedies available to the unpaid seller are:

- an action for the price (s 49); and
- damages for non-acceptance of the goods (s 50).

Action for the price

Where, under a **contract of sale**, the property in the goods has passed to the buyer and he wrongfully neglects or refuses to pay for the goods according to the terms of the contract, the seller may commence an action against him for the price of the goods (s 49(1)).

Where, under a **contract of sale**, the price is payable on a **day certain** irrespective of **delivery** and the buyer wrongfully neglects or refuses to pay such price, the seller may maintain an action for the price, although the property in the goods has not passed and the goods have not been appropriated to the contract (s 49(2)).

In Chapter 4 ('Retention of title clauses', p 45) we discussed the effects of the Court of Appeal's decision in *FG Wilson (Engineering) Ltd v John Holt & Co (Liverpool) Ltd* (2014) where the seller was denied a claim for the price because of a **retention of title** clause whereby the seller had retained ownership of the goods until payment. The court held that the seller could not bring an action for the price under s 49(1) because that remedy is only available where property in the goods has passed to the buyer. Furthermore, the court held that s 49(1) provided an exclusive (rather than a permissive) remedy for the price which meant that no claim for the price could be brought unless s 49 applied. Sellers should, therefore, consider the effect of s 49(2) and make the price payable on a **day certain**, irrespective of delivery, so as to ensure they do not fall foul of the protection they thought they had secured when incorporating a **retention of title** clause into their contract of sale. It would also be prudent for sellers to provide expressly in the contract that the price is payable even though property has not passed.

> ### ✅ *Looking for extra marks?*
>
> Section 49(2) applies in cases where the parties have agreed that payment will be made upon the occurrence of a specific event rather than on a particular date. This is known as a payment on a **day certain**. The event might be something like the completion of the manufacturing stage of the goods or some other stage in the process that the parties have agreed should be the **day certain** for the purpose of payment (*Workman Clark & Co Ltd v Lloyd Brazileno* (1908)).
>
> Because an action for the price is a debt claim, it has a distinct advantage over a claim in damages. This is because concepts such as remoteness, causation, and mitigation do not arise in debt claims; neither do questions of assessment or contributory negligence.

Damages for non-acceptance of the goods

The unpaid seller is entitled to commence an action against the buyer for damages if he wrongfully neglects or refuses to accept and pay for the goods (s 50(1)). This is known as an action in damages for non-acceptance.

The measure of damages—the general rule

The measure of damages is the estimated loss directly and naturally resulting, in the ordinary course of events, from the buyer's breach of contract (s 50(2)).

Where there is an available market

The method used for calculating the seller's loss 'directly and naturally resulting in the ordinary course of events from the buyer's breach of contract' is explained in s 50(3). This provides that where there is an available market for the goods in question, the measure of damages is prima facie to be ascertained by the difference between the contract price and the market or current price at the time or times when the goods ought to have been accepted or (if no time was fixed for acceptance) at the time of the refusal to accept.

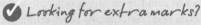 ✔ Looking for extra marks?

Don't forget the provisions of s 54 SGA which provides that the seller may *also* be entitled to claim *special damages* based on the loss arising from any special circumstances of which the parties were aware at the time the contract was made.

What amounts to an 'available market' for the purpose of s 50(3) is more difficult to explain. At one time, it was said to refer to something like a Corn Exchange or Cotton Exchange where 'there was a fair market where they could have found [another] purchaser' (*Dunkirk Colliery Co v Lever* (1878)). But times have now moved on and Upjohn J stated in *Thompson Ltd v Robinson (Gunmakers) Ltd* (1955) that had the matter been *res integra* (a point not governed by an earlier decision, or by a rule of law), he would have found that an 'available market' merely meant that the situation in the particular trade in the particular area was such that the particular goods could freely be sold, and that there was a demand sufficient to absorb readily all the goods that were thrust on it, so that if a purchaser defaulted, the goods in question could readily be disposed of. This now appears to be how an available market will today be defined.

Disapplication of the available market rule

Section 50(3) only lays down a 'prima facie' rule for the measurement of damages. This prima facie rule refers to an available market. The available market rule could, in certain circumstances, result in an incorrect or unfair assessment of damages and it can therefore be displaced when there is no means of readily disposing of the goods that were contracted to be sold or otherwise where it would be unjust to apply the rule (*Thompson Ltd v Robinson (Gunmakers) Ltd* (1955)). *Thompson* can be contrasted with *Charter v Sullivan* (1957), a case similar to *Thompson* except that the car in question was a Hillman Minx, which the seller acknowledged they could sell as many as they could get hold of. They were, therefore, only entitled to nominal damages.

Revision tip

Section 50(3) sets out the prima facie measure for the calculation of damages in an available market. It should go without saying that if there is no available market then s 50(3) will not apply. In such a situation, the measure of damages will depend on whether the seller had, at the time →

Key cases
✱✱✱✱✱✱✱✱✱✱

> ➡ the buyer wrongfully refused to take delivery of the goods, already manufactured or procured the goods in question. If he has, then the prima facie measure of damages will likely be the difference between the contract price and the value of the goods at the time of the buyer's breach (*Harlow & Jones Ltd v Panex (International) Ltd* (1967)).

The available market rule and unique goods

The market price rule in s 50(3) will not apply to unique goods. This is because with unique goods the seller can only sell them once and he will not be allowed to make more than one profit. The sale of second-hand cars has been held to fall into the unique goods rule where no available market within the meaning of s 50(3) exists and the damages recoverable will be limited to the particular loss sustained on the particular transaction (*Lazenby Garages Ltd v Wright* (1976)).

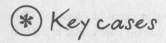 **Looking for extra marks?**

We saw above ('Damages for non-acceptance of the goods', p 120) that s 50(1) provides that the unpaid seller is entitled to commence an action against the buyer for damages if he wrongfully neglects or refuses to accept and pay for the goods. You should also consider the position if the buyer refuses to take delivery of the goods. **Section 37 SGA** provides that when the seller is ready and willing to deliver the goods and requests the buyer to take delivery of them, and the buyer does not within a reasonable time after such request take delivery of the goods, he is liable to the seller for any loss occasioned by his neglect or refusal to take delivery, and also for a reasonable charge for the care and custody of the goods.

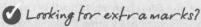 **Key cases**

Case	Facts	Held/Principle
Charter v Sullivan [1957] 2 QB 117	The buyer failed to accept delivery of a Hillman Minx car which he had contracted to buy from the seller. Shortly after the buyer's breach, the seller resold the car for the same price to another purchaser, the retail price having been fixed by the manufacturer. The seller claimed the loss of profit on the repudiated sale. Demand for Hillman Minxes exceeded the supply which the seller was able to obtain. In other words,	The Court of Appeal held that on the facts of the case the seller had failed to prove any loss arising from the buyer's breach. The case was one to which s 50(2) of the (1893) **SGA** should be applied in preference to s 50(3). **Section 50(2)** explains that the measure of damages is the estimated loss directly and naturally resulting, in the ordinary course of events, from the buyer's breach of contract. The seller was entitled to recover only nominal damages. Sellers LJ explained that where a seller can prove that a profit has been

Case	Facts	Held/Principle
	the number of sales of Minxes the seller could make was limited to the number of the cars he could obtain. He, therefore, did not lose a sale or any profit.	irretrievably lost on a sale of goods by the buyer's default it would be recoverable as damages in accordance with **s 50(2)**. But where there has been a resale of the goods, the seller has the burden of proving a loss of profit beyond that which on the face of it has been recouped by the resale.
FG Wilson (Engineering) Ltd v John Holt & Co (Liverpool) Ltd [2014] 1 WLR 2365	Wilson was a manufacturer and seller of generators and parts. Wilson's standard terms included **a retention of title** clause providing that title to the purchased goods did not pass until Holt had paid in full. When Holt failed to pay a number of invoices, Wilson brought proceedings for the price.	The Court of Appeal held that a claim for the price under the contract meant a claim falling within **s 49 SGA**. Wilson could not have a claim for the price independently of that section. Wilson's claim had to comply with the condition in **s 49(1)** that property in the goods had to have passed to Holt. The court observed that if an action for the price could be maintained whenever the obligation to pay had arisen, **s 49** would be largely otiose, which indicated that the section was intended to specify the only circumstances in which a seller could maintain an action for the price. Thus, unless Wilson could establish that property in the goods had passed to Holt, it would have no claim for the price. That was an inherent result of a **retention of title** clause, and it showed the dangers, as well as its benefits, of such clauses. As title in the goods had not passed to Holt, Wilson did not have a valid action for the price. This could have been avoided by the seller stipulating that the price is payable on a **day certain** irrespective of delivery, thereby bringing it within the scope of **s 49(2)** and giving it an entitlement to bring an action for the price. Section **49(2)** applies irrespective of whether or not delivery has been made or title has passed.
Harlow & Jones Ltd v Panex (International) Ltd [1967] 2 Lloyd's Rep 509	The buyer agreed to buy 10,000 tons of steel. The goods were to be delivered Free-on-Board (F.O.B.) during August/September at the seller's option. The seller notified the buyer in July that the goods would be ready at the beginning of August and requested him to arrange a vessel. The buyer failed to reply but on 1 August notified the seller that they would be calling forward half the goods in mid-August with the remainder to	Roskill J held that the buyer was liable. The only term that was necessary to imply was that the seller would notify the buyer when the seller expected to load and then the buyer would be under the normal duty under a F.O.B. contract to provide the vessel at the correct time. The seller's only obligation was to give the notice they had given, but which the buyer had ignored. As there was no available market in the steel, the measure of damages was, according to **s 50(2)** of the (1893) **SGA**, the difference on 30 September between

Case	Facts	Held/Principle
	be loaded by the end of August. On 3 August, the buyer told the seller that due to non-confirmation the mid-August stem vessel had been missed, and that as a consequence the buyer could not now ship in August. On 11 August, the buyer demanded a reply within 24 hours as to whether the seller could guarantee all the goods ready for loading between 20 and 27 August. On 22 August, the buyer informed the seller that they accepted the seller's conduct as repudiation of the contract. The seller claimed against the buyer alleging wrongful failure to accept the goods on or before 30 September.	the contract price of the goods and the then value to the seller. The seller had taken back 1,500 tons of the steel and the measure of damages would be the loss of profit equal to the difference between the price at which the seller bought and the price he would have got from the buyer.
Lazenby Garages Ltd v Wright [1976] 1 WLR 459	The claimant car dealers bought a second-hand BMW car in February 1974 for £1,325. A few days later, W agreed to buy it from them for £1,670 and to take delivery on 1 March. He then told the dealers that he did not wish to proceed with the purchase and refused to accept delivery. About six weeks later the dealers sold the same car to another buyer for £1,770. Despite that more profitable sale, the dealers claimed damages from W for what they described as their 'loss of profit' of £345, being the difference between the £1,325 they had paid and the £1,670 agreed with the defendant. W's defence was that the dealers had not suffered any loss by his refusal to accept delivery.	The Court of Appeal held that where the subject matter of a repudiated sale was a unique article like a second-hand car for which there was no available market within the meaning of **s 50(3)** of the (1893) **SGA**, the sellers could recover as damages only the particular loss sustained on the transaction, and nothing more. In this case, as the sellers had resold the very car at a higher price, they had not suffered any loss and therefore were not entitled to recover any damages.
Re Charge Card Services Ltd (No 2) [1989] Ch 497	The company operated a charge card scheme with garages whereby the garages accepted its credit cards and charged the company the price of petrol and other products supplied to its cardholders. In return, the company	The Court of Appeal held that since it could not have been intended that the cardholder was liable to pay twice (to the company and the garage), payment by card was an absolute discharge of the cardholder's liability to the garage. Browne-Wilkinson LJ explained that 'the

Case	Facts	Held/Principle
	undertook to pay the garages the price of the goods, less its commission. The company issued cards to account holders who authorised the company to pay for fuel and debit them accordingly. The company went into voluntary liquidation owing sums to the garages and being owed debts from cardholders. Transactions involving credit or charge cards involved pre-existing schemes of separate bilateral contracts between the company and the suppliers and the company and the cardholders whereby the suppliers agreed to accept cards in payment for goods and the cardholders were entitled to use the cards to commit the company to honour its obligation to pay the suppliers. In turn, the cardholders were liable to pay the company the price charged by the suppliers.	cardholder is liable to pay the company whether or not the company has paid the garage . . . Payment by credit card is normally to be taken as an absolute, not a conditional, discharge of the buyer's liability'. Subject to the terms of the contract, the buyer ordinarily discharges his obligation to the seller fully on paying by credit or charge card, and if the credit company cannot pay the seller, the seller has no redress against the buyer. The cardholders discharged their obligations absolutely to the garages when they obtained fuel using their cards.
Thompson Ltd v Robinson (Gunmakers) Ltd [1955] Ch 177	The buyer contracted to purchase a new Standard Vanguard car from the seller but wrongfully failed to take delivery when it was available. The price of the car was fixed by the manufacturers. The seller mitigated its loss by persuading its supplier to take the car back without penalty. The seller then brought a claim against the buyer for their loss of profit amounting to £61. The buyer argued that as there was no difference between the market price of the car and the selling price the seller was only entitled to nominal damages. Their case was that **s 50(3) SGA** applied because there was an available market for that particular car and that the price for the car had been fixed by the manufacturer. The seller had mitigated its loss and therefore had suffered no loss. The court rejected this argument.	Upjohn J held that an 'available market' in **s 50(3)** is not limited to a market such as the Cotton Exchange or Baltic or Stock Exchange, but merely means that the situation in the trade in the particular area is such that the goods can freely be sold if a purchaser defaults. If there is not a demand which can readily absorb all the goods available for sale, so that if a purchaser defaults the sale is lost, there will not be an 'available market' within the meaning of the subsection. In such a case the seller's loss is the loss of his bargain, and he will be entitled by way of damages to the profit which he would have made but for the buyer's wrongful failure to take delivery. The judge stated that even if there had been an available market, **s 50(3)** provided only a prima facie rule and, if it was unjust to apply it, it was not to be applied. As a result, the measure of damages was the seller's loss of profit amounting to £61.

Exam question

Case	Facts	Held/Principle
Workman Clark & Co Ltd v Lloyd Brazileno [1908] 1 KB 968	The seller contracted with the buyer for the construction of a steamer, the price for which was to be paid by the buyer by five instalments, which were respectively to become due at different stages of the construction of the vessel. The contract provided for the hull and materials of the vessel to become the absolute property of the buyer upon payment of the first instalment subject only to the seller's lien for any unpaid sums. When the first payment instalment remained unpaid, the seller sued the buyer.	The Court of Appeal held that this case fell within the meaning of **s 49(2)** of the (1893) **SGA** and that all the seller had to show in order to entitle them to payment of the instalment claimed was that they had fulfilled the conditions upon which this instalment was, by the contract, payable.

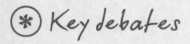

(✳) Key debates

Topic	Damages and the available market
Viewpoint	Examines the definition of an available market within the meaning of **s 50(3) SGA** and assesses how the appropriate level of damages might be calculated where the market price of the goods is inapplicable.
Source	(2004/5) Dec/Jan, *Buyer* 1

Topic	Liability for loss of goods
Viewpoint	Considers whether the burden of proof of a loss of profits claim was on the seller to show that it could not have obtained a re-order from the buyer or on the third party to show that the seller could have done so.
Source	(2008/9) Dec/Jan, *Buyer* 1

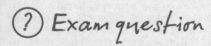

(?) Exam question

Questions on the remedies available to a seller and buyer will frequently be asked together. For this reason, please see Chapter 10, 'Exam questions', p 143.

#10

Remedies of the buyer

Key facts

- This chapter discusses the various remedies that are available to a buyer under a contract of sale of goods.

- There is an *additional* hierarchy of rights available to consumer buyers by virtue of the **Sale and Supply of Goods to Consumers Regulations 2002**.

- The remedies include (where applicable) the right to:

  - reject the goods;

  - sue for non-delivery or late delivery of the goods;

  - sue for damages following the seller's breach of warranty;

  - where the buyer is a consumer, require the seller to repair or replace the goods or claim from him a reduction in the price or rescind the contract.

Introduction

This chapter sets out the remedies available to a buyer under a sale of goods contract. The buyer's harshest remedy in respect of the seller's breach of contract is to reject the goods, terminate the contract of sale, and, where applicable, sue the seller for damages.

A buyer will only be entitled to terminate the contract if the seller has committed a breach of **condition** of the contract. A mere breach of **warranty** will only entitle the buyer to sue for damages. As we will see, in certain circumstances, a buyer will be obliged to (or may choose to) treat the seller's breach of condition as a breach of warranty.

If the seller's breach relates to the *quality* of the goods, then different rules as to damages apply. This kind of breach is known as a breach of warranty of quality.

Some of the remedies differ depending upon the circumstances, such as, whether the buyer was dealing as a consumer or whether the goods were bought for the purpose of resale.

The buyer's right to reject the goods

The buyer may reject the goods in the following circumstances:

If the seller has breached a condition of the contract

If the term that has been breached is a condition (for example, a breach of a statutory implied term as to the quality of the goods), the buyer may treat the contract as at an end and sue for damages, unless:

1. he has accepted the goods (see Chapter 8, 'Acceptance', p 107, for the rules on when a buyer is deemed to have accepted the goods). If the buyer has accepted the goods, then he will no longer be entitled to reject them for breach of condition but will be obliged to treat the breach as a breach of **warranty** only, unless there is an express or implied term of the contract to that effect (s 11(4) SGA). However, the right to reject goods after they have been accepted is still available for a breach of s 12(1) SGA;

2. he did not deal as a consumer (i.e. he is a commercial buyer) and the breach is so slight that it would be unreasonable for him to reject the goods. In such a case, he will have to treat the breach as a breach of **warranty** only (s 15A SGA). It is for the seller to show that the breach is so slight that he should be entitled to rely on this subsection (s 15A(3)); or

3. he has waived the condition, or elected to treat the breach of the condition as a breach of **warranty** and not as a ground for treating the contract as repudiated (s 11(2) SGA).

Where the buyer does not deal as a consumer

Section 15A modifies the remedies available to a buyer for breach of condition in cases where the buyer does not deal as a consumer. It provides that, unless the parties agree otherwise, in the case of a contract of sale of goods, where the buyer would have the right to reject the goods by reason of the seller's breach of a term implied by ss 13, 14, or 15 (see Chapter 2, 'Statutory implied terms', p 8) but where that breach is so slight that it would be unreasonable for him to reject them, then, if the buyer does not deal as a consumer, the breach is not to be treated as a breach of **condition** but may be treated as a breach of **warranty**.

Example

An example of how s 15A operates might be helpful.

Sue owns a furniture shop. She buys her sofas from Wally who is a wholesaler. One sofa is defective but the defect is so slight that it would be unreasonable for her to reject it. Sue then sells the sofa to Norman, who does not inspect it before purchase but notices the defect a short time later. The same breach occurs in both contracts but the remedies may be very different. Because Norman has dealt as a consumer he may be entitled to treat the contract as repudiated and reject the sofa. However, because Sue did not deal as a consumer when she purchased the goods from Wally, she cannot treat her contract with him as repudiated and may only bring a claim against him in damages for breach of **warranty**.

We discussed *Re Moore and Landauer* (1921) in Chapter 2 ('The description must amount to a term of the contract', p 14) where the buyer was entitled to reject the goods even though the breach was extremely minor. At that time, there was no statutory equivalent of s 15A. It seems very likely that had s 15A SGA been in force at that time, the court would have held that the breach was so slight that it would have been unreasonable for the buyer to have rejected the goods.

Revision tip

Don't forget that s 15A SGA applies to ss 13, 14, and 15, but not to s 12(1) SGA. The rule is different in cases where the buyer deals as a consumer. A consumer for these purposes is defined in UCTA (see Chapter 5, 'When does a buyer deal as a consumer?', p 63). Because s 15A does not apply to s 12(1), any buyer (whether or not he is dealing as a consumer) will be entitled to treat the seller's breach of condition as a repudiation of the contract. Also don't forget that s 15A is irrelevant in so far as ss 12(2)(a) or 12(2)(b) are concerned and that these sections imply warranties in any event.

✅ Looking for extra marks?

The rules discussed above explain the circumstances when a buyer may be entitled to reject the goods. These rules naturally apply only to contracts of sale of goods. In other kinds of contract (such as **hire purchase** or contracts to provide a service) the buyer may also choose to accept the seller's breach of **condition** or repudiation and treat the contract as at an end. The buyer's right to treat the contract as terminated will be lost if he *affirms* the contract (just as it would be lost in a **contract of sale** where the buyer *accepts* the goods). Although there are no statutory rules on what →

The buyer's right to reject the goods
****

→ amounts to affirmation, a buyer will be deemed to have affirmed the contract where, with full knowledge of the breach, he indicates to the supplier that he will not be treating the contract as repudiated. Once the buyer has done this, similar to the situation in a contract of sale, he will then only be entitled to sue the supplier for damages.

If the seller delivers the wrong quantity of goods

The buyer may reject the goods if the seller has delivered the wrong quantity (s 30) although a buyer who does not deal as a consumer will not be entitled to reject them if the breach is so slight that it would be unreasonable to reject (s 30(2A)). This was discussed in Chapter 8, 'Delivery of the wrong quantity', p 104.

Where a term in the contract of sale gives the buyer the right to reject

Where the **contract of sale** expressly gives the buyer the right to reject the goods for a specific event, then upon the occurrence of that event the buyer may reject the goods.

Where the seller has committed a repudiatory breach of the contract

If the seller commits a repudiatory breach of the **contract of sale**, the buyer may accept such breach as bringing the contract to an end.

Where the seller breaches an innominate term of the contract which deprives the buyer of substantially the entire benefit of the contract

You should recall from Chapter 2, 'Classification of terms', pp 9–10, that an innominate term is one where the *consequences or seriousness* of the breach determine whether or not it takes effect as a **condition** or a **warranty**. In this way, if the consequences of the breach are so fundamental that the innocent party has been deprived of substantially the entire benefit of the contract he will be entitled to treat the contract as repudiated and sue for damages. If, on the other hand, the effects of the breach are only minor, it will be treated as a breach of warranty (see *Hong Kong Fir Shipping Co Ltd v Kawasaki Kisen Kaisha Ltd* (1962)).

Damages for non-delivery

Revision tip

Where the seller wrongfully neglects or refuses to deliver the goods to the buyer, the buyer will be entitled to purchase similar goods from another supplier. In general terms, if the replacement goods cost more, then the buyer can claim this difference from the seller in damages. Conversely, where the buyer pays the same price or less for the replacement goods then, prima facie, his damages will be only nominal. In both situations, it is the market price of the goods at the time of the breach that is relevant.

Section 51(1) provides that where the seller wrongfully neglects or refuses to deliver the goods to the buyer, the buyer may sue him for damages for non-delivery. The measure of damages is the estimated loss directly and naturally resulting, in the ordinary course of events, from the seller's breach of contract (s 51(2)).

Was there an available market for the goods?

Where there is an available market for the goods in question the measure of damages is prima facie to be ascertained by the difference between the contract price and the market or current price of the goods at the time the goods ought to have been delivered or (if no time was fixed) at the time of the refusal to deliver (s 51(3)).

Where there is no available market for the goods, then the damages are calculated in accordance with s 51(2). This means that the damages will be assessed under common law in accordance with the first limb or rule in *Hadley v Baxendale* (1854). This provides that the damages which the buyer ought to receive in respect of the breach of contract should be the loss which would arise naturally 'according to the usual course of things', from the breach (per Alderson B). The buyer is, of course, under a duty to take reasonable steps to mitigate his loss and will only be entitled to recover damages for the loss actually suffered as a result of the seller's breach.

The fact that the buyer bought the goods for the purpose of resale is generally ignored for the purpose of calculating damages for non-delivery and the prima facie rule noted above prevails. However, in *R&H Hall Ltd v WH Pim Junior & Co Ltd* (1928), the House of Lords made four exceptions, which, if all of them are present, will displace the prima facie rule and the court will instead take account of the buyer's resale of the goods and any loss which the buyer sustains in connection with the resale will be recoverable:

- the parties to the first contract must have contemplated that the buyer was to resell the goods. Therefore, the first seller will have known that his buyer would sustain loss in the event of non-delivery;
- the resale contract must have been made before the delivery due date on the first contract;

Damages for non-delivery

✱✱✱✱✱✱✱✱✱✱✱

- the resale contract must be for the exact same (not just similar) goods as were to be supplied under the first contract; and
- the resale contract must be in accordance with the market and not be an extravagant or unusual bargain.

Revision tip

You should also refer to Chapter 9, 'Where there is an available market', p 121, for a discussion of the rules on available market. Also, don't forget the provisions of s 54 SGA which provide that the buyer may, in addition to claiming damages under the market rule, *also* be entitled to claim *special damages* based on the loss arising from any special circumstances of which the parties were aware at the time the contract was made. This refers to damages under the second limb or rule in *Hadley v Baxendale*.

Rejected goods and non-delivery

Where the buyer lawfully rejects the goods and treats the seller's breach as a repudiation of the contract he must make the goods available for collection. Unless the parties have agreed otherwise, s 36 SGA provides that where goods are delivered to the buyer, and he refuses to accept them, having the right to do so, he is not bound to return them to the seller, but it is sufficient if he intimates to the seller that he refuses to accept them. Even though the goods will already have been delivered to him, the buyer can claim damages for non-delivery under s 51 SGA. This is in addition to reclaiming the price paid. This might at first glance appear to be rather odd but the reason for it is because any delivery that the seller has made will be deemed not to have been made because the buyer has treated the contract as repudiated as the goods contracted for were not delivered. However, the buyer's right to claim damages for non-delivery will not be available if he has waived the **condition**, or elected to treat the breach of the condition as a breach of **warranty** rather than as a ground for treating the contract as repudiated (s 11(2) SGA), and in such a case his claim will be limited to a claim in damages for breach of warranty under s 53 SGA.

Example

Norman buys a sofa from Sue's shop. Immediately he sits on it, it feels lumpy, and there is a large tear in one of the seats. He rejects it straight away and terminates the contract under s 14 SGA (see Chapter 2, 'Statutory implied terms', p 8). Although he must make the sofa available for collection, he is under no obligation to return it to the shop, it being sufficient that he intimates to Sue that he has rejected it (s 36). He is entitled to the return of the money paid. He is also entitled to claim damages for non-delivery under s 51.

Damages for late delivery of the goods

Late delivery of the goods usually amounts to a breach of condition entitling the buyer to reject the goods and sue for non-delivery under s 51.

The buyer may, however, choose to accept late delivery of the goods or the late delivery may only be a breach of **warranty**. In this case, the damages for late delivery will be assessed under common law adopting the two limbs or rules in *Hadley v Baxendale*. We looked at the first of these rules under 'Was there an available market for the goods?', p 131. The second rule in *Hadley v Baxendale* provides that the damages should be the loss 'as may reasonably be supposed to have been in the contemplation of the parties at the time when they made the contract, as the probable result of the breach of it' (per Alderson B).

There will be a difference in the calculation of damages for late delivery depending on whether the goods were bought for the purpose of resale.

Goods not bought for the purpose of resale

Where the buyer buys the goods for his own consumption then his measure of damages will be the loss, if any, he has suffered as a result of the late delivery. The usual measure of damages will be the market value of the goods on the date the goods should have been delivered less the market price, if lower, on the date they were actually delivered. Of course, if the market value of the goods is higher on the date of actual delivery, then the buyer has suffered no loss in this regard. In addition, the buyer ought to be able to claim damages to compensate him for any losses sustained as a result of him being deprived of the goods during the period of delay. He is, of course, under a duty to mitigate his loss and this might require him, where reasonably practicable, to hire similar goods until the arrival of the delayed goods. If he does hire goods during this period, he ought to be able to recover the reasonable cost of the hire.

Goods bought for the purpose of resale

Where the buyer buys the goods for the purpose of resale, and their market value decreased by the time they were eventually delivered compared to their value when they ought to have been delivered, then the buyer is entitled to be compensated for this loss. The general rule is that the buyer's entitlement to damages is calculated as the difference between the market price of the goods at the time they should have been delivered and their market price at the time they were in fact delivered. The contract price is irrelevant. However, in *Wertheim v Chicoutimi Pulp Co* (1911), the Privy Council held that the buyer was entitled only to the difference between the market price at the time the goods ought to have been delivered and the price at which the buyer managed to resell the goods which, in this case, was considerably less than the measure of damages noted above as being the general rule. This resulted in the original buyer receiving a much lesser sum than he would have been awarded had the general rule been followed.

Damages for breach of warranty

Damages for 'breach of warranty' and 'breach of warranty of quality' distinguished

In Chapter 2, 'Classification of terms', pp 9–10, we discussed the difference between a breach of **warranty** and a breach of **condition** and it is worth briefly looking over the difference again. In short, unless any of the exceptions discussed under 'If the seller has breached a condition of the contract', p 128, apply (in which case what *would* have been a breach of condition will *then* be treated as a breach of warranty) a breach of condition entitles the innocent party to treat the contract as at an end, whereas a breach of warranty entitles him to sue for damages only.

Breach of warranty

Where the seller either commits a breach of **warranty** or where the buyer chooses (or is compelled) to treat a breach of a **condition** by the seller as a breach of warranty, then the buyer is not entitled to reject the goods. Instead, he may claim from the seller damages for breach of warranty or alternatively deduct the amount of these damages from the price either to reduce the price or to extinguish it (**s 53(1) SGA**).

Just because the buyer has set up the breach of warranty in diminution or extinction of the price does not prevent him from suing the seller for the same breach of warranty if he has suffered further loss (**s 53(4)**).

The measure of damages for breach of warranty is the estimated loss directly and naturally resulting, in the ordinary course of events, from the breach of warranty (**s 53(2)**). As noted above, this means that the damages will be assessed under common law in accordance with the first limb or rule in *Hadley v Baxendale*.

Breach of warranty of quality

Section 53(3) introduces a different expression of 'breach of warranty of quality'. If the seller's breach relates to the *quality* of the goods then s 53(3) provides that his loss is prima facie the difference between the value of the goods at the time of delivery to the buyer and the value they would have had if they had fulfilled the **warranty** (i.e. conformed to the contract). In many cases, the value of the goods had they fulfilled the warranty (i.e. had there been no breach of warranty) would be the same as the contract price.

However, where any defect would not be detected until after the buyer had resold the goods to his own customers, damages should be assessed on the basis of the buyer's liability to the ultimate customer and not under the prima facie rule in s 53(3) SGA which should be displaced (*Bence Graphics International Ltd v Fasson UK Ltd* (1998)).

Revision tip

At first glance, the term 'breach of warranty of quality' might appear to contradict the terms as to quality in the SGA which categorise them as conditions. They are indeed conditions and s 53(3) does not change that. Section 53(3)—and indeed the entirety of s 53—only deals with remedies for breach of warranty. Therefore, a breach of **condition** (even one in respect of quality) is unaffected by s 53. What s 53(3) is referring to is the situation where the breach of condition is to be treated as a breach of **warranty** for one of the reasons discussed under 'If the seller has breached a condition of the contract', p 128.

Example

Let's go back to the example shown under 'Rejected goods and non-delivery', p 132, to see how s 53(3) might affect Norman's treatment of the sofa. Instead of rejecting the sofa for a breach of s 14 (which is a **condition**), Norman may decide to treat the breach of condition as a breach of **warranty** and sue for damages. (Of course, he does not need to do this and can maintain his action for breach of condition.) As this breach relates to the quality of the goods, and Norman has chosen to treat what would have been a breach of condition as a breach of warranty, his damages will be prima facie the difference between the value of the goods at the time of delivery and the value they would have had if there had been no breach of warranty (s 53(3)). Let us assume that the contract price of the sofa was £1,000 and that, because of the defect, it is now only worth £800. Norman's damages, therefore, would prima facie be £200 under s 53(3) and he keeps the sofa. However, had he not chosen to treat the breach of condition as a breach of warranty, he would have been entitled to the return of his £1,000 and he would also be entitled to claim damages for non-delivery under s 51.

Summary of s 53 SGA

See Figure 10.1 on p 136. The seller has either breached a **warranty** or the buyer is treating (or is required to treat) the seller's breach of **condition** as a breach of warranty.

Figure 10.1 Summary of s 53 SGA

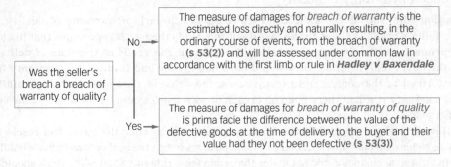

Additional rights of buyers in consumer cases—Sale and Supply of Goods to Consumers Regulations 2002

The Sale and Supply of Goods to Consumers Regulations 2002 came into force on 31 March 2003. They make amendments to the sale of goods legislation by inserting new ss 48A–F into the SGA and provide *additional* remedies to a buyer who 'deals as a consumer'. *It is important to appreciate that these remedies are additional to the pre-existing regime contained in the SGA that is available to all buyers.*

For the purposes of the 2002 Regulations a consumer is '. . . any natural person who . . . is acting for purposes which are outside his trade, business or profession' (reg 2). Clearly, a company cannot be a consumer as it is not a natural person. In most cases, it will be fairly obvious whether or not this definition has been satisfied; the focus being on whether the predominant purpose for the purchase was private or otherwise. Some cases will be more difficult to determine: for example, a sole trader who purchases goods such as a computer for his work and private use.

Section 48A SGA applies to a buyer (who must deal as a consumer) if the goods do not conform to the **contract of sale** at the time of **delivery**. Goods will not conform to the contract if there is, in relation to the goods, a breach of an express term of the contract or a term implied by ss 13, 14, or 15 SGA (s 48F).

Revision tip

Two requirements must be satisfied in order for a buyer to rely on these additional remedies:

1. the buyer must be dealing as a consumer; and
2. the goods must fail to conform to the contract in respect of a term implied by ss 13, 14, or 15 SGA or in respect of an express term of the contract. If the breach relates to a different implied undertaking, for example, the implied term as to title in s 12 SGA, then these additional remedies will not apply.

Additional rights of buyers in consumer cases

✳︎✳︎✳︎✳︎✳︎✳︎✳︎✳︎✳︎

It is important to note the effect of s 48A(3), as this reverses the burden of proof in relation to these new remedies. Goods which do not conform to the contract at any time within six months from the date of delivery will be presumed not to have conformed at the date of actual delivery, unless (s 48A(4)):

(a) it is established that the goods did so conform at that date; or

(b) the presumption is incompatible with the nature of the goods or the nature of the lack of conformity. The presumption will be incompatible with the nature of the goods if the goods are not intended to survive six months, such as with perishable foodstuffs. The nature of the lack of conformity relates to the circumstances which show that the lack of conformity is inconsistent with the application of the six-month presumption because it is more likely that the thing complained about was caused by the consumer. This would occur if, for example, the consumer complained about a dent in the goods after, say, five months of ownership.

If s 48A applies then the buyer will have the right to:

- require the seller to repair the goods (s 48B(1)(a)); or
- require him to replace the goods (s 48B(1)(b)); or
- require him to reduce the purchase price of the goods by an appropriate amount (s 48C(1)(a)); or
- **rescind** the contract (s 48C(1)(b)).

If the buyer requires the seller to repair or replace the goods, then the seller must repair or replace them within a reasonable time without causing significant inconvenience to the buyer. The seller must also bear any necessary costs incurred in doing so, including the cost of any labour, materials, or postage (ss 48B(2)(a) and 48B(2)(b)). However, the buyer will not be entitled to the repair or replacement remedies if such remedies are either impossible to perform or disproportionate in comparison to any of the other remedies not chosen (including price reduction or **rescission** (s 48B(3) SGA).

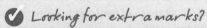

✓ Looking for extra marks?

One remedy is likely to be disproportionate in comparison to another if the one chosen by the buyer imposes costs on the seller which, in comparison to those that might be imposed on him by another remedy, are unreasonable, taking into account the value which the goods would have if they conformed to the contract, the significance of the lack of conformity, and whether the other remedy could be effected without significant inconvenience to the buyer. Any question as to what is a reasonable time or significant inconvenience is to be determined by reference to the nature of the goods and the purpose for which the goods were bought.

If the buyer requires the seller to repair or replace the goods then, until he has given the seller a reasonable time in which to repair or replace them, he will not be able to reject the goods and terminate the contract for breach of **condition** nor choose a different remedy—for example, requiring the seller to replace the goods when he first required him to repair them (s 48D; *Lowe v W Machell Joinery Ltd* (2011)). In cases where the consumer has successfully rescinded the contract, the seller may reduce the amount of the price reimbursed 'to take account of the use he has had of the goods since they were delivered to him' (s 48C(3) SGA).

Revision tip

The additional remedies available to a buyer by virtue of the amendments to the SGA made by the 2002 Regulations *co-exist* with and are *alternatives* to those contained in the pre-amended parts of the SGA. They also operate in a *hierarchical* manner (repair, replacement, price reduction then **rescission**) but also note the rules in relation to time, impossibility, etc. The buyer may choose to enforce one regime of remedies or the other. The pre-amended parts of the SGA do not require the buyer to allow the seller the opportunity to repair or replace the goods. This means that where there is a breach of **condition** and the buyer has decided he does not want the goods he is best advised (provided he is entitled so to do) to reject the goods under the pre-amended parts of the SGA. Because of the hierarchical manner of the newer remedies it is not possible for the buyer to do this straight away under s 48A. We have seen (Chapter 8, 'Lapse of reasonable time', pp 108–9) that a buyer only has a short time in which to reject the goods for a breach of condition and that there is great uncertainty about the length of time he has before the right to reject is lost. Therefore, this additional right of rescission will, in appropriate cases, provide the buyer with a final chance of 'rejecting' the goods where the repair and replacement route has either failed, taken too long, or caused significant inconvenience to him. Finally, don't forget that the reverse burden of proof does not apply to the pre-amended remedies of damages and rejection.

Specific performance

Revision tip

Don't forget that the usual remedy for breach of contract is rejection and/or an award of damages. There are, however, occasions where a monetary award will not provide the buyer with an adequate remedy. This gap is filled by an award of **specific performance** which can be found in s 52 SGA.

Specific performance is only available to a buyer and is at the discretion of the court. **Section 52** explains that the remedy is available only in respect of a breach of contract to deliver **specific** or **ascertained goods**. If successful, the court will order that the contract be performed specifically.

Specific performance, therefore, compels the seller to complete their obligations under the contract. It is especially usual when the subject matter of the contract is unique (such as with the sale of land or antiques) where an award of damages will clearly not compensate the buyer appropriately. It will not be awarded when an award of damages will suffice and will not be an easy remedy to secure.

✅ *Looking for extra marks?*

Specific performance is an equitable remedy and, is therefore, a discretionary remedy. The usual equitable maxims apply and it will be impressive to quote one or two of them ('he who comes to equity must come with clean hands', or 'he who seeks equity must do equity'). These maxims ➡

➡ simply mean that the remedy will not be available if the party seeking it (in this case, the buyer) has not behaved appropriately, as it is a general rule that equity does not aid a party at fault.

An award of **specific performance** 'applies to all cases where the goods are specific or ascertained, *whether the property has passed to the buyer or not*' (per Lord Hanworth MR in *Re Wait* (1927)). Therefore, even where the property in the goods has already passed to the buyer (but clearly not possession) a claim under s 52 can be made.

Although Lord Hanworth MR made it plain in *Re Wait* that specific performance applies whether or not the property in the goods had passed to the buyer, it seems that the courts are more likely to make the order for specific performance to protect the party that *owns* the goods rather than the party who merely has a *contractual right* in them (*Redler Grain Silos Ltd v BICC Ltd* (1982)).

Specific performance and consumer cases

It was noted above that **specific performance** is not an easy remedy to secure. However, in consumer cases, the power of the court to order specific performance is contained in s 48E(2) SGA and the additional remedies of repair and replacement available to the consumer buyer (s 48B) will now be easier to secure via an order for specific performance.

Summary of remedies for breach of s 13 SGA

See diagram in Chapter 2, 'Summary of s 13', p 15, for a summary of how s 13 may be breached. Figure 10.2 assumes that there has been a breach of s 13.

Figure 10.2 Remedies for breach of s 13 SGA

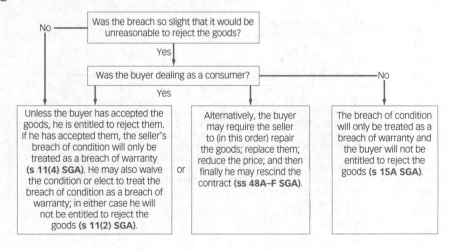

Summary of remedies for breach of s 14(2) SGA

See diagram in Chapter 2, 'Summary of s 14(2)', pp 19–20, for a summary of how s 14(2) may be breached. Figure 10.3 assumes that there has been a breach of s 14(2).

Figure 10.3 Remedies for breach of s 14(2) SGA

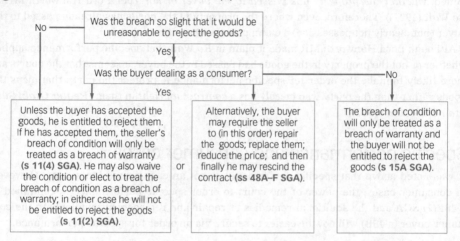

Summary of remedies for breach of s 14(3) SGA

See Chapter 2, 'Summary of s 14(3)', p 22, for a summary of how s 14(3) may be breached. Figure 10.4 assumes that there has been a breach of s 14(3).

Figure 10.4 Remedies for breach of s 14(3) SGA

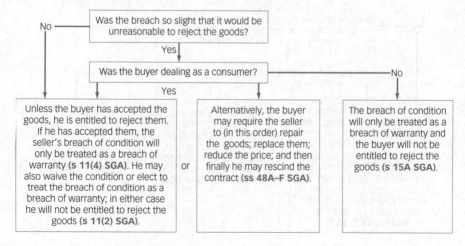

Summary of remedies for breach of s 15 SGA

See diagram in Chapter 2, 'Summary of s 15', pp 24–25, for a summary of how s 15 may be breached. Figure 10.5 assumes that there has been a breach of s 15.

Figure 10.5 Remedies for breach of s 15

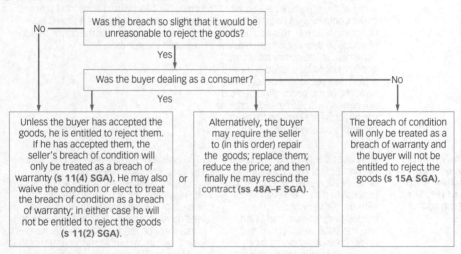

No ——— Was the breach so slight that it would be unreasonable to reject the goods?

Yes

Was the buyer dealing as a consumer? ——————— No

Yes

| Unless the buyer has accepted the goods, he is entitled to reject them. If he has accepted them, the seller's breach of condition will only be treated as a breach of warranty (**s 11(4) SGA**). He may also waive the condition or elect to treat the breach of condition as a breach of warranty; in either case he will not be entitled to reject the goods (**s 11(2) SGA**). | or | Alternatively, the buyer may require the seller to (in this order) repair the goods; replace them; reduce the price; and then finally he may rescind the contract (**ss 48A–F SGA**). | The breach of condition will only be treated as a breach of warranty and the buyer will not be entitled to reject the goods (**s 15A SGA**). |

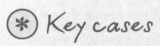

(✳) Key cases

Case	Facts	Held/Principle
***Bence Graphics International Ltd v Fasson UK Ltd* [1998] QB 87**	F manufactured a vinyl product which was sold to B who printed identification marks on it for resale to customers for use in labelling bulk containers. It was a condition of the contract that the vinyl would remain in good condition for five years. However, owing to a defect, it degraded, resulting in the marks becoming illegible. B sought to recover the whole of the purchase price or alternatively an indemnity against claims from customers.	The Court of Appeal held that in the circumstances of the case, where F would have known that any defect would not be detected until after B had sold on the subject matter of the contract, it was appropriate that damages should be assessed on the basis of B's liability to the ultimate consumer and not under the prima facie rule in **s 53(3) SGA** which should be displaced. Where the buyer sustains no loss, then damages will not be awarded.

Case	Facts	Held/Principle
Re Moore and Landauer [1921] 2 KB 519	The sellers contracted to sell a quantity of tinned fruit which were to be packaged in cases each containing 30 tins. The overall correct quantity was delivered but some of the tins were packed in cases containing 24 tins. The Court of Appeal held that this was a sale of goods by description and that the statement in the contract that the goods were to be packed 30 tins to a case was part of the description. As some of the goods tendered did not correspond with that description the buyers were entitled to reject the entire consignment.	This case was discussed in Chapter 2, 'The description must amount to a term in the contract', p 14. The breach was exceptionally minor. It seems very likely that had **s 15A** SGA been in force at that time, the court would have held that the breach was so slight that it would have been unreasonable for the buyer to have rejected the goods.
R&H Hall Ltd v WH Pim Junior & Co Ltd [1928] All ER Rep 763	The buyer bought a consignment of corn. Before the due date for delivery, he resold the corn at a profit. When the vessel arrived with the delivery of corn the market price of corn had fallen and the seller refused to deliver. Under the normal prima facie rule for calculating damages for non-delivery of goods it is the market price itself that determines loss and the fact that the buyer buys the goods for the purpose of resale is generally ignored for the purpose of calculating damages for non-delivery.	The House of Lords made four exceptions to the prima facie rule, which if all are present, will see it displaced and the court will instead take account of the buyer's resale of the goods and any loss which the buyer sustains in connection with the resale will be recoverable. (1) The parties to the first contract must have contemplated that the buyer was to resell the goods. Therefore the first seller will have known that his buyer would sustain loss in the event of non-delivery. (2) The resale contract must have been made before the delivery due date on the first contract. (3) The resale contract must be for the exact same (not just similar) goods as were to be supplied under the first contract. (4) The resale contract must be in accordance with the market and not be an extravagant or unusual bargain.
Wertheim v Chicoutimi Pulp Co [1911] AC 301	The contract of sale was to deliver 3,000 tons of moist wood pulp to the buyer between 1 September and 1 November 1990. The contract price of the goods was 25s per ton. The buyer had resold the goods for 65s per ton. The market price of the goods when delivery should have been made was 70s per ton but had dropped to 42s 6d by the time delivery had actually been made.	The general intention of the law in giving damages for breach of contract is that C should be placed in the same position as he would have been in if the contract had been performed. In the case of late delivery the measure of damages in order to indemnify the purchaser is the difference between the market price at the respective dates of due and actual delivery of the goods purchased. However, in cases where the purchaser has resold them at a price in excess of that prevailing at the date of

Case	Facts	Held/Principle
	The buyer claimed 27s 6d a ton, which was the difference between the market price at the due date of delivery (70s) and the market price at the date of actual delivery (42s 6d).	actual delivery then he must give credit for that excess when estimating his damages. The Privy Council held that since he had sold the goods at 65s a ton his loss was only 5s a ton and that was all he was entitled to recover.

(99) Key debates

Topic	The Sale and Supply of Goods to Consumers Regulations
Author/Academic	Chris Willett, Martin Morgan-Taylor, and Andre Naidoo
Viewpoint	Discusses the **Sale and Supply of Goods to Consumers Regulations 2002** and considers the implications of taking into account public statements in assessing satisfactory quality; the conformity with Council Directive 1999/44; amendments to the rules on risk; remedies including repair, replacement, price reduction, and **rescission**.
Source	[2004] Jan *Journal of Business Law* 94

Topic	Specific performance—a regular remedy for consumers?
Author/Academic	D Harris
Viewpoint	Discusses the amendments to the **Sale of Goods Act 1979** providing the buyer with four remedies where goods fail to conform to the **contract of sale** at the time of **delivery**, including **specific performance**. Examines the power of the court under **s 48E(2)** to make an order requiring specific performance including the court's discretion to make an order. Discusses the scope of the power and the use of specific performance to compel the seller to repair.
Source	(2003) 119 *Law Quarterly Review* 541

(?) Exam questions

Problem question

Helen recently acquired the following items and now seeks your advice about any remedies she might have, and any legal issues that might arise, as a result of the following problems:

(a) A plasma television set bought from a High Street store for which she paid £600. The TV never worked but because of the pressures of work she only managed to return it to the store 12 months later.

Exam questions
✳✳✳✳✳✳✳✳✳

(b) A new Playstation which she exchanged for an old one. She bought this at the same time and from the same store as the television. This never worked.

(c) A second-hand wristwatch which she bought from a car boot sale and paid £30 by cheque. It was described as 'waterproof' and the leaflet advertising it claimed it kept excellent time. When she got it home she found that it was not waterproof and also that it lost more than one minute in time every week.

(d) A skirt for a dinner party she was planning. In a rush, she picked up the wrong size from the shelf.

(e) Some roofing tiles from a local builders' merchant. The tiles were mostly cracked and unusable. Helen was in a hurry when she bought them and only had a quick look at them. She hadn't noticed they were cracked.

Essay question

Unless a private seller makes an express promise or representation to the buyer when selling goods, the buyer will have no remedy if those goods turn out to be defective.

Critically evaluate the rules relating to defective goods in the light of this statement.

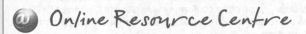 Online Resource Centre

To see an outline answer to this question visit www.oup.com/lawrevision/

#11

Consumer credit

Key facts

- The principal piece of legislation is the **Consumer Credit Act 1974**.

- This has been amended by the **Consumer Credit Act 2006** which has made a number of important changes to the legislation.

- The legislation provides rights to borrowers who take credit under a 'regulated agreement'.

- The extortionate credit bargain provisions have been replaced by a test which considers whether there was an unfair relationship between the borrower and the lender.

- There are strict formalities for completing regulated agreements. An improperly executed regulated agreement is enforceable against the borrower or hirer only by order of the court.

- A regulated agreement *may* be a cancellable agreement.

- In certain circumstances, the borrower will have a like claim against the lender for the supplier's misrepresentation or breach of contract.

- Since the closure on 1 April 2014 of the Office of Fair Trading, responsibility for the regulation of consumer credit activities has transferred to the Financial Conduct Authority.

- Although the **Consumer Credit Act 1974** (as amended) remains in force it no longer provides the statutory framework for the *regulation* of consumer credit. The regulatory regime now falls under the **Financial Services and Markets Act 2000** by virtue of the **Financial Services and Markets Act 2000 (Regulated Activities) (Amendment) (No 2) Order 2013**.

Introduction

Many businesses and individuals require credit. The party providing the credit was previously known as the **creditor** and the party who borrows or owes the money was known as the **debtor**. These parties are now known as the lender and the borrower.

The Consumer Credit Act 1974 was gradually implemented over the course of 11 years until it was fully in force on 19 May 1985. Despite its title, the CCA 1974 does not just deal with consumer credit; it also deals with parties who are provided with credit in the course of a business.

Until 1 April 2014, the CCA 1974 required most businesses that lent money to consumers, or offered goods or services on credit terms, or engaged in certain ancillary credit activities, to be licensed by the Office of Fair Trading. Trading without a licence in such cases amounted to a criminal offence which could, on conviction, result in a fine and/or a term of imprisonment. The OFT closed on 1 April 2014, from which date responsibility for the regulation of consumer credit activities transferred to the Financial Conduct Authority.

From 1 April 2014, by virtue of the Financial Services and Markets Act 2000 (Regulated Activities) (Amendment) (No 2) Order 2013 (FSMA RAO), entering into consumer credit or consumer hire agreements or carrying on activities including credit brokerage or debt collection are now regulated activities for the purposes of the Financial Services and Markets Act 2000. Any person carrying on credit-related or hire-related activities by way of business is now required to be authorised and regulated by the FCA, or hold 'interim permission' to do so, in order to carry on such activities lawfully and avoid breaching the 'general prohibition' under s 19 FSMA which may amount to a criminal offence.

The CCA 1974 (as amended) gives rights to borrowers who take credit under a regulated agreement.

This chapter explains some of the key common law and statutory provisions relating to consumer credit agreements and the common issues that arise.

Table 11.1 shows which provisions of the new FSMA RAO correspond to the provisions of the CCA.

Table 11.1 Destination table comparing CCA to the new (FSMA RAO) regime provisions

CCA (section)	FSMA RAO (article)	Comments
8(1) *Consumer credit agreement*	60B(3)	Definition of credit agreement has not changed
9(1) *Meaning of credit*	60L(1)	See definition
9(3) *Hire purchase agreement treated as fixed-sum credit*	60L(8)	

10 *Running-account credit and fixed-sum credit*	60L(1)	Minor drafting changes, including use of 'borrower' and 'lender' rather than 'debtor' and 'creditor'
11 *Restricted-use credit and unrestricted-use credit*	60L(1) and 60L(2)	
12 *Debtor-creditor-supplier agreements*	60L(1)	'debtor-creditor-supplier' is now 'borrower-lender-supplier'
13 *Debtor-creditor agreements*	60L(1)	'debtor-creditor' is now 'borrower-lender'
14 *Credit-token agreements*	Not applicable	Not carried forward as not relevant to **FSMA** provisions
15 *Consumer hire agreements*	60N	
16(1) to (4) *Exempt agreements where creditor is specified or of a description specified by Secretary of State*	60E(1) to (4) and (7)	FCA (rather than Secretary of State) to maintain list of persons/class of persons to whom exemption applies
16(5)(a) *Exemption by reference to number of payments*	60F	
16(5)(b) *Exemption by reference to total charge for credit*	60G	
16(5)(c) *Exemption by reference to a country outside the UK*	60C(8)	
16(6) *Exemption for consumer hire agreements in relation to electricity, gas, or water linked to metering equipment*	60P	
16(6A), (6B) *Exemption for housing authorities*	60E(5) and (7)	
16(6C) to (6E) *Exemption for regulated mortgage contracts and home purchase plans*	60C(2)	
16A *Exemption for high net worth individuals*	60H and 60Q	FCA (rather than Secretary of State) now deals with the declaration and statement for high net worth individuals

16B *Exemption relating to businesses*	60C(3) to (7) and 60O	FCA now deals with exemption for businesses
16C *Exemption relating to investment properties*	60D	
20 *Total charge for credit*	60M	FCA (rather than Secretary of State) now deals with provision in rules as to the total charge for credit
189(1) *Definitions*	60L(1)	'Individual' is now 'relevant recipient of credit'

Regulated agreements

The CCA 1974 and CCA 2006 provide rights to borrowers who have taken credit under a **regulated agreement**. Unless an agreement is a regulated agreement then, in general terms, the CCA 1974 will not operate to provide rights to borrowers.

A **regulated agreement** is defined by s 189(1) CCA 1974 as 'a *consumer credit agreement*, or *consumer hire agreement*, other than an *exempt agreement*'. The words highlighted in italics need considering.

In *Nram plc v McAdam* (2014) the lender represented that an unsecured loan of more than £25,000 was to be regulated by the CCA 1974. The court held that the rights and remedies available under the CCA were therefore imported into the (unregulated) agreement so that the borrower was entitled to redress in the form of repayment under s 77A of sums wrongly debited on account of interest and default sums for non-compliance.

Consumer credit agreement

Under FSMA RAO 60B(3):

- a 'credit agreement' means an agreement between an individual or relevant recipient of credit ('A') and any other person ('B') under which B provides A with credit of any amount;
- an 'exempt agreement' means a credit agreement which is an exempt agreement under articles 60C–60H; and
- a 'regulated credit agreement' means any credit agreement which is not an exempt agreement.

Therefore, a **consumer credit agreement** is a **regulated agreement** provided that none of the exemptions apply.

Who is a 'relevant recipient of credit'?

A 'relevant recipient of credit' is defined in **FSMA RAO 60L** as:

(a) a partnership consisting of two or three persons not all of whom are bodies corporate, or

(b) an unincorporated body of persons which does not consist entirely of bodies corporate and is not a partnership.

This replaces the previous requirement for the debtor to be 'an individual' within the meaning of **s 189(1) CCA**.

The meaning of *'credit'* is a broad one and includes 'a cash loan and any other form of financial accommodation' under which the borrower is given time to pay **(FSMA RAO 60L(1))**. A hire purchase agreement falls within the meaning of *'credit'*.

Removal of the £25,000 financial limit

If the agreement was made before 6 April 2008 a **consumer credit agreement** had to be for no more than £25,000 (excluding interest and other charges). This limit was removed by **s 2 CCA 2006** for agreements made after this date and the Act will then apply to lending up to any amount unless exempted from its application.

Consumer hire agreement

A **consumer hire agreement** is defined in **FSMA RAO 60N(3)** as:

> an agreement between a person ('the owner') and an individual or relevant recipient of credit ('the hirer') for the bailment or, in Scotland, the hiring, of goods to the hirer which:
>
> (a) is not a hire-purchase agreement, and
>
> (b) is capable of subsisting for more than three months.

This replaces the previous definition in **s 15(1) CCA**.

A consumer hire agreement is a **regulated agreement** provided that none of the exemptions apply.

You will see from the above definition that a **consumer hire agreement** must be *capable* of subsisting for more than three months. There is no requirement that it *must* subsist for more than this period. In *Dimond v Lovell* (2002) the hire agreement stated that it could not last for more than 28 days. It was therefore not a consumer hire agreement.

Exempt agreements

Agreements that are exempt used to be found in **s 16 CCA 1974** and the **Consumer Credit (Exempt Agreements) Order 1989**. The meaning of exempt agreements can now be found in **FSMA**. These can conveniently be grouped as follows:

Regulated agreements

(a) exemptions relating to the nature of the agreement

A credit agreement is an exempt agreement if:

- it is a regulated mortgage contract or a regulated home purchase plan (**FSMA RAO 60C(2)**);
- the lender provides the borrower with credit exceeding £25,000 *and* the agreement is entered into by the borrower wholly or predominantly for the purposes of a business carried on, or intended to be carried on, by the borrower (**FSMA RAO 60C(3)**);
- the lender provides the borrower with credit of £25,000 or less and the agreement is entered into by the borrower wholly for the purposes of a business carried on, or intended to be carried on, by the borrower, *and* the agreement is a Green Deal plan (within the meaning of **s 1 of the Energy Act 2011**) (**FSMA RAO 60C(4)**);
- it is made in connection with trade in goods or services between the UK and a country outside the UK, within a country, or between countries outside the UK, and the credit is provided to the borrower in the course of a business carried on by the borrower (**FSMA RAO 60C(8)**).

(b) exemptions relating to the purchase of land for non-residential purposes

A credit agreement is an exempt agreement if:

- at the time it is entered into, any sums due under it are secured by a legal mortgage on land and less than 40% of the land is used, or is intended to be used, as or in connection with a dwelling by the borrower or a related person of the borrower, or in the case of credit provided to trustees, by an individual who is a beneficiary of the trust or a related person of a beneficiary (**FSMA RAO 60D**).

(c) exemptions relating to the nature of the lender

A credit agreement is an exempt agreement if:

- it relates to the purchase of land and if the lender is specified, or of a description specified, in rules made by the FCA under **paragraph 3**, or a local authority. The **paragraph 3** rules are that the FCA may make rules specifying any of the following: (a) an authorised person with permission to effect or carry out contracts of insurance; (b) a friendly society; (c) an organisation of employers or organisation of workers; (d) a charity; (e) an improvement company (within the meaning given by **section 7 of the Improvement of Land Act 1899**); (f) a body corporate named or specifically referred to in any public general Act; (g) a body corporate named or specifically referred to in, or in an order made under, a relevant housing provision; (h) a building society (within the meaning of the **Building Societies Act 1986**); (i) an authorised person with permission to accept deposits (**FSMA RAO 60E(1)-(3)**);
- it is secured by a legal mortgage on land and that land is used or is intended to be used as or in connection with a dwelling, and the lender is a housing authority (**FSMA RAO 60E(5)**);

- the lender is an investment firm or a credit institution, and the agreement is entered into for the purpose of allowing the borrower to carry out a transaction relating to one or more financial instruments (**FSMA RAO 60E(6)**).

(d) **exemptions relating to number of repayments to be made**

A credit agreement is an exempt agreement if:

- (with limited exceptions) the agreement is a borrower-lender-supplier agreement for fixed-sum credit, and the number of payments to be made by the borrower is not more than, four and those payments are required to be made within a period of 12 months or less (beginning on the date of the agreement), and the credit is secured on land or provided without interest or other significant charges (**FSMA RAO 60F(2)**);

- (with limited exceptions) the agreement is a borrower-lender-supplier agreement for running-account credit and the borrower is to make payments in relation to specified periods which must be, unless the agreement is secured on land, of three months or less, and the number of payments to be made by the borrower in repayment of the whole amount of credit provided in each such period is not more than one, and where the credit is secured on land, or provided without interest or other significant charges (**FSMA RAO 60F(3)**);

- the agreement is a borrower-lender-supplier agreement financing the purchase of land, and the number of payments to be made by the borrower is not more than four, and where the credit is secured on land, or provided without interest or other charges (**FSMA RAO 60F(4)**);

- the agreement is a borrower-lender-supplier agreement for fixed-sum credit, and the credit is to finance a premium under a contract of insurance relating to land or anything on land, and the lender is the lender under a credit agreement secured by a legal mortgage on that land, and the credit is to be repaid within the period (which must be 12 months or less) to which the premium relates, and in the case of an agreement secured on land there is no charge forming part of the total charge for credit under the agreement other than interest at a rate not exceeding the rate of interest from time to time payable under the agreement, and in the case of an agreement which is not secured on land the credit is provided without interest or other charges, and the number of payments to be made by the borrower is not more than 12 (**FSMA RAO 60F(5)**);

- the agreement is a borrower-lender-supplier agreement for fixed-sum credit and the lender is the lender under a credit agreement secured by a legal mortgage on land, and the agreement is to finance a premium under a contract of whole life insurance which provides, in the event of the death of the person on whose life the contract is effected before the credit referred to above has been repaid, and for payment of a sum not exceeding the amount sufficient to meet the amount which, immediately after that credit has been advanced, would be payable to the lender in respect of that credit (including interest from time to time payable under that agreement), and in the case of an agreement secured on land there is no charge forming part of the total charge for credit under the agreement other than interest at a rate not exceeding the rate of interest from time to time payable under the agreement, and in the case of an agreement which is not secured on land, the credit is provided without interest or other charges, and the number of payments to be made by the borrower is not more than 12 (**FSMA RAO 60F(6)**).

(e) **exemptions relating to the total charge for credit**

A credit agreement is an exempt agreement if:

- it is a borrower-lender agreement and the lender is a credit union and the rate of the total charge for credit does not exceed 42.6% (**FSMA RAO 60G(2)**);

- (with limited exceptions) it is a borrower-lender agreement and it is an agreement of a kind offered to a particular class of individual or relevant recipient of credit and not offered to the public generally and it provides that the only charge included in the total charge for credit is interest, and interest under the agreement may not at any time be more than the sum of 1% and the highest of the base rates published by the banks specified on the date 28 days before the date on which the interest is charged (**FSMA RAO 60G(3)**);

- (with limited exceptions) it is a borrower-lender agreement and an agreement of a kind offered to a particular class of individual or relevant recipient of credit and not offered to the public generally and it does not provide for or permit an increase in the rate or amount of any item which is included in the total charge for credit and the total charge for credit under the agreement is not more than the sum of 1% and the highest of the base rates published by the banks specified on the date 28 days before the date on which the charge is imposed (**FSMA RAO 60G(4)**).

(f) **exemptions relating to the nature of the borrower**

A credit agreement is an exempt agreement if:

- the borrower is an individual and the agreement is either secured on land, or for credit which exceeds £60,260, and the agreement includes a declaration made by the borrower which provides that the borrower agrees to forgo the protection and remedies that would be available to the borrower if the agreement were a regulated credit agreement and which complies with rules made by the FCA for these purposes, and a statement has been made in relation to the income or assets of the borrower which complies with rules made by the FCA for these purposes, and the connection between the statement and the agreement complies with any rules made by the FCA for these purposes (including as to the period of time between the making of the statement and the agreement being entered into), and a copy of the statement was provided to the lender before the agreement was entered into (**FSMA RAO 60H**).

Unfair relationship between lender and borrower

The concept of the unfair relationship was introduced by the **CCA 2006** which made amendments to the **CCA 1974**. This was introduced to remedy some of the problems with the now repealed **ss 137–140** where the court had the power to reopen a credit agreement if it was held to be 'extortionate'. The statutory test of 'extortionate' was a high one: the payments required to be made must have been 'grossly exorbitant'. As a result of this harshness, **ss 137–140** were repealed and replaced by **ss 140A–D** whereby, on application by the borrower, the court could reopen a credit agreement where there was an 'unfair relationship' between the lender and the borrower.

Revision tip

The new unfair relationship test that replaced the extortionate credit bargain provisions applies to all new consumer lending transactions and not just to agreements regulated by the **CCA**.

By **s 140A(1) CCA 1974** the court may make an order (under **s 140B**) in connection with a credit agreement if it determines that the relationship between the lender and the borrower arising out of the agreement is unfair to the borrower because of one or more of the following:

- any of the terms of the agreement or of any related agreement;
- the way in which the lender has exercised or enforced any of his rights under the agreement or any related agreement; or
- any other thing done (or not done) by, or on behalf of, the lender either before or after the making of the agreement or any related agreement.

Although the court may take account of any of matters noted in **s 140A(1)** as well as any other matters it considers to be relevant (**s 140A(2)**), it is important to appreciate that the question for determination is whether or not the *relationship* arising out of the credit agreement between the lender and the borrower is unfair (*Patel v Patel* (2009)).

✅ *Looking for extra marks?*

A question in this area might state that the relationship between the lender and the borrower has ended. You should explain that under **s 140A(4)** a court may still make a determination under this section in relation to a relationship notwithstanding that the relationship may have ended.

Once the borrower (or a surety) alleges that the relationship between the lender and the borrower is unfair to the borrower, **s 140B(9) CCA 1974** states that it is then for the lender to prove that the relationship is not unfair.

Unfair relationship between lender and borrower

As noted above, s 140B sets out the powers of the court to make an order in relation to an unfair relationship between the lender and the borrower. The powers of the court are wide in this regard. Where the court is satisfied that an unfair relationship has arisen under s 140A(1) it may make an order to:

- require the lender (or any associate or former associate of his) to repay, in whole or in part, any sum paid by the borrower or by a surety by virtue of the agreement or any related agreement (whether paid to the lender, the associate, or the former associate, or to any other person);
- require the lender (or any associate or former associate of his) to do or not to do (or to cease doing) anything specified in the order in connection with the agreement or any related agreement;
- reduce or discharge any sum payable by the borrower or by a surety by virtue of the agreement or any related agreement;
- direct the return to a surety of any property provided by him for the purposes of a security;
- otherwise set aside, in whole or in part, any duty imposed on the borrower or on a surety by virtue of the agreement or any related agreement;
- alter the terms of the agreement or of any related agreement;
- direct accounts to be taken between any persons.

In *Scotland v British Credit Trust Ltd* (2014) the Court of Appeal held that the negotiations and misrepresentation by a double-glazing salesman about the need to purchase payment protection insurance when taking out a loan were deemed to have been conducted by the double-glazing company as agent for the finance company, and their conduct was therefore relevant as 'things done (or not done) by, or on behalf of, the creditor' in determining whether the relationship between the lender and the borrower was unfair for the purposes of s 140A. As the borrower would not have purchased the payment protection policy but for the misrepresentation and breaches of the Insurance Conduct of Business rules these matters created an unfair relationship, and the judge properly exercised her discretion under s 140B to require the finance company to repay the loan payments referable to the policy and to vary the loan agreement so as to excuse the borrower from repaying the rest of the loan so far as it related to the policy.

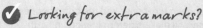

✅ Looking for extra marks?

Since the concept of the unfair relationship was introduced by the CCA 2006 it is interesting to note that the word 'unfair' remains undefined. Given that the courts adopted rather strict interpretations of 'extortionate' and 'grossly exorbitant' under the old provisions (ss 137 and 138), the absence of any definition of unfair will provide them with considerably greater flexibility when determining whether the relationship was unfair.

Having said that, the Supreme Court has now handed down its first judgment on what amounts to an unfair relationship for the purposes of ss 140A–D CCA (*Plevin v Paragon Personal Finance Ltd* (2014).

In *Plevin v Paragon Personal Finance Ltd* (2014) Mrs Plevin took out a personal loan through LLP Processing (UK) Ltd. LLP proposed that she borrow £34,000 from Paragon repayable in instalments over 10 years, and that she take out a payment protection insurance policy for five years with Norwich Union, who was Paragon's designated insurer. The PPI premium of £5,780 was payable at the outset and added to the amount of the loan. 71.8% of the premium was taken in commission: LLP retained £1,870 and Paragon retained £2,280. Although the Financial Industry Standards Association guide which LLP gave to Mrs Plevin told her that 'commission is paid by the lending company' she was not told the amount of the commission or the identity of the recipients. Mrs Plevin argued that the relationship between herself and Paragon was unfair under s 140A(1)(c) because of the non-disclosure of the commissions and also because of the failure of anyone involved to advise on the suitability of the PPI policy for her needs. Insofar as LLP committed these defaults, Mrs Plevin says it did so 'on behalf of' Paragon. The Insurance Conduct of Business Rules (which are the statutory rules regulating the insurance industry) do not require insurance intermediaries to disclose commissions to their customers but do require an insurance intermediary which makes a 'personal recommendation' to a customer to buy an insurance contract to take reasonable steps to ensure that the recommendation is suitable for the customer's demands and needs. Lord Sumption held that the non-disclosure of the amount of commissions and the identity of the recipients did make Mrs Plevin's relationship with Paragon unfair under s 140A(1)(c) but the failure to conduct a needs assessment of Mrs Plevin did not. He stated that at some point the commissions may become so large that the relationship cannot be regarded as fair if the customer is kept in ignorance and concluded that Mrs Plevin would have questioned whether the PPI policy represented value for money if she had been aware of the commission amounts and might not have taken out the policy at all. This unfairness was the responsibility of Paragon, the only party which knew the size of both commissions.

The documentation and signatures

Section 60(1) CCA 1974 sets out the essential form and content of documents embodying regulated agreements so as to ensure the borrower or hirer is made aware of:

- the rights and duties conferred or imposed on him by the agreement;
- in the case of a **consumer credit agreement**, the amount and rate of the total charge for credit. This includes the Annual Percentage Rate, or APR;
- the protection and remedies available to him under the CCA 1974; and

- any other matters which it is desirable for him to know about in connection with the agreement.

Section 61(1) goes on to explain that a regulated agreement will not be properly executed unless:

- a document in the prescribed form itself containing all the prescribed terms and conforming to the requirements of s 60(1) is signed in the prescribed manner both by the borrower or hirer and by or on behalf of the lender or owner;
- the document embodies all the terms of the agreement (other than implied terms); and
- the document is, when presented or sent to the borrower or hirer for signature, in such a state that all its terms are readily legible.

Furthermore, the Consumer Credit (Agreements) Regulations 2010 require further information to be contained in the documents embodying a regulated consumer credit agreement. This further information is set out in Schedule 1 of these Regulations and includes, where appropriate:

- the right to a copy of the agreement in good time to consider whether the borrower wishes to proceed with it. If the lender did not provide a copy then he can only enforce it with a court order;
- if the agreement is secured on land then the borrower must be provided with a notice explaining that his home may be repossessed if he fails to maintain repayments on a mortgage or other debt secured on it;
- an explanation of the right to cancel the agreement; and
- an explanation of the right to the repossession of the goods in the event of outstanding repayments.

In cases where the agreement was entered into prior to 6 April 2007, the lender will not be able to enforce it if the strict requirements contained in (the now repealed) ss 127(3)–(5) were not complied with. The court had no discretion in this regard. These requirements were in relation to the signing of an agreement which failed to contain certain minimum basic terms and to cancellable agreements where certain requirements were not met.

An agreement that has not been properly signed will not be properly executed (s 61(1) CCA 1974). An improperly executed regulated agreement is enforceable against the borrower or hirer only by order of the court (s 65) although the court does have a general discretion to permit the lender to enforce the agreement. In exercising its discretion, the court will have regard to the following factors noted in s 127:

- any prejudice caused to any person by the contravention in question;
- the degree of culpability for the contravention; and

- its power to reduce or discharge any sum payable by the borrower or hirer so as to compensate him for prejudice suffered as a result of the contravention in question.

✅ Looking for extra marks?

Although in certain circumstances an agreement may not be enforceable against the borrower, it is important to appreciate that the borrower should not be penalised for the lender's failure to ensure the agreement was properly executed. For this reason, therefore, the borrower can, if he wishes, enforce such an agreement as against the lender or supplier in the event, for example, that the goods supplied under a **hire purchase** agreement are not of satisfactory quality.

Where the agreement was unenforceable by virtue of the CCA 1974 the courts would not enforce it even if this meant that the borrower was, as a result, unjustly enriched. This is because the Act itself contemplated that a borrower might benefit from the improper execution of such an agreement (*Dimond v Lovell* (2002)). Furthermore, in *Wilson v First County Trust Ltd (No 2)* (2004), the House of Lords held that the unenforceability of a regulated agreement did not breach the lender's rights under the Human Rights Act 1998, as that Act had not yet come into force, and that s 127(3) CCA 1974 did not contravene Art 6(1) or Protocol 1 Art 1 of the European Convention on Human Rights 1950.

✅ Looking for extra marks?

The simple technical error that rendered unenforceable the agreement in *Wilson* resulted in the loan being unrecoverable. Although the House of Lords in *Wilson* correctly applied the law, there was certainly no justice in that case for the lender. To cure such an injustice in future cases, the CCA 2006 repealed ss 127(3)–127(5) of the 1974 Act resulting in the court explicitly having discretion in cases concerning the enforceability of improperly executed agreements. It is likely, therefore, that cases such as *Dimond* and *Wilson* would now be decided differently, thus depriving borrowers from being unjustly enriched merely as a result of a minor technical infringement of the requirements.

Cancellation rights

A regulated agreement *may* be a cancellable agreement. Section 67 CCA 1974 provides that a regulated agreement may be cancellable by the borrower or hirer provided that:

- the antecedent negotiations included oral representations made in the presence of the borrower or hirer;
- it was not secured on land; and
- it was signed by the borrower away from the trade premises of the lender or supplier.

Cooling-off period

To provide greater protection to the borrower or hirer, s 68 provides for a general five-day cooling-off period (which in some circumstances is 14 days) starting from when he receives a copy of the signed cancellable agreement.

Small agreements

A small agreement is defined by s 17(1) CCA 1974 and is either:

- a regulated **consumer credit agreement** for credit not exceeding £50, other than a **hire purchase** or conditional sale agreement; or

- a regulated **consumer hire agreement** which does not require the hirer to make payments exceeding £50, in either case, being an agreement which is either unsecured or secured by a guarantee or indemnity only (whether or not the guarantee or indemnity is itself secured).

Revision tip

The main significance of a small agreement is that it is exempt from the majority of the provisions on formalities and cancellation.

Borrower-Lender-Supplier (B-L-S) and Borrower-Lender (B-L) agreements (formerly, Debtor-Creditor-Supplier (D-C-S) and Debtor-Creditor (D-C) agreements)

Prior to the amendments made by the FSMA, D-C-S and D-C agreements were defined in ss 12 and 13 CCA 1974, respectively. Both were regulated **consumer credit agreements**. The distinction between the two was straightforward. A **D-C-S agreement** was where the **creditor** was also the supplier or had a business connection with the supplier. Here, the agreement was made by the creditor under pre-existing arrangements, or in contemplation of future arrangements, between himself and the supplier, or which was financing a transaction between the **debtor** and the creditor. Typical D-C-S agreements were credit sales or where the payment was made by credit card. A **D-C agreement** was where the creditor was not also the supplier and had no business connection with the supplier. The creditor merely provided the credit for the transaction. Here, the agreement was not made under pre-existing arrangements or in contemplation of future arrangements between the creditor and the supplier. The CCA 1974 does not apply to the agreement between the debtor and the supplier.

Borrower-Lender-Supplier (B-L-S) and Borrower-Lender (B-L) agreements

Following the implementation of the **FSMA**, a D-C-S agreement is now a Borrower-Lender-Supplier agreement (B-L-S) and a D-C agreement is now a Borrower-Lender agreement (B-L) under **FSMA RAO 60L(1)**.

Borrower-Lender-Supplier agreements and Borrower-Lender agreements

A Borrower-Lender-Supplier agreement is defined by **FSMA RAO 60L(1)** as:

(a) a credit agreement to finance a transaction between the borrower and the lender, whether forming part of that agreement or not;

(b) a credit agreement:

(i) to finance a transaction between the borrower and a person ('the supplier') other than the lender, and

(ii) which is made by the lender under pre-existing arrangements, or in contemplation of future arrangements, between the lender and the supplier, or

(c) a credit agreement which is:

(i) an unrestricted-use credit agreement, and

(ii) made by the lender under pre-existing arrangements between the lender and a person ('the supplier') other than the borrower in the knowledge that the credit is to be used to finance a transaction between the borrower and the supplier.

A Borrower-Lender agreement is defined by **FSMA RAO 60L(1)** as:

(a) a credit agreement:

(i) to finance a transaction between the borrower and a person ('the supplier') other than the lender, and

(ii) which is not made by the lender under pre-existing arrangements, or in contemplation of future arrangements, between the lender and the supplier,

(b) a credit agreement to refinance any existing indebtedness of the borrower, whether to the lender or another person, or

(c) a credit agreement which is:

(i) an unrestricted-use credit agreement, and

(ii) not made by the lender:

(a) under pre-existing arrangements between the lender and a person other than the borrower ('the supplier'), and

(b) in the knowledge that the credit is to be used to finance a transaction between the borrower and the supplier.

Revision tip

The practical difference between a **D-C-S** and a **D-C agreement** is that with a D-C-S agreement both the supplier and the **creditor** are potentially liable to the **debtor** for misrepresentation and breach of contract by the supplier. The same applies to B-L-S and B-L agreements.

Liability of the lender for the seller's misrepresentation or breach of contract

Revision Lip

The situation discussed here concerns a customer who has two separate contracts: one with the supplier and the other with the lender who provides credit for the purchase. At common law, only the party with whom the contract is made can be liable for a breach of that contract. **Section 75 CCA 1974** is, therefore, a very valuable provision, as it explains that where the borrower has any claim against the supplier in respect of a **misrepresentation** or breach of contract, he shall have a like claim against the lender, who, with the supplier, shall be jointly and severally liable to the borrower. The section only applies to **debtor-creditor-supplier** or borrower-lender-supplier agreements. In short, this is where there exists some business connection between the lender and the supplier: it must fall within **s 12(b) CCA 1974**, which means it must be made under preexisting arrangements or in contemplation of future arrangements between the lender and the supplier.

Where there exists a business connection between a supplier of goods and a lender who provides finance for a commercial transaction to sell a single item costing between £100 and £30,000 (s 75(3)(b)), then a borrower who uses such finance under a regulated agreement is protected by s 75. Provided the transaction falls between the above figures, then it does not matter that the borrower only pays for part of it using credit. The borrower will still be protected and the lender's liability will be for the whole amount.

The lender and supplier must be different parties. The protection provided by s 75 is that the lender is jointly and severally liable for the supplier's:

- misrepresentation; or
- breach of contract.

This liability is known as connected lender liability. Because the lender and supplier are jointly and severally liable, then the borrower is entitled to sue either or both of them.

It is not possible to exclude the provisions of s 75 (s 173(1)).

In *Durkin v DSG Retail Ltd and HFC Bank Plc* (2014) the Supreme Court had to consider whether the 'like claim' provision in s 75 entitled a consumer to terminate a credit agreement where the goods purchased were defective or not in accordance with the contract of sale so as to relieve him from the obligation to make any further payments under the credit agreement. The court held that the consumer was entitled to rescind the credit agreement but not as a result of the 'like claim' provision in s 75(1) but via an altogether different and less obvious route. At paragraph 26 of the judgment, Lord Hodge explained that:

> It is inherent in a debtor-creditor-supplier agreement under section 12(b) of the 1974 Act, which is also tied into a specific supply transaction, that if the supply transaction which it financed is in effect

brought to an end by the debtor's acceptance of the supplier's repudiatory breach of contract, the debtor must repay the borrowed funds which he recovers from the supplier. In my view, in order to reflect that reality, the law implies a term into such a credit agreement that it is conditional upon the survival of the supply agreement. The debtor on rejecting the goods and thereby rescinding the supply agreement for breach of contract may also rescind the credit agreement by invoking this condition. As the debtor has no right to retain or use for other purposes funds lent for the specific transaction, the creditor also may rescind the credit agreement. It appears to me that similar reasoning would apply to a section 12(c) agreement where the credit agreement tied the loan to a particular transaction.

Second cardholders

The problem with a second cardholder (the authorised user) can be simply stated. Section 75 (and for that matter s 56 discussed under 'Misrepresentation', p 162) confer rights only on the *debtor/borrower*. The authorised user (typically the husband or wife of the principal cardholder) is not liable to pay the debts incurred and he or she is not (in ordinary parlance anyway) the debtor/borrower. However, s 189 defines 'debtor' rather widely as 'the individual receiving credit under a consumer credit agreement . . . '. Credit 'includes a cash loan and any other form of financial accommodation' (s 9 (1)). It could be argued, therefore, that the authorised user is a debtor for the purpose of s 75 (and s 56) although it could also be argued that since it is only the principal cardholder who is liable for the debts incurred, he is the person who receives the financial accommodation. There are, as yet, no decided cases on the matter and it is therefore uncertain whether or not a second cardholder will receive the same protection under s 75 as if he were the principal cardholder.

Foreign transactions

After some doubt whether s 75 provided protection in respect of foreign transactions it was held by the House of Lords in *Office of Fair Trading v Lloyds TSB Bank Plc* (2008) that it does, subject to the credit agreement being a UK credit agreement. This decision makes it plain that s 75 can assist a customer who makes a purchase abroad using his UK credit card.

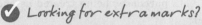 **Looking for extra marks?**

You should explain that since s 75 imposes joint and several liability on both the lender and supplier, s 75 is especially beneficial to customers where the supplier becomes insolvent, cannot be traced, or otherwise where he considers a claim against the lender might be more fruitful, for example in the case of a foreign transaction where the **contract of sale** is governed by the law of another country.

Liability of the lender for the seller's misrepresentation/breach
✳✳✳✳✳✳✳✳✳✳

Extent of the lender's liability

The lender's liability under s 75 is not limited to the amount of the credit. A lender will be liable for all losses provided they are not too remote.

Lender's indemnity

The lender may, if he wishes, join the seller as a party into any claim brought by the borrower and to claim an indemnity from him (ss 75(2) and 75(5)).

Misrepresentation

Regulated agreements

Where there exists a business connection between a supplier of goods and a lender who provides finance for the transaction, the supplier is treated as the lender's agent with regard to any antecedent negotiations (s 56 CCA 1974). As a result of this statutory agency, the lender will be liable for statements made by the supplier during any antecedent negotiations leading to a regulated agreement. Antecedent negotiations start as soon as the supplier and the customer first start communicating with one another, and this includes communication by advertisement (s 56(4)).

Revision tip

There will be a connection between the supplier and the lender in the following situations:
- when the customer uses a credit card to pay for the goods;
- when the customer takes goods on **hire purchase**.

The significance of s 56 is that any **misrepresentations** made by the supplier about the goods will enable the borrower customer to pursue the lender. Not only will the lender be liable for the supplier's misrepresentations but the borrower will be entitled to rescind the regulated agreement. As the supplier is treated as the lender's agent, the borrower may, if he wishes, just give notice of such **rescission** to the supplier (s 102).

The antecedent negotiations referred to in s 56 whereby a supplier will be deemed to be the agent of the lender are those 'in relation to' goods sold or proposed to be sold (s 56(1)(b)). Therefore, a supplier's promise to settle a buyer's existing debt was an antecedent negotiation 'in relation to' a subsequent purchase, both purchases being treated as one transaction (*Forthright Finance Ltd v Ingate* (1997)).

It is not possible to exclude the provisions of s 56 (s 173(1)).

Unregulated agreements

Where the supplier sells goods to the finance company under an unregulated agreement he is not generally treated as the finance company's agent unless exceptional circumstances apply (*Branwhite v Worcester Works Finance Ltd* (1969)).

Liability of the creditor in linked credit agreements

Section 75A applies from 1 February 2011. It supplements s 75 although its function is quite different. It only applies to linked credit agreements.

Revision Tip

A linked credit agreement means a regulated **consumer credit agreement** which serves exclusively to finance an agreement for the supply of **specific goods** or the provision of a *specific* service and where either the lender uses the services of the supplier in connection with the preparation or making of the credit agreement or the *specific* goods or provision of a *specific* service are explicitly specified in the credit agreement itself. Because of this requirement, credit card payments will almost always be excluded from the section because the agreement under which a credit card is provided relates to the payment of goods or services *generally* rather than to the supply of *specific* goods or services.

Section 75A will normally apply where:

- the goods or services were purchased under a linked credit agreement;
- the credit agreement falls *outside* the scope of s 75 but *within* the scope of the **Consumer Credit Directive**;
- there has been a breach of contract by the supplier in relation to the goods or services. Unlike s 75 it does not apply to misrepresentations;
- the borrower has taken all reasonable steps with the supplier to obtain satisfaction before making a claim against the lender under s 75A.

However, the section does not apply where:

- the cash value of the goods or service is £30,000 or less;
- the credit agreement is for credit which exceeds £60,260;
- the credit agreement is entered into by the borrower wholly or predominantly for the purposes of a business carried on, or intended to be carried on, by him.

To pursue a claim directly against the lender under s 75A the following conditions must be met:

- the supplier cannot be traced;
- the borrower has contacted the supplier but the supplier has not responded;
- the supplier is insolvent;
- the borrower has taken reasonable steps (but not necessarily litigation) to pursue his claim against the supplier but has not obtained satisfaction for his claim. A borrower is to be deemed to have obtained satisfaction where he has accepted a replacement product or service or other compensation from the supplier in settlement of his claim.

Retaking of protected goods

If the borrower is in breach of a regulated **hire purchase** or a regulated conditional sale agreement relating to goods and has already paid to the lender one-third or more of the total price of the goods and the property in the goods remains in the lender, then the lender will not be entitled to recover possession of the goods from the borrower without an order of the court (s 90(1)). The phrase 'protected goods' simply refers to the goods under this section. If goods are recovered by the lender in contravention of s 90, then the regulated agreement, if not previously terminated, shall terminate, and the borrower shall be released from all liability under the agreement, and shall also be entitled to recover from the lender all sums paid by him under the agreement (s 91).

Borrower's right to complete payments ahead of time

A borrower under a regulated **consumer credit agreement** is entitled at any time, upon notice to the lender and the payment to him of all sums owing under the agreement, to discharge his indebtedness under the agreement (s 94(1)). In order to understand how much remains owing under the agreement, the borrower is entitled to require the lender to set out the amount of the payment required to discharge his indebtedness, together with particulars showing how the amount is arrived at (s 97(1)).

Non-commercial agreements

A non-commercial agreement is defined by s 189(1) CCA 1974 as 'a consumer credit agreement or a consumer hire agreement not made by the creditor or owner in the course of a business carried on by him'. Agreements between family members or friends are usually non-commercial agreements (*Hare v Schurek* (1993)).

The Financial Conduct Authority Consumer Credit Sourcebook (CONC)

The consumer credit chapter of the FCA Consumer Credit Sourcebook ('CONC') provides detailed rules and guidance for consumer credit firms on matters such as financial promotion, advising, selling, debt collection as well as conduct generally. Under the provisions of the FSMA, in the event of a breach of the rules set out in CONC, a private person has a statutory right of action in damages where that person can demonstrate loss as a result of the rule breach in question (s 138D Financial Services and Markets Act 2000). This demonstrates the broader range of remedies afforded to borrowers under the FSMA regime.

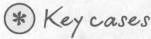

Key cases

Case	Facts	Held/Principle
***Durkin v DSG Retail Ltd and HFC Bank Plc* [2014] UKSC 21**	Durkin visited a PC World store (DSG) in Scotland to purchase a laptop computer, making clear that he wanted one with an internal modem. A sales assistant identified a laptop but said that he was unsure whether it had an internal modem. He agreed that Durkin could take the computer home and return it if it did not. Durkin paid a £50 deposit and signed a credit agreement with HFC for the balance of £1,449. The following day he found that the computer did not have an internal modem so he returned it to the store and asked for his deposit back and for the credit agreement to be cancelled. The store manager refused to accept his rejection of the goods and took no steps to cancel the credit agreement. Durkin did not pay any money to HFC under the credit agreement explaining to them that he had rejected the laptop and had rescinded both his contract of sale and the credit agreement. HFC warned him that if he did not make payments he might have difficulty obtaining future credit and threatened to serve a default notice on him under the CCA 1974. Without making any enquiries, HFC issued a default notice and intimated to credit reference agencies that he had been in default of his obligations under the credit agreement. Although Durkin recovered his £50 deposit in an out-of-court settlement he claimed that the adverse credit register entries caused him loss. Durkin sought a **declarator** that he had validly rescinded both the contract of sale and the credit agreement and also claimed damages. The Sheriff declared	For present purposes, three key issues arose which were heard by the Supreme Court: • whether there was a valid loan agreement between Durkin and HFC • whether the right to rescind the loan agreement was a 'like claim' under **s 75(1) of the CCA 1974**. If not, did the loan agreement survive rescission of the supply agreement? • what obligations did HFC have to investigate the existence of the debt or dispute? Lord Hodge (who delivered the judgment of the court) held that Durkin was entitled to rescind the credit agreement and validly did so when he gave notice to HFC. His Lordship held, however, that this was not as a result of the 'like claim' provision in **s 75(1)** as this section conferred no such right but via an altogether different and less obvious route. At paragraph 26 of the judgment, Lord Hodge explained that 'It is inherent in a debtor-creditor-supplier agreement under section 12(b) of the 1974 Act, which is also tied into a specific supply transaction, that if the supply transaction which it financed is in effect brought to an end by the debtor's acceptance of the supplier's repudiatory breach of contract, the debtor must repay the borrowed funds which he recovers from the supplier. In my view, in order to reflect that reality, the law implies a term into such a credit agreement that it is conditional upon the survival of the supply agreement. The debtor on rejecting the goods and thereby rescinding the supply agreement for breach of contract may also rescind the credit agreement by invoking this condition. As the debtor has no right to retain or use for other purposes funds lent for the specific transaction, the creditor also may rescind the credit agreement. It appears to me that similar reasoning would apply to a **section 12(c)** agreement where the credit agreement tied the loan to a particular transaction.'

Key cases

****

Case	Facts	Held/Principle
	that he had validly rescinded the contract of sale (this was not challenged on appeal). Although his claim succeeded Durkin appealed the quantum of damages awarded and HFC cross-appealed against the decree of **declarators**.	As to the conduct of HFC, since it knew of Durkin's assertion that the credit agreement had been rescinded it was under a duty to investigate that assertion in order reasonably to satisfy itself that the credit agreement remained enforceable before reporting to the credit reference agencies that he was in default. HFC made no such enquiries, accepting without question DSG's position that Durkin had not been entitled to rescind the contract of sale. Lord Hodge held that HFC was under an obligation to investigate whether a debt properly existed prior to making any report to credit reference agencies. In the case of a disputed debt it should not have made a report to the credit agencies until the existence of the debt was determined. For practical purposes this means that creditors must not threaten to report bad debts to the credit agencies as a means of forcing payment from consumers until the existence of any such debt has been properly established.
Dimond v Lovell [2002] 1 AC 384	D's car was damaged as a result of an accident caused by L. Her insurance company suggested that she hire a car from a company specialising in hiring cars to victims of car accidents. Under this agreement, the company would have conduct of any litigation and the costs of the hire would not be payable until the conclusion of the case on the proviso that she would be under no liability for the hire charges even if they could not be recovered from L. The terms of the hire agreement stated that it could not last for more than 28 days. As **s 15(1) CCA 1974** requires that a consumer hire agreement must be capable of subsisting for more than three months, the agreement was not a consumer hire agreement. L's insurer refused to pay the hire charges asserting that it was an unenforceable consumer credit agreement.	The House of Lords held that as the terms of the agreement stipulated that the company's right to recover the hire charges was to be deferred, credit had been granted to D with the result that the agreement was a regulated agreement for the purposes of CCA 1974. As the agreement had been improperly executed and was therefore unenforceable by the company against D, D had not been unjustly enriched by not having to pay the hire charges since the CCA contemplated that a debtor might benefit from the improper execution of an agreement. In the circumstances, D was not entitled to recover damages for the hire as she was not obliged to pay for it.

Case	Facts	Held/Principle
Forthright Finance Ltd v Ingate [1997] 4 All ER 99	The buyer entered into an agreement with a dealer to purchase a car to be financed by F. One year later he agreed to purchase a newer model from a second dealer. This dealer agreed to take the first car in part-exchange and to discharge the balance that was outstanding to F. A new agreement was made with a second creditor for the second car. The second dealer went into liquidation, having failed to pay F as promised. F sought to recover the money directly from the buyer. The buyer argued that **s 56 CCA 1974** meant that the second creditor was bound by the second dealer's promise to discharge the amount owed to F and therefore he had no liability.	The Court of Appeal held that where goods which would be the subject of a D-C-S agreement were sold or proposed to be sold by a broker, then any negotiations relating to those goods would be deemed to have been made by the negotiator as agent for the creditor. The second creditor was therefore liable.
Hare v Schurek [1993] CCLR 47	C was a car dealer who did not usually extend credit to his customers. He sold a car to his friend and entered into a 'one-off' hire purchase agreement with him. The case concerned whether he needed a consumer credit licence.	The Court of Appeal held that a person who enters into occasional regulated agreements is not carrying on a consumer credit or a consumer hire business by virtue of **s 189(2) CCA 1974**, which provides that a person is not to be treated as carrying on a particular type of business merely because occasionally he enters into transactions belonging to a business of that type. Therefore, as he did not carry on a consumer credit or consumer hire business he did not need a consumer credit licence.
Office of Fair Trading v Lloyds TSB Bank Plc [2008] 1 AC 316	L was an issuer of credit cards. The question for the appeal was whether the protection provided under **s 75 CCA 1974** applied also to foreign transactions. L argued that if it did apply to foreign transactions, the implications would be that it would make UK credit card issuers the potential guarantors of some 29 million foreign suppliers with whom they would not have any direct contractual relations.	The House of Lords held that **s 75**, consistent with the policy behind the Act of protecting consumers, was applicable as much to foreign as to domestic supply transactions, and contained no words of territorial limitation. Therefore, **s 75** governed agreements between UK credit card issuers and their customers without territorial limitation. The sole limitation on the territorial scope of **s 75** was that the credit agreement had to be a UK credit agreement.

Case	Facts	Held/Principle
Plevin v Paragon Personal Finance Ltd [2014] UKSC 61	Mrs Plevin took out a personal loan through LLP Processing (UK) Ltd. LLP proposed that she borrow £34,000 from Paragon repayable in instalments over 10 years, and that she take out a payment protection insurance policy for 5 years with Norwich Union who was Paragon's designated insurer. The PPI premium of £5,780 was payable at the outset and added to the amount of the loan. 71.8% of the premium was taken in commission: LLP retained £1,870 and Paragon retained £2,280. Although the Financial Industry Standards Association guide which LLP gave to Mrs Plevin told her that 'commission is paid by the lending company' she was not told the amount of the commission or the identity of the recipients. Mrs Plevin argued that the relationship between herself and Paragon was unfair under **s 140A(1)(c)** because of the non-disclosure of the commissions and also because of the failure of anyone involved to advise on the suitability of the PPI policy for her needs. Insofar as LLP committed these defaults, Mrs Plevin says it did so 'on behalf of' Paragon. The Insurance Conduct of Business Rules, which are the statutory rules regulating the insurance industry, do not require insurance intermediaries to disclose commissions to their customers but do require an insurance intermediary which makes a 'personal recommendation' to a customer to buy an insurance contract to take reasonable steps to ensure that the recommendation is suitable for the customer's demands and needs.	The Supreme Court has now handed down its first judgment on what amounts to an unfair relationship for the purposes of **ss 140A–D CCA**. Lord Sumption (who delivered the sole judgment) held that the non-disclosure of the amount of commissions and the identity of the recipients did make Mrs Plevin's relationship with Paragon unfair under **s 140A(1)(c)** but the failure to conduct a needs assessment of Mrs Plevin did not. Lord Sumption stated that the non-disclosure of the commissions did make the relationship between Paragon and Mrs Plevin an unfair one. He stated that at some point, the commissions may become so large that the relationship cannot be regarded as fair if the customer is kept in ignorance and concluded that Mrs Plevin would have questioned whether the PPI policy represented value for money if she had been aware of the commission amounts and might not have taken out the policy at all. This unfairness was the responsibility of Paragon, the only party which knew the size of both commissions. However, the court held that Paragon's failure to conduct their own needs assessment of Mrs Plevin did not make its relationship with her unfair. The absence of a regulatory duty under the ICOB Rules was not conclusive although it was highly relevant: Paragon could not reasonably be expected to perform a duty which the relevant statutory code assigned to someone else, namely LLP. LLP's failure to conduct a needs assessment of Mrs Plevin could not be treated as something done 'by or on behalf of' Paragon, because LLP was not acting as Paragon's agent. The ordinary and natural meaning of the words 'on behalf of' imports agency, and that is how the courts have ordinarily construed them. Nothing in this case demands a broader interpretation. The phrase 'by or on behalf of' suggests that the act or omission must be done by the creditor itself, or by someone else whose acts and omissions engage the creditor's responsibility as if the creditor had done or not done it itself. Further, the **Consumer Credit Act 1974** makes extensive use of the technique of imputing responsibility to the creditor for the acts or omissions of other parties who are not (or not necessarily) the creditor's agents, including in **s 140A(3)**, and when it does so, it does so in clear terms. Finally, there would be no coherent criteria for determining what connection other

Case	Facts	Held/Principle
		than agency would be required between the creditor and the acts or omissions causing the unfairness. In the result, the case was remitted to the Manchester County Court to decide what, if any, relief under **s 140B** should be ordered.
Wilson v First County Trust Ltd (No 2) [2004] 1 AC 816	W borrowed £5,000 from a pawnbroker using her car as security. The agreement was a regulated agreement and was correctly documented save that a documentation fee of £250 was erroneously entered in the wrong box and thereby noted as part of the loan. This had the effect of misstating the total charge for credit. The Court of Appeal held that as the document fee was not credit within the meaning given in the **CCA 1974**, one of the prescribed terms had been incorrectly stated and, pursuant to **s 127(3)**, the agreement was unenforceable. As a result, W was entitled to keep the loan amount, pay no interest, and also recover her car. The Secretary of State appealed arguing that the restriction on the enforcement of improperly executed credit agreements given in **s 127(3)** was incompatible with the **Human Rights Act 1998**.	The House of Lords upheld the Court of Appeal's decision. The fact that a regulated agreement was not enforceable unless a document containing all the prescribed terms was signed by the debtor constituted a restriction on the scope of the rights a creditor acquired under a regulated agreement but did not bar access to the court to decide whether the case was caught by the restriction. The inability of the court to make an enforcement order was a limitation on the substantive scope of a creditor's rights but did not offend the rule of law or the separation of powers. The **Human Rights Act 1998** did not apply as it was not in force at the material time and the court's inability to enforce the agreement did not engage **Art 6(1) European Convention on Human Rights** which guarantees procedural fairness. Further, if the court's inability to enforce the agreement deprived the lender of its rights under the **First Protocol Art 1** then that interference was justified. As Lord Nicholls of Birkenhead explained, 'one would not expect a statute promoting human rights values to render unlawful acts which were lawful when done. That would be to impose liability where none existed at the time the act was done'.

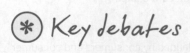

✳ Key debates

Topic	House of Lords' ruling ends shopper uncertainty
Author/Academic	Andrew Digwood
Viewpoint	Discusses the House of Lords' ruling in *Office of Fair Trading v Lloyds TSB Bank Plc* on whether, under **s 75 CCA 1974**, consumers may claim refunds from their credit card companies for purchases made abroad as well as in the UK.
Source	(2007) 157 *New Law Journal* 1555

Exam questions

★★★★★★★★★★

Topic	**The Consumer Credit Act and human rights issues**
Author/Academic	Sylvia Elwes
Viewpoint	Examines the House of Lords' ruling in *Wilson v First County Trust Ltd (No 2)*, concerning the enforceability of a consumer credit agreement which misstated the full amount of credit advanced. Outlines the judicial approaches to whether the **Human Rights Act 1998** had retrospective effect; whether **s 127(3) CCA 1974** contravened the **European Convention on Human Rights 1950**; and whether a lender who lost the right to enforce an agreement could obtain a restitutionary remedy for unjust enrichment.
Source	(2004) 25(2) *Business Law Review* 28

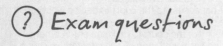 Exam questions

Problem question

Alf got married two years ago to Veronica. Veronica used to live in France where she still has family. They now both live in England. For the past 10 years, Alf has had a credit card with Eastern Bank plc. He uses it only for convenience and always settles his bill as soon as the monthly statement arrives. Since they married, Alf made Veronica an authorised user on his card. Last Christmas, Veronica visited her family in France. Whilst she was there, she bought eight silver-plated dinner place mats using the credit card. Each mat cost (when converted from Euros to Stirling) £15. The total charge was therefore £120. She particularly liked the mats because of their unique pattern in that when placed together they made a picture of the Eiffel Tower although when used separately they didn't look out of place. The shop told Veronica that the mats were dishwasher proof. However, the first time Veronica washed them in the dishwasher the silver plating came away and she has since learned that they are not suitable for washing in a dishwasher. Unfortunately, the shop has now gone out of business.

Advise Veronica of any rights she might have against the credit card company.

Essay question

Section 75 of the **Consumer Credit Act 1974** has been applauded by consumers and consumer groups yet criticised severely by the credit industry arguing that it is unjust and flawed.

Critically evaluate s 75 in the light of the above.

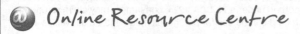 Online Resource Centre

To see an outline answer to this question visit www.oup.com/lawrevision/

#12

The creation of agency and the agent's authority

Key facts

- The word 'agent' has a specific legal meaning and the law attaches special rules to the relationship of agency.

- Agency is crucial for the commercial world to operate.

- An agent can alter the legal position of his principal, most notably by entering into contracts on his principal's behalf.

- There are three main parties in the case of agency: the agent, the principal, and the third party.

- Broadly, the principal will take on the rights and liabilities created by contracts made by the agent provided the agent had authority to act.

- The authority of the agent is therefore critical in understanding whether or not the principal will be bound by his acts.

- Authority need not be with the principal's consent or agreement.

- A principal may, in certain circumstances, ratify the acts of an agent who was not authorised to act.

Figure 12.1 The agency relationship

Introduction

The primary purpose of agency is for the **agent** to bring the **principal** and the third party into direct contractual relations. The negotiations are between the agent and the third party but the contract is formed between the principal and the third party. This can be seen from the diagram in Figure 12.1 and is encapsulated by the Latin maxim *qui facit per alium facit per se* (he who acts through another acts for himself).

The words 'agent' and 'agency' have specific legal meanings. They must not be confused with the words as used in everyday language such as 'estate agent' or 'Sony agent' which are unlikely to be agents in the strict legal sense. An estate agent will generally not have the authority, without more, to bring the seller and buyer into direct contractual relations so as to conclude the contract on behalf of a seller. A shop displaying a notice saying, for example, 'Sony agent' is merely an authorised distributor or reseller of the manufacturer's goods rather than an agent in the legal sense.

> ✅ *Looking for extra marks?*
>
> You should explain that the word '**agent**' has a specific legal meaning and that the misuse of the word is nothing new. In *Kennedy v De Trafford* (1897) Lord Herschell stated that:
>
> No word is more commonly and constantly abused than the word 'agent'. A person may be spoken of as an 'agent', and no doubt in the popular sense of the word may properly be said to be an 'agent', although when it is attempted to suggest that he is an 'agent' under such circumstances as create the legal obligations attaching to agency that use of the word is only misleading.

The nature of agency

Many contracts are concluded by **agents**. This is because many contracts are made with limited companies which, being separate legal personalities, cannot act without the intervention of a human being. Thus, the sales assistant in your local store will act as agent when making a contract with the store (the **principal**). Even if the contract is not made with a limited company, then unless the owner makes the contract personally it will be made by a member of his staff who will, in law, be an agent. Partners in a legal partnership will be agents for the partnership and for each other when transacting business on behalf of the partnership.

Creation of agency

In the majority of cases, agency is the result of an agreement between **principal** and **agent**. This agreement may be express or implied. The majority of agency agreements will be contractual but as we will see, this is not always necessary. For example, agency can arise as a matter of law or may be implied from the circumstances of the case. The same principles might also show that an agency relationship does not arise. For example, in *Spearmint Rhino Ventures (UK) Ltd v Commissioners for H.M. Revenue and Customs* (2007), Mann J held that the lap-dancers who entertained customers at Spearmint Rhino's clubs were acting on their own behalf as principals and not as agents for the club when negotiating and receiving fees from customers. Accordingly, the club owner was not liable to account for VAT on the supply of the services provided by the dancers.

Agency may also be imposed where one party has acted on behalf of another during an emergency. This is known as 'agency of necessity' and will be considered later.

In the majority of cases, agency may be created without any formalities. This means that (unless exceptions apply) an agency may be created informally even where the purpose of the agency is for the agent to perform some act on behalf of the principal which itself must conform to some formality, such as where the act must be in writing or evidenced in writing.

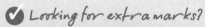

✅ **Looking for extra marks?**

You should explain that as it is the **principal** who is contracting with the third party, the principal himself must possess the legal capacity to perform the transaction that his **agent** performs on his behalf. This simply means that provided the principal has capacity to act, then it does not matter that his agent does not. Therefore, a principal, with full capacity, may perfectly properly appoint a minor to contract on his behalf even though the minor himself lacks capacity in his own right.

The agent's authority

Revision tip

Questions on agency tend to focus on the extent of the **agent's** authority and how this affects any transactions made by him for his **principal**. You must be clear in your answer how the agent's authority arises, what kind of authority he has, and how this might affect the transaction concerned.

An **agent** can only bind his principal if he has some kind of authority to do so, otherwise the **principal** will not be bound to the contract with the third party. Provided there is some authority for the agent to act, then the principal will be bound to the third party and will be liable to him for his agent's acts.

The agent's authority
✳✳✳✳✳✳✳✳✳✳

Authority is a legal concept. You should note that authority might exist even without the consent of the principal. It is important, therefore, to consider on what basis the agent has the authority to bind his principal and what happens where he acts without authority or where he exceeds his authority.

There are several kinds of authority which will be discussed below. It is important to appreciate that an agent's authority can exist either with or without the principal's consent or agreement (see Figure 12.2).

Actual authority

Actual authority is where the **principal** gives the **agent** actual authority to enter into the arrangement with the third party on his behalf. This can either be express or implied.

Figure 12.2 The agent's authority

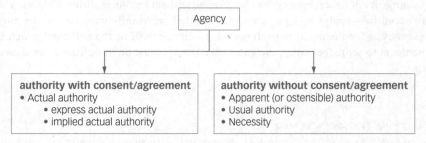

Express actual authority

This is the most straightforward situation and arises where the relationship of agency is created by express agreement. This agreement, which need not be in writing, should also set out the scope of the agent's authority. In *Freeman & Lockyer v Buckhurst Park Properties (Mangal) Ltd* (1964), Diplock LJ explained actual authority as:

> . . . a legal relationship between principal and agent created by a consensual agreement to which they alone are parties. Its scope is to be ascertained by applying ordinary principles of construction of contracts, including any proper implications from the express words used, the usages of the trade, or the course of business between the parties.

The words 'any proper implications' refer to the other kind of actual authority, 'implied actual authority'.

Implied actual authority

As the word 'implied' suggests, this kind of authority comes about by implication rather than by express words. It is still actual authority, in that there is agreement between principal and agent that the latter shall have authority, but the *scope* of the authority will be more difficult to determine. It will be left to the court to decide whether or not it had been agreed between the principal and the agent that the agent was authorised to do the act in question. It typically arises out of the *relationship* between principal and agent, or as a result of the conduct of the parties. This can be seen from the following case:

Hely-Hutchinson v Brayhead Ltd [1968] 1 QB 549

The chairman of a company acted as its managing director although he had never been appointed to that role. He signed, on behalf of the company, contracts of guarantee and indemnity in favour of a third party's debts. When the company tried to avoid this liability it was held that it was bound by the contracts because it had, by conduct, granted to the chairman the implied authority of a managing director to bind the company in such a way. Lord Denning MR explained that:

> *It is implied when it is inferred from the conduct of the parties and the circumstances of the case, such as when the board of directors appoint one of their number to be managing director. They thereby impliedly authorise him to do all such things as fall within the usual scope of that office.* (emphasis added)

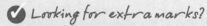 **Looking for extra marks?**

It will be impressive to demonstrate your understanding of the concept of implied actual authority by referring to the above decision of Lord Denning and, in particular, to quote the words emphasised in italics.

You should note that where the **principal** has expressly instructed an **agent** not to act in a particular way, then the agent will not have implied actual authority to act in that way as it is in direct contravention of the principal's instructions (*Waugh v HB Clifford and Sons Ltd* (1982)).

Apparent (also referred to as ostensible) authority

In *Freeman & Lockyer v Buckhurst Park Properties (Mangal) Ltd* (1964), Diplock LJ defined **apparent authority** as:

> a legal relationship between the principal and the [third party] created by a representation, made by the principal to the [third party], intended to be and in fact acted upon by the [third party], that the agent has authority to enter on behalf of the principal into a contract of a kind within the scope of the 'apparent' authority, so as to render the principal liable to perform any obligations imposed upon him by such contract . . . The representation, when acted upon by the [third party] by entering into a contract with the agent, operates as an estoppel, preventing the principal from asserting that he is not bound by the contract. It is irrelevant whether the agent had actual authority to enter into the contract.

The agent's authority

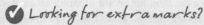

Whereas **actual authority** derives from an *agreement* between the principal and the agent, apparent authority arises where the principal makes a representation so as to give an impression to the third party that the agent has authority to act on his behalf. In other words, apparent authority arises where the third party has been induced into entering the contract with the principal by an agent who *appears* to have authority to act but in fact has no such authority.

Apparent authority is not authority in the strict meaning of the word. It is no more than an illusion of authority created by the principal's representation. It is the authority of the agent as it *appears* to the third party. It was described by Toulson J in *ING Re (UK) Ltd v R&V Versicherung AG (2006)* in the following terms:

> The doctrine of apparent or ostensible authority is based on estoppel by representation. Where a principal (P) represents or causes it to be represented to a third party (T) that an agent (A) has authority to act on P's behalf, and T deals with A as P's agent on the faith of that representation, P is bound by A's acts to the same extent as if A had the authority which he was represented as having.

Where apparent authority arises, the principal is estopped from denying that the agent had the authority to make it with the result that the contract with the third party will be enforced against the principal. In other words, the principal is prevented (estopped) from asserting that he is not bound by the contract. The agent need not be aware of the existence of the representation, although he is likely to be aware of it.

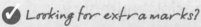

The representation that creates **apparent authority** may take a variety of forms. The most common is representation by conduct; that is, by permitting the **agent** to act in the conduct of the **principal**'s business with third parties. By so doing, the principal is representing that the agent has his authority to enter into contracts with third parties of the kind which an agent usually has **actual authority** to make.

There are three requirements for apparent authority to exist (per Slade J in *Rama Corporation Ltd v Proved Tin and General Investments Ltd* (1952)):

1. The **principal**, or someone authorised by him, must have represented to the third party that the **agent** had authority to act on behalf of the principal. This representation, which may be of fact or law, may be made by words or conduct or may be implied by previous dealings between the parties or from the principal's conduct. In *Armagas Ltd v Mundogas SA* (1986), the House of Lords confirmed that the representation must come from the principal and not the agent.

2. The third party must have relied on the representation.

3. The third party must have altered his position although not necessarily to his detriment. This third requirement appears nowadays to be satisfied simply by the third party entering into the contract itself (see, for example, the judgment of Diplock LJ in *Freeman & Lockyer v Buckhurst Park Properties (Mangal) Ltd* (1964)).

A situation might arise where the third party knows, or ought to know, that the **agent** has no authority to do certain things. In this situation it will be unlikely that the agent will have **apparent authority** to carry out those things.

First Energy (UK) Ltd v Hungarian International Bank Ltd [1993] 2 Lloyd's Rep 194

The Bank appointed a senior manager (the **agent**) to one of its branches. The manager told the third party customer that he did not have the authority to grant a loan facility and that only his head office had such authority. Some time later, he told the customer that head office had authorised the loan. In fact, the manager had been mistaken and the head office had not granted the loan. The Court of Appeal held that by the Bank appointing the senior manager to his role, the Bank had represented to the customer that the manager had **apparent authority** to communicate to his customer the lending decisions of his head office. He did not have authority to grant the loan himself and made this plain to his customer. This means that had he told his customer that he had himself authorised the loan then no question of apparent authority would have arisen.

Revision tip

You should always consider whether or not the **agent** has **actual authority** (express or implied) before going on to consider other kinds of authority. If the agent has actual authority, you should then explain that there will generally be no need to consider the other kinds of authority.

Usual authority

Whether 'usual authority' exists as a kind of authority in its own right has been the subject of much debate. In the majority of cases, usual authority can be seen as emanating from other kinds of authority, particularly implied **actual authority** and **apparent authority**, and is little more than an extension of these kinds of authority.

The agent's authority

✱✱✱✱✱✱✱✱✱✱

We saw under 'Implied actual authority', pp 174–175, that in *Hely-Hutchinson v Brayhead Ltd* (1968), Lord Denning MR stated that when the board of directors appoints one of their number to be managing director 'they thereby impliedly authorise him to do all such things as fall within the usual scope of that office'. Therefore, in cases where an agent belongs to a particular class of trade or profession he will normally have the usual authority to do whatever is necessary in order for him to fulfil his express authority as **agent**.

A case that illustrates usual authority in the context of **apparent authority** is *Panorama Developments (Guildford) Ltd v Fidelis Furnishing Fabrics Ltd* (1971).

Panorama Developments (Guildford) Ltd v Fidelis Furnishing Fabrics Ltd [1971] 2 QB 711

A company secretary hired vehicles purportedly for his company but which were in fact for his own private use. The company refused to pay, arguing that it was not bound by the hire contracts. The Court of Appeal held that as company secretary he had **apparent authority** to enter into contracts that were connected with the administrative side of the business from which he had usual authority for tasks such as the hiring of vehicles. Because these sorts of contracts were within the usual authority of a company secretary the company was therefore bound by these contracts and liable for the debt.

These cases illustrate usual authority as extensions of implied **actual authority** and **apparent authority**. But does usual authority exist as an independent category of authority? The importance of this question can be seen in *Watteau v Fenwick* (1893) (the facts of which can be found under 'Key Cases', p 183) where the court had to consider whether an **agent** could bind his **principal** to a contract in circumstances where he acts outside of his actual authority (for example, because his act was prohibited in the agency agreement) and no question of apparent authority arises (because the principal had not represented to the third party that the agent had authority to act on his behalf). The court held that usual authority was an independent category of authority in its own right and that the agent had usual authority to act on his principal's behalf and to bind him to a contract even though the principal had expressly forbidden him to make it.

✓ *Looking for extra marks?*

It will be impressive to explain the bizarre decision in *Watteau v Fenwick*, which was described by Bingham J in *Rhodian River Shipping Co SA v Halla Maritime Corp (The Rhodian River and The Rhodian Sailor)* (1984) as 'a somewhat puzzling case' and that its 'true ratio is not altogether easy to perceive'. *Watteau v Fenwick* has been strongly criticised yet has never been overruled. Notwithstanding that the judgment was couched in terms of agency, it has been impressively argued that the decision can be justified on orthodox legal principles 'provided one gets away from the idea that the law of agency has anything to do with it' (see Andrew Tettenborn, 'Agents, Business Owners and Estoppel' [1998] *CLJ* 274).

Revision tip

You should have in mind that the decision in *Watteau v Fenwick* is unlikely to be followed and in any event is restricted to the following circumstances:

1. the third party must be unaware of the existence of a '**principal**' and must think that the '**agent**' is acting on his own behalf rather than as agent for some principal;
2. the 'agent' has no actual authority to do the act because he has been forbidden to do so by the 'principal'; and
3. the contract made by the 'agent' must be usual for an agent in his position.

A good answer will explain:

- why there was no **actual authority** (because the 'agent' had been forbidden to do the act);
- why there was no **apparent authority** (because the 'principal', or someone authorised by him, had not represented **to the third party** that the 'agent' had authority to act on his behalf. This must be the case because the third party must be unaware of the existence of a 'principal' and must think that the 'agent' is acting on his own behalf rather than as agent for some principal); and
- that even if the above criteria are met, it is still unlikely that the decision will be followed given the amount of criticism it has received.

Agency of necessity

An **agency of necessity** might be imposed where one party (the **agent**) has acted on behalf of another (the **principal**) during an emergency. The emergency must have posed such an imminent threat to the principal's property or other interests that the agent needed to have acted immediately without there having been any time for him to have sought his principal's instructions. The agent's acts are, therefore, for the benefit of his principal.

✔ Looking for extra marks?

You should explain that with modern methods of communication there are now much fewer instances where the agent cannot communicate with the principal in order to gain his express instructions and therefore an agency of necessity is now much less likely to arise.

The following conditions must be satisfied before the law will impose an **agency of necessity**:

1. the **agent** must be in control of his **principal**'s property;
2. the agent's intervention must be a necessity;
3. it must be impossible (or at the very least, not reasonably practicable) for the agent to contact his 'principal' so as to get his instructions;
4. the agent's actions must be bona fide and in the interests of his principal;

Ratification

5. the agent's actions must be reasonable and prudent in all the circumstances; and

6. the principal must be competent when the agent intervened.

A good example of a case concerning agency of necessity is *Springer v Great Western Railway Co* (1921).

Springer v Great Western Railway Co [1921] 1 KB 257

Bad weather and a strike delayed the delivery by sea of a consignment of tomatoes. The **agent** felt that he had to sell them before they perished. Because he could have communicated with the **principal** before selling the consignment the court refused to impose an **agency of necessity** and he was therefore liable to the owners for the losses.

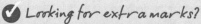 **✓ Looking for extra marks?**

Agency of necessity is highly likely to be restricted to maritime cases although the door was left open by the Court of Appeal in *Surrey Breakdown Ltd v Knight* (1999) as to whether this kind of agency could extend to cases on land. Despite this, the courts have consistently refused to extend it beyond the maritime cases.

Ratification

If an **agent** carries out an act in the name of a **principal** for which he was not authorised, the principal may decide to ratify the transaction. If the principal decides to ratify the transaction then he adopts the agent's unauthorised acts which then become authorised *ab initio*. In other words, **ratification** is equivalent to antecedent authority and the agent will be regarded as having retrospective **actual authority**.

In *Koenigsblatt v Sweet* (1923), Lord Sterndale MR explained ratification in the following terms:

> Once you get a ratification it relates back; it is equivalent to an antecedent authority: *mandato priori æquiparatur*; and when there has been ratification the act that is done is put in the same position as if it had been antecedently authorised.

✓ Looking for extra marks?

You should explain that **ratification** is an all-or-nothing principle. Therefore, a **principal** who ratifies only part of a transaction will be held to have ratified the whole: 'A party wishing to ratify a transaction must adopt it in its entirety' (*Smith v Henniker-Major & Co* (2003), per Robert Walker LJ).

The following factors are important:

- Only the person on whose behalf the **agent** has acted may ratify. An undisclosed **principal** cannot ratify (*Keighley, Maxted & Co v Durant* (1901)).

- The principal must have been in existence at the time the contract was made. This requirement clearly relates to agents who are acting on behalf of companies. It means that if an agent acts for a 'company' before it has been incorporated, the company once incorporated cannot then ratify the transaction (*Kelner v Baxter* (1866–67)).

- The principal must himself have been competent to perform the act at the time the agent acted on his behalf. This rule demonstrates that **ratification** relates to the time that the agent purported to act for the principal. Therefore, the principal must himself have had the capacity to have performed the act at that time (*Boston Deep Sea Fishing and Ice Co Ltd v Farnham* (1957)).

- The principal must also be competent to perform the act at the time of ratification. Following on from the above rule, it might appear rather strange that the principal also needs to have capacity at the point he wishes to ratify the agent's act. After all, the theory underpinning ratification is that the principal is deemed to have made the contract at the time the agent made it and, that being the case, it should not matter what his capacity to contract is at some later time. Nevertheless, it is established that the principal must *also* have capacity at the time of ratification (*Grover & Grover Ltd v Mathews* (1910)). There will be limited application for this rule and it is likely to be restricted to cases such as where an agent, without authority, enters into an insurance contract for the principal and that after the insured property has been destroyed the principal seeks to ratify the contract. He will not be allowed to do so.

- The principal will not be permitted to wait and see whether the transaction is advantageous to him before deciding whether to approve it (*SEB Trygg Holding Aktiebolag v Manches* (2005)) (reversed on other grounds).

- The principal must ratify within a reasonable time of the agent's act. Lapse of time is relevant to whether ratification should be inferred. The longer the principal stands by and does nothing, while action is taken by the contracting third party (and others) under a false impression as to the agent's authority, the more compelling the inference of ratification becomes, irrespective of whether the principal came under any positive duty to speak (*SEB Trygg Holding Aktiebolag v Manches*) (reversed on other grounds).

- A void contract cannot be ratified.

✅ Looking for extra marks?

It will be beneficial to explain the potential absurdity which requires the **principal** to have legal capacity both at the time the **agent** made the contract as well as when he seeks to ratify it. You should explain this by pointing out that it is merely a legal fiction that the principal makes the contract from the outset. The reality is that he adopts the contract that the agent made some time earlier.

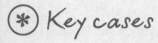

Case	Facts	Held/Principle
Boston Deep Sea Fishing and Ice Co Ltd v Farnham [1957] 1 WLR 1051	A trawler owned by a French company was at an English port when France became occupied by enemy forces during the war. The English company carried on trade by using the trawler during the war period, purporting to act as agents of the French company, although without authority from them for whom they had previously acted as managers. At the end of the war the French company purported to ratify the English company's activities.	The principal must himself have been competent to perform the act at the time the agent acted on his behalf. It was held that the French company could not effectively ratify the English company's activities during the hostilities as the French company was at that time an alien enemy. Harman J explained that 'at the time the acts were done the French company was an alien enemy at common law. It was therefore not a competent principal because it could not have done the act itself'.
Freeman & Lockyer v Buckhurst Park Properties (Mangal) Ltd [1964] 2 QB 480	The company's directors allowed one of their number to act as managing director but had not formally appointed him to that role. He then engaged a firm of architects to carry out some work for the company even though he had no actual authority to do so. The company refused to pay the architect firm's invoice arguing that they were not bound by the agreement because the director lacked actual authority to make the contract.	It was held that the company had represented to third parties that the director had authority. This form of authority is known as apparent or ostensible authority. The company was therefore bound by the contract with the architects.
Grover & Grover Ltd v Mathews [1910] 2 KB 401	An agent, without proper authority, insured a factory on behalf of the owner (the principal). After the factory was destroyed by fire the principal sought to ratify the insurance contract so as to take its benefit. Clearly, the owner could not have insured the factory after it had been destroyed and for the same reason it was held that he could not ratify the policy.	The principal must also be competent to perform the act at the time of ratification. Hamilton J held that where a contract of insurance is made by one person on behalf of another without authority, it cannot be ratified by the party on whose behalf it was made after and with knowledge of the loss of the thing insured.
Keighley, Maxted & Co v Durant [1901] AC 240	The agent purchased a consignment of wheat but did so outside the scope of his authority. He used his own name and did not disclose that he was acting as agent for a principal. The principal then decided he would ratify the contract but later changed his mind.	Only the person on whose behalf the agent has acted may ratify. An undisclosed principal cannot ratify. The House of Lords held that a contract made by a person intending to contract on behalf of a principal, but without his authority, cannot be ratified by the 'principal', where the person who made the contract did not state at the time of making it to be acting on behalf of a principal.

Case	Facts	Held/Principle
Watteau v Fenwick [1893] 1 QB 346	H was the manager of F's pub. H's name appeared on the licence and was also painted above the door. F's existence was concealed. F expressly prohibited H from purchasing certain goods for the pub unless F supplied them. In contravention of this prohibition, H bought from W cigars on credit terms. W thought that H was the owner. F refused to pay for the cigars arguing that he was not bound by the contract to purchase them as he had expressly prohibited H from doing so.	F was liable for the debt notwithstanding that he expressly prohibited H from purchasing the cigars. Wills J held that H had usual authority to make the contract: 'the principal is liable for all the acts of the agent which are within the authority usually confided to an agent of that character, notwithstanding limitations as between the principal and the agent put upon that authority'. This case suggests that where the 'principal', whose existence is concealed from the third party, restricts the usual authority of his 'agent', then the third party will be entitled to assume that the 'agent' has the authority that is usually possessed by such a person and will not be bound by the restriction placed on the 'agent' by the 'principal'.
Waugh v HB Clifford and Sons Ltd [1982] Ch 374	A firm of solicitors settled an action contrary to their client's express instructions. The Court of Appeal held that the settlement agreement was binding on its client.	The solicitors were agents of their client. They clearly didn't have express actual authority to act as they did. Solicitors would ordinarily have implied actual authority to settle a case for their client but no such authority arose in this case because of their client's contrary express instructions. The solicitors did, however, have apparent authority and therefore the settlement agreement was binding.

⟨⟩⟩ Key debates

Topic	The agent's apparent authority: paradigm or paradox?
Author/Academic	Ian Brown
Viewpoint	Considers the basis of **apparent authority** and asks whether the concept has been distorted by artificial methods of ascertaining the existence and extent of the **principal's** liability.
Source	[1995] *Journal of Business Law* 360

Exam question

✳✳✳✳✳✳✳✳✳

Topic	The significance of general and special authority in the development of the agent's external authority in English law
Author/Academic	Ian Brown
Viewpoint	This article traces the development of an agent's external authority under English law, highlighting the decline in the concept of general authority in favour of apparent authority.
Source	[2004] *Journal of Business Law* 391

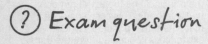 Exam question

Questions on the creation of agency, the agent's authority, and the relations created by the agency will frequently be asked together. For this reason, please see Chapter 13, 'Exam questions', p 202.

#13

The relationships created by agency—the rights and liabilities of the parties

Key facts

- The distinction between a disclosed and an undisclosed agency is important because this might affect the parties' rights and liabilities.

- The rights and liabilities of the various parties are discussed in this chapter.

- An agent owes two kinds of duty to his principal: contractual and fiduciary.

- In addition to the situations where the agent may be liable to the third party it is also important to note that he may also be liable for breach of warranty of authority. This would arise where the agent claims (warrants) to have authority to make the contract when he in fact has no such authority.

- A different species of agent, known as the 'commercial agent', was created by the **Commercial Agents (Council Directive) Regulations 1993**, and has many of its own rules.

- It is important to understand the different ways an agency can be terminated as well as the consequences of bringing it to an end.

Introduction

In Chapter 12, 'The creation of agency and the agent's authority', p 171, we looked at the creation of agency. This chapter considers the relationships that are created by agency, namely the rights and liabilities of the parties involved.

One of the first things to consider is whether the agency is disclosed or undisclosed, because this might affect the parties' rights and liabilities.

The rights and liabilities of the parties

We will consider separately the rights and liabilities of the **principal**, the third party, and of the **agent**.

The rights and liabilities of the principal on the contract made by the agent

Disclosed agency

Where the agent has actual authority

In cases where an **agent** has **actual authority** (express or implied) to make a contract for a **disclosed principal** then:

- the **principal** is entitled to enforce the agreement against the third party; and
- the third party may likewise enforce it against the principal.

This is because the contract takes effect as between the principal and the third party in the same way as if they had made the contract directly.

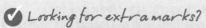
✅ *Looking for extra marks?*

We saw in Chapter 12, 'Ratification', p 180, that where a **principal** ratifies a contract made by an **agent** acting without **actual authority**, then the act of **ratification** has the effect of giving the agent retrospective actual authority. You should explain that in cases where the agent has ratified the contract, the principal is entitled to enforce the agreement against the third party and the third party may likewise enforce it against the principal in the same way as if the agent had the principal's actual authority in the first place.

Where the agent has apparent authority

Where the **agent** has apparent (but not actual) authority then:

- the **principal** cannot enforce the contract against the third party; but
- the third party may enforce it against the principal.

The only exception to the rule preventing the principal enforcing the contract against the third party is where the principal is entitled to, and does, ratify the contract.

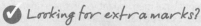 **Looking for extra marks?**

We discussed *Watteau v Fenwick* (1893) in Chapter 12, 'Usual authority', p 177. You should recall that in that case the **agent** had neither **actual** nor **apparent authority** and made the contract in his own name. A number of consequences arise from such a situation. The **principal** would not be able to enforce the contract against the third party, although the third party could enforce it against the principal. You should also note that because the agent had neither actual nor apparent authority and made the contract in his own name, **ratification** would not have been possible.

Undisclosed agency

It is essential to appreciate that in the case of an **undisclosed principal**, he (the undisclosed principal) can sue the third party on a contract made by the **agent** even though the third party did not know that the agent contracted on the principal's behalf. However, an undisclosed principal will only be able to bring a claim against the third party if the agent had actual authority to make the contract.

✅ **Looking for extra marks?**

It might appear rather unfair to allow an **undisclosed principal** to sue a third party on a contract where the third party was unaware that the **agent** had contracted on the **principal's** behalf. The justification for this was explained by Lord Lindley in *Keighley, Maxted & Co v Durant* (1901) as little more than mere 'convenience'.

Notwithstanding that in most situations a concealed, **undisclosed principal** will be entitled to sue or may be sued on contracts his **agent** has concluded on his behalf, in the following situations the **principal** will not be entitled to sue the third party or otherwise intervene in the agent's contract:

1. Where an *express* **term** of the contract made between the agent and the third party excluded the relationship of agency, for example, by excluding the intervention of an undisclosed principal.

   This is the most straightforward situation. It makes sense that where the agent expressly undertakes that he is not acting for any other person, then an undisclosed principal cannot intervene in the contract.

2. Where, by *implication*, there is a term in the contract made between the agent and the third party that excludes the intervention of an undisclosed principal.

   Rather than there being an *express* term in the contract that excludes the intervention of an undisclosed principal, in this situation the contract may, *by implication*, exclude the intervention of an undisclosed principal. In many cases, this will be apparent by the way the agent's role was described in the contract.

> **Humble v Hunter** (1848) 12 QB 310
>
> An **agent** entered into a charterparty on behalf of an **undisclosed principal** and signed the document indicating that he was the owner of the ship. The principal then sought to intervene in the contract but was unsuccessful because the agent, by signing as owner, had impliedly indicated that there was no (undisclosed) principal.

3. Where the third party intended to contract with the agent personally and not as agent. This would arise, for example, where the agent's identity was of particular importance to the third party who wished to contract with the agent to the exclusion of any other party.

    Where there is a personal contract, for example, for a famous musician to perform at a concert, an undisclosed principal will not be permitted to intervene and substitute himself in place of the contracted agent.

A similar situation arises where it is the identity or personality of the undisclosed principal that is of particular importance to the third party:

> **Said v Butt** [1920] 3 KB 497
>
> Said, a theatre critic, wished to attend the first night of a play. He knew that, in consequence of his having made certain comments against some members of the theatre staff, he would not be allowed to purchase a ticket in his own name. He therefore asked a friend (the **agent**) to buy a ticket for him which he did without disclosing that it was for Said (the **principal**). Butt, the theatre's managing director, refused Said entry. McCardie J held that in the case of an undisclosed agency with a 'strikingly present' personal element, an **undisclosed principal** will not be allowed to intervene on the agent's contract by seeking to enforce it.

The rights and liabilities of the third party on the contract made by the agent

Disclosed agency

Where the agent has actual authority

Where the **agent** has **actual authority** and makes a contract on behalf of the **principal** then:

- the third party will be entitled to enforce it against the principal; similarly
- the principal will be entitled to enforce it against the third party.

Where the agent has apparent authority

Where the **agent** has apparent (but not actual) authority then:

- the third party will be entitled to enforce the contract against the **principal**; however
- the principal will not be able to enforce the contract against the third party.

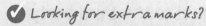
> ✔ **Looking for extra marks?**
>
> You should explain that the reason the **principal** will not be able to enforce the contract against the third party is because (even though he made a representation to the third party) the third party made no representation to him.

Settlement with the agent

Where the **agent** is acting on behalf of a **disclosed principal** and the third party settles with the agent then he will be deemed to have settled with the **principal**, provided the agent had either actual or **apparent authority** to accept monies on behalf of the principal. A typical example of this can be seen in the retail environment. Where the purchaser (third party) pays the shop assistant (agent) for goods or services he has purchased he is deemed to have settled with the owner (principal). Authority was discussed in Chapter 12, 'The agent's authority', p 173. In the above example, the agent is likely to have actual authority to accept the third party's settlement on his principal's behalf and will certainly have apparent authority to do so.

Undisclosed agency

Where the **agent** is acting on behalf of an **undisclosed principal** the third party is entitled to sue the agent on the contract as soon as the contract is made. The position is different once the undisclosed principal is revealed, and in this situation, the third party then has the choice of suing either the principal or the agent. However, once the third party has unequivocally elected to sue either the principal or the agent, then he must keep to that choice and may not then sue the other. The issuing of proceedings does not of itself amount to an election to pursue the remedy against that party to the exclusion of the other, but it is strong evidence of an election, which if not rebutted by the circumstances will show an election (*Clarkson Booker Ltd v Andjel* (1964)).

Settlement with an undisclosed agent

Where the third party settles with an undisclosed agent then he will be deemed to have settled with the **principal**. This will be the case even if the **agent** then fails to account to the principal for this money. For example, an agent sells to a third party a vehicle on behalf of an **undisclosed principal**. The agent then disappears without paying the sale money to the principal. The third party will be deemed to have settled with the principal in the same way as he would had he paid the money directly to the principal (which, of course, he could not do because the principal in this example was undisclosed).

> ✔ **Looking for extra marks?**
>
> You should explain that the reason for the above rule is that by allowing an undisclosed agent to act for him, the **principal** is deemed to have made a representation to the third party that the third party may settle with the **agent**. It therefore doesn't matter to the third party what the agent then does with the money. This is said to be a form of estoppel. This is hardly convincing, because it is hard to imagine how a principal, who is undisclosed, is capable of making a representation to any third party who, by the very fact he is undisclosed, is unaware of his existence.

The rights and liabilities of the agent to the third party on the contract made by the agent

Disclosed agency

The general rule with a **disclosed agency** is that the **agent** cannot sue or be sued on the contract made with the third party. This is simply because it is not the agent's contract (*Montgomerie & Others v United Kingdom Mutual Steamship Association Limited* (1891)). This rule is subject to certain exceptions, in particular where either the contract itself or the circumstances show that the agent accepts personal liability in the contract. Even in such circumstances, with a disclosed agency, the **principal** is also likely to be liable.

Undisclosed agency

With an **undisclosed agency**, it is important to consider the position both from when the principal remains undisclosed and then when he is revealed.

While the principal remains undisclosed

The **agent** is liable to the third party. This is because the third party thought he was contracting directly with the agent.

When the undisclosed principal is revealed

Once the hitherto **undisclosed principal** is revealed he also becomes liable on the contract. You should note that even in this situation the agent's liability to the third party continues and the third party can choose whether to sue the **principal** or the **agent**. The rule in *Clarkson Booker Ltd v Andjel* (1964) ('Undisclosed agency', p 187) also applies here.

Breach of warranty of authority

It is important to note that the **agent** may also be liable to the third party for breach of **warranty** of authority. This would arise where the agent claims (warrants) to have authority to make the contract when he in fact has no such authority. In such a situation, he will be liable to the third party if the third party relies on the warranty and suffers a loss as a result (*Yonge v Toynbee* (1910)).

The rights of the agent against his principal

Unlike the relatively sizeable number of duties owed by an **agent** to his **principal**, the principal's duties towards his agent are more limited. This is owing to the view taken by the common law that it is the principal who needs protecting from his agent and not the other way around.

As against his principal, and depending upon the circumstances, an agent might have the following rights:

Remuneration

Provided there is a term in the agency agreement to this effect, and the **agent** acts within his authority (or the **principal** has ratified an agent's unlawful act), then the agent will be entitled to be remunerated by the principal. Otherwise, no such entitlement will arise. The term as to the right to remuneration may be express or implied, although a court will be slow to imply a term into the agency agreement which entitles an agent to remuneration where the agreement is silent on this point (*Attorney General of Belize v Belize Telecom Ltd* (2009)). Alternatively, the agent may be entitled to be paid on a *quantum meruit* basis. Commercial agents, as defined by the **Commercial Agents (Council Directive) Regulations 1993**, operate differently and will be considered under 'Commercial Agents (Council Directive) Regulations 1993', p 196.

An indemnity

At common law, an **agent** is entitled to be indemnified by his **principal** for expenses, losses, and liabilities that he reasonably incurs whilst executing his duties as agent within the scope of his actual authority (*Thacker v Hardy* (1878–79)). An **express term** in the agency agreement to the effect that the agent is not entitled to an indemnity will mean that no indemnity will be paid.

The principal's duty to indemnify his agent might also arise in cases where the agent is liable in tort (*Adamson v Jarvis* (1827)).

A lien

Where an **agent** is owed money by his **principal** he is entitled to retain possession of the principal's property until he has been paid. The **lien** is not a general lien and arises only in respect of the particular property for which the money is owed (*Bock v Gorrissen* (1860)). The right of lien can be excluded by contract between the agent and principal and, in any event, will only exist where property belonging to the principal is in the agent's possession (*Bryans v Nix* (1839)).

The agent's duties to his principal

An **agent** owes two kinds of duty to his **principal**:

1. a contractual duty; and
2. a **fiduciary** duty.

The agent's contractual duties to his principal

The **agent** owes three different contractual duties to his **principal**:

The agent's duties to his principal
✳✳✳✳✳✳✳✳✳✳

A duty to obey his principal's lawful instructions

This duty arises out of a *bilateral* **agreement** between the **agent** and his **principal**. That is, in return for payment to the agent, the agent undertakes to carry out the principal's instructions:

> **Turpin v Bilton** (1843) 5 Man & G 455
>
> An **agent** undertook to insure his **principal's** ship but failed to do so. The ship was destroyed and the agent was held liable for the principal's loss for failing to obey his instructions.

In the case of a *unilateral* **agreement** between the **agent** and his **principal**, the agent will not be liable if he fails to obey his principal's lawful instructions. This is because with unilateral agreements the agent will not have made a contractual promise to perform and he is therefore under no legal obligation to do so. For example, if the principal promises to pay his agent £100 if the agent sells his watch, the agent will be under no contractual obligation to sell it, and will therefore not be in breach of his duty to obey his principal's instructions by not selling it.

Just as an agent will not be liable for failing to obey his principal's lawful instructions under a unilateral agreement, an agent will not be liable if he is a mere *gratuitous* agent; that is, an agent who acts for a principal without payment. This is because the principal does not provide consideration. A gratuitous agent can still be liable to his principal under the law of tort if he is in breach of a duty of care owed to his principal.

A duty to act with due care and skill in the performance of his duties

An **agent** is required to exercise the degree of care, skill, and diligence that is to be expected of an agent carrying out the particular role. The standard required will be case-specific and will depend on all of the circumstances.

Where an agent performs a service in the course of a business, this duty is implied by virtue of the **Supply of Goods and Services Act 1982, s 13** (see Chapter 2, 'Sections 12–16 SGSA', p 26).

A *gratuitous* agent will also owe this duty but (as there is no contract) only in tort (*Chaudhry v Prabhakar* (1989)).

> ✅ *Looking for extra marks?*
> Don't forget that any attempt to exclude or restrict this duty will be subject to the **Unfair Contract Terms Act 1977** which was considered in Chapter 5, 'Unfair Contract Terms Act 1977 (UCTA)', p 62.

A duty to perform his obligations personally

Because of the **fiduciary** nature of the parties' relationship, an **agent** must not delegate his duties to a sub-agent unless:

- the principal expressly or impliedly authorises it. If an agent delegates his duties without authority, then the sub-agent's acts will not be valid and will not bind the principal (*John McCann & Co v Pow* (1974)). The principal may, however, ratify the agent's delegation;

- it is the usual practice in the trade or profession to which the agent belongs to delegate the authority and it is neither unreasonable to do so nor inconsistent with the terms of the agent's contract with his principal (*Solley & Others v Wood* (1852));

- the nature of the agency requires that it be performed either wholly or partly by a sub-agent (*The Quebec and Richmond Railroad Company v Quinn* (1858));

- the delegation is necessitated by an unforeseen circumstance; and

- the duty is purely 'ministerial' and does not require particular confidence and discretion.

Del credere agents

It is a general principle of agency law that 'a person who makes a contract ostensibly as an agent cannot afterwards sue or be sued upon it, subject to . . . where there is a *del credere* agency' (**Phonogram Ltd v Lane (1982)**, per Shaw LJ).

Although cases involving *del credere* agencies can be traced back to the 1800s, they are now quite rare because of the range of alternative methods of credit that are nowadays available.

The agent's fiduciary duty to his principal

An **agent** owes a **fiduciary** duty to his **principal**. You should explain that this is due to the fact that the agent has the power to affect the legal relations between his principal and the third party and therefore occupies a position of trust and confidence. As a result, equity imposes fiduciary duties on agents to protect their principals. An agent will owe these fiduciary duties to his principal whether he is paid or acts gratuitously.

The fiduciary duties owed by an agent to his principal are:

A duty to avoid a conflict of interest

An **agent** must avoid situations where his personal interest conflicts, or possibly conflicts, with his duty to his **principal** (*Aberdeen Rail Co v Blaikie Brothers* (1843–60)).

An agent must not, without his principal's consent, use the principal's property to secure a profit for himself or use any information or knowledge for his own benefit which he has acquired by virtue of his position as agent (*Boardman v Phipps* (1967)).

Agents might have certain interests that might conflict with (or might be seen to conflict with) the interests of their principal. In such situations, an agent can avoid placing himself in a conflict situation by disclosing any potential conflict to his principal who may then, if he so wishes, permit the agent to continue to act for him in full knowledge of the potential conflict (*Clark Boyce v Mouat* (1994)).

The agent's duties to his principal

****

A duty not to make a 'secret profit' or to accept a bribe

A secret profit is made where an **agent**, whilst acting for his **principal**, receives some profit over and above that agreed with the principal. An agent is not allowed to accept commission from a third party without his principal's approval (*Imageview Management Ltd v Jack* (2009)).

> **Hippisley v Knee Brothers [1905] 1 KB 1**
>
> An auctioneer advertised for sale certain goods belonging to his **principal**. He paid a reduced trade price for the advertising but charged his principal the full non-trade rate. The court held that he had committed a breach of his **fiduciary** duty to his principal not to make a secret profit.

A duty to account to the principal for payments received

An **agent** has two key duties in respect of payments he receives that are intended for his **principal**:

1. He must keep such monies separate from his own money unless he is permitted by the agency agreement to mix the funds.

2. He must keep and maintain accurate accounts of transactions and furnish his principal with them when his principal requests them (*Turner v Burkinshaw* (1867)). The duty to furnish his principal with accounts upon his principal's request survives the termination of the agency agreement (*Yasuda Fire & Marine Insurance Co of Europe Ltd v Orion Marine Insurance Underwriting Agency Ltd* (1995)).

An agent who fails to maintain proper accounts of transactions made on his principal's behalf will put his own funds at risk because there is a presumption that any monies that the agent cannot prove to be his own will be deemed to belong to his principal (*Lupton v White* (1808)).

A duty to preserve confidentiality

An **agent** is under an absolute duty to preserve his **principal's** confidentiality. This includes not disclosing any confidential information to any third parties. This duty is higher than merely taking reasonable precautions with the principal's information and survives the termination of the agency agreement (*Bolkiah v KPMG* (1999)).

Remedies for breach of fiduciary duty

The court has wide discretion when awarding remedies to a **principal** where his **agent** has committed a breach of a **fiduciary** duty. Where the agent makes a profit as a result of his breach of a fiduciary duty, the following remedies might be available to the principal:

- he may dismiss the agent summarily without notice;
- he may recover any profits made by the agent as a result of the agent's breach;
- he may rescind the contract made with the third party; and

- where the agent has received a bribe, he may recover from the agent the amount of the bribe or bring a claim in damages against the agent or the party paying the bribe to recover any losses he has sustained as a result of the bribe.

> ## ✅ Looking for extra marks?
>
> When awarding damages to the **principal** for his **agent's** breach of **fiduciary** duty, the court will take account of the circumstances of the agent's breach. If the breach is of a minor or technical nature (such as in *Hippisley v Knee Brothers*, discussed above) then the court is likely to order the agent to account to the principal for the profit wrongly made. However, where the agent's breach of fiduciary duty is fraudulent, then the court will take a more serious view. This can be seen from the Privy Council's decision in *Attorney General for Hong Kong v Reid* (1994) where it held that the property that was purchased using money obtained from bribery was held on trust for the principal who was also entitled to dismiss the agent.

Termination of agency

We will now consider how an agency may be terminated, and the effects of termination.

Termination by agreement

- *As between **principal** and **agent***, an agency can be terminated by agreement just as it can be created by one.
- An agency may also come to an end when the specific task given to the agent has been completed. It may also end on the date fixed by the agreement.

However, this might not have the same effect as between *principal and the third party* and just because the agent's actual authority has been terminated or restricted it does not necessarily mean that the agent's acts can no longer bind the principal in relation to third parties if the third party is unaware of the agent's lack of authority.

Termination by operation of law

Independently of the wishes of the parties, an agency will normally be held to have been terminated in any of the following circumstances:

Where the principal or agent loses legal capacity, such as with death or mental incapacity

This rule is said to be justified because of the personal nature of the agency agreement and the particular importance given to the specific identity of the principal and the agent.

Death

> ### *Campanari v Woodburn* (1854) 15 CB 400
>
> Campanari (the **agent**) agreed to sell a picture on behalf of Woodburn (the **principal**) for which he was to receive £100 commission upon the conclusion of the sale. Before the agent was able to sell the picture, his principal died. The agent was unaware of the death and continued to sell the picture. Jervis CJ held that the agent was not entitled to his commission because the agency had automatically terminated on the principal's death but he was entitled to his reasonable expenses incurred in carrying out his duties.

Mental incapacity

The supervening mental incapacity of the agent automatically terminates the agency because the **agent** is unable to comprehend the nature and character of the acts his **principal** requires of him (*Boughton v Knight* (1872–75)). Similarly, the principal's mental incapacity terminates the agency because 'where such a change occurs as to the principal that he can no longer act for himself, the agent whom he has appointed can no longer act for him' (*Drew v Nunn* (1878–79)).

Where the principal or agent become insolvent

Where the **principal** becomes insolvent the agency automatically terminates on the ground that insolvency equates to legal incapacity. Generally, where it is the **agent** who becomes insolvent, the agency will terminate, although this might depend on the terms of the agency agreement itself.

Where the contract between the principal and agent becomes frustrated

Where the agency agreement is embodied in a contract, certain intervening events may frustrate the contract. These events include those that would render performance of the contract impossible or illegal (*Marshall v Glanvill & Another* (1917)).

Commercial Agents (Council Directive) Regulations 1993

In addition to the traditional relationship of **agent** that is largely governed by common law, there is another distinct species of agent known as the 'commercial agent'. Commercial agents are governed by the **Commercial Agents (Council Directive) Regulations 1993**. The Regulations only govern the relationship between the commercial agent and the **principal** and do not apply to the rights and obligations involving the third party which remain to be governed by common law.

Provided the Regulations apply (and they will only apply if the definition of 'commercial agent' in **reg 2** is satisfied) then the duties owed to the principal are contained in **reg 3**. It has been said that these duties are broadly similar to those owed under common law (*Cureton v Mark Insulations Ltd* (2006)).

Regulation 2(1) defines a commercial agent as:

Reg 2 of the Commercial Agents (Council Directive) Regulations 1993:

a self-employed intermediary who has continuing authority to negotiate the sale or purchase of goods on behalf of another person (the 'principal'), or to negotiate and conclude the sale or purchase of goods on behalf of and in the name of that principal.

A person who has power to enter into commitments on behalf of a company in his capacity as an officer of a company is not a commercial agent. Neither is a partner acting as a partner in his firm or a person who acts as an insolvency practitioner.

The Regulations also only apply to commercial agents *whose activities are paid*.

The duties of a commercial agent to his principal

Regulation 3 sets out the duties of a commercial agent to his principal. These are that:

Reg 3(1) of the Commercial Agents (Council Directive) Regulations 1993:

in performing his activities a commercial agent must look after the interests of his principal and act dutifully and in good faith.

In addition, **reg 3(2)** sets out that a commercial agent must:

- make proper efforts to negotiate and, where appropriate, conclude the transactions he is instructed to take care of;
- communicate to his principal all the necessary information available to him; and
- comply with reasonable instructions given by his principal.

The duties of a principal to his commercial agent

Regulation 4 sets out the duties of the **principal** to his commercial **agent**. This provides that the principal 'must act dutifully and in good faith' **(reg 4(1))**.

In particular, **reg 4(2)** explains that the principal must:

- provide his commercial agent with the necessary documentation relating to the goods concerned; and
- obtain for his commercial agent the information necessary for the performance of the agency contract, and notify his commercial agent within a reasonable period once he anticipates that the volume of commercial transactions will be significantly lower than that which the commercial agent could normally have expected.

In addition, **Regulation 4(3)** sets out that the principal shall:

Reg 4(3) of the Commercial Agents (Council Directive) Regulations 1993:

inform his commercial agent within a reasonable period of his acceptance or refusal of, and of any non-execution by him of, a commercial transaction which the commercial agent has procured for him.

Unlike an agency governed by common law, **reg 5** provides that the parties to a commercial agency governed by the Regulations cannot contract out of the above duties.

The remuneration of commercial agents

During the period of the agency

Part III of the Regulations deals with remuneration. The first thing to note is that if there is no agreement as to remuneration (which as a matter of good practice there ought to be) the **agent** is entitled to remuneration customarily allowed to agents for the type of goods involved in the area where the agent carries on his activities. If there is no such customary practice, the agent is entitled to a reasonable remuneration taking into account all the aspects of the transaction (**reg 6**).

Regulation 7 sets out the commercial agent's entitlement to commission. He shall be entitled to commission on commercial transactions concluded during the period covered by the agency contract:

(a) where the transaction has been concluded as a result of his action; or

(b) where the transaction is concluded with a third party whom he has previously acquired as a customer for transactions of the same kind.

A commercial agent shall also be entitled to commission on transactions concluded during the period covered by the agency contract where he has an exclusive right to a specific geographical area or to a specific group of customers and where the transaction has been entered into with a customer belonging to that area or group.

After the termination of the agency

Regulation 8 provides that a commercial **agent** shall be entitled to commission on commercial transactions concluded after the agency contract has terminated if:

(a) the transaction is mainly attributable to his efforts during the period covered by the agency contract and if the transaction was entered into within a reasonable period after that contract terminated; or

(b) the order of the third party reached the **principal** or the commercial agent before the agency contract terminated. The principal must also provide the commercial agent with statements of commission quarterly and the commercial agent must be provided with all available information which he needs to check the amount of commission due to him (reg 12).

Duration of the agency agreement

The **agent** and the **principal** are entitled to receive from the other on request a signed statement setting out the terms of the agency (reg 13).

An agency agreement for a fixed period which continues to be performed by both parties after that period has expired shall be deemed to be converted into an agency contract for an *indefinite* period (reg 14).

Termination of the agency agreement

Where the agency agreement is for an indefinite period, either party may terminate it by notice. The periods of notice are set out in reg 15:

- one month for the first year;
- two months during the second year; and
- three months during the third and subsequent years.

Shorter notice periods may not be agreed, but longer ones can be. However, if longer notice periods are agreed, the notice to be given by the **principal** may not be shorter than the notice to be given by the **agent**.

These rules do not prevent the immediate termination of the agency agreement either where one party fails to carry out all or part of his obligations under the contract or for exceptional circumstances that might arise where the law permits immediate termination (reg 16).

Compensation or indemnity due to the commercial agent on termination of the agency

Regulation 17 provides that on the termination of the agency agreement the **agent** is entitled either to be compensated for damage or indemnified, and that unless the agency agreement provides otherwise he is entitled to be compensated rather than indemnified. This is also the position where the agreement expires rather than being terminated (*Tigana Ltd v Decoro Ltd* (2003)).

Where the commercial agent is entitled to be *compensated*, he is entitled to compensation for the damage he suffers as a result of the termination of his relations with his **principal**.

Commercial Agents (Council Directive) Regulations 1993

✳✳✳✳✳✳✳✳✳✳✳✳

Damage is deemed to occur particularly when termination takes place in either or both of the following circumstances:

- circumstances which deprive the commercial agent of the commission which proper performance of the agency contract would have procured for him whilst providing his principal with substantial benefits linked to the activities of the commercial agent; and

- circumstances where the commercial agent has not been enabled to amortise the costs and expenses that he had incurred in the performance of the agency contract on the advice of his principal.

Where the commercial agent is entitled to be *indemnified*, the entitlement to an indemnity applies if he has brought in new customers or alternatively he has significantly increased the volume of business with existing customers and the principal continues to derive substantial benefits from ongoing business with these customers. The amount of indemnity the commercial agent is likely to receive is whatever is equitable having regard to all the circumstances and, in particular, the commission lost by the agent on the business transacted with those customers. Having said that, the indemnity will not exceed one year's average annual remuneration calculated over the previous five years of the agreement or, if it lasted for less than five years, over the entire agreement.

The commercial agent is also entitled to this compensation if the contract ends because of his death.

The commercial agent must notify his principal within 12 months following the end of the agreement that he intends to make a claim, failing which he will lose his right to pursue a claim.

The commercial agent's right to receive compensation and/or an indemnity will be lost in the following circumstances:

- where the principal terminates the agreement where he could have justified immediate termination because of the agent's default;

- where the commercial agent terminates the agreement, except where such termination is justified because of the principal's default or where the commercial agent terminated it because owing to his age, infirmity, or illness, he could not reasonably have been expected to carry on; or

- where the commercial agent assigns the agreement to another person with the agreement of his principal.

The parties are not allowed to contract out of the rules for compensation and indemnity if this would be to the detriment of the agent.

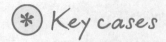 Key cases

Case	Facts	Held/Principle
Armstrong v Jackson [1917] 2 KB 822	A stockbroker acting as agent for his principal was instructed by his principal to purchase 600 shares in a company. The stockbroker already owned 600 of these shares which he transferred to his principal.	The stockbroker's conduct placed himself in a position whereby his duty to his client (principal) conflicted with his own personal interest. The principal was entitled to rescind the entire transaction even though the shares had by then decreased in value.
Attorney General for Hong Kong v Reid [1994] 1 AC 324	Reid (the agent) was working as a customs officer. In breach of his fiduciary duty to the Crown (the principal), he accepted bribes with which he purchased a number of properties.	The Privy Council held that a gift accepted by a person in a fiduciary position as an incentive for his breach of duty constituted a bribe and, although in law it belonged to the fiduciary, in equity he not only became a debtor for the amount of the bribe to the person to whom the duty was owed but he also held the bribe and any property acquired therewith on constructive trust for that person.
Boardman v Phipps [1967] 2 AC 46	A solicitor, acting as agent for the trustees of an estate, attended annual general meetings of a company in which the estate held a small interest. The solicitor thereby obtained information about the company from which he concluded that its shares were undervalued. The trustees of the estate did not wish to purchase more of the shares. The solicitor, using his own personal money then purchased a controlling interest in the company. The solicitor made a substantial personal gain from this investment. The estate also benefited from the increase in the value of the shares it held.	The House of Lords held that the solicitor must account to the estate for the personal profit he had made because the information he acquired whilst attending the company's annual general meetings belonged to the estate. It did not matter that he was acting in good faith nor that his actions also produced a financial benefit for the estate.
Hippisley v Knee Brothers [1905] 1 KB 1	An auctioneer advertised for sale certain goods belonging to his principal. He paid a reduced trade price for the advertising but charged his principal the full non-trade rate.	The court held that he had committed a breach of his fiduciary duty to his principal not to make a secret profit but as he had acted without fraud and as the advertising contract was incidental to and severable from the primary contract of sale of goods, he was still entitled to his commission for the sale of his principal's goods.

Case	Facts	Held/Principle
***Imageview Management Ltd v Jack* [2009] EWCA Civ 63**	A football agent negotiated the transfer of a player. His fee was to be 10% of the player's salary. At the same time, the agent agreed a separate deal with the club for arranging a work permit for the player. This separate deal was not declared to the player. When the player eventually found out that his agent had made a secret profit he stopped paying him the agreed 10% of his salary.	The law imposes high standards on agents whose personal interests come second to the interests of their clients. If an agent undertakes to act for a man he has to act for him as if he were him and not allow his own interest to get in the way without telling the client. The Court of Appeal held that in making an undisclosed private deal with a football club to obtain a work permit for a foreign footballer, a football agent had acted in breach of his fiduciary duty to the footballer. The footballer did not have to pay any more fees to the agent and was entitled to the repayment of commission already paid as well as the fee received by the agent for the secret deal.

Key debates

Topic	**The (fiduciary) duty of fidelity**
Author/Academic	Robert Flannigan
Viewpoint	Discusses the distinction between a duty of fidelity and a **fiduciary** duty as it might apply to an **agent.**
Source	(2008) 124 *Law Quarterly Review* 274

Topic	Undisclosed principals and contract
Author/Academic	Tan Cheng-Han
Viewpoint	Discusses whether a basis for the doctrine of the **undisclosed principal** exists which can be reconciled with the rules on privity of contract.
Source	(2004) 120 *Law Quarterly Review* 480

Exam questions

Problem question

Sue appoints Ian as her agent to buy furniture and to sell it to her trade customers. She informs her suppliers and customers of Ian's appointment. Sue tells Ian that he is not to buy any red sofas as she doesn't think they are good sellers. Unbeknown to Sue, Ian is a thief and has recently served a term of imprisonment for dishonesty. Ian visits Sofas Ltd, one of Sue's main suppliers and, purporting to act for Sue, agrees to purchase 20 red sofas for £15,000. In fact, Ian knows that he can sell these sofas to his friend Bob for £20,000 and keep the profit for himself. The following day, Ian enters into an agreement with Bob to sell the sofas for £20,000 without telling Bob that he is Sue's agent. Shortly afterwards, Sofas Ltd find out what Ian was up to and tells Sue that they will not honour the agreement to sell the red sofas. Fearing a loss of business, Sue then purports to ratify the purchase with Sofas Ltd as well as the sale to Bob.

Advise the parties.

Essay question

The duties owed by agents to their principals are to be found in the express terms of their contract.

Critically evaluate this statement.

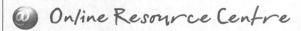

To see an outline answer to this question visit www.oup.com/lawrevision/

Exam essentials

Plan, plan, plan

- Don't leave your revision too late. The later you leave it the more rushed you will be and the more you will panic.
- As soon as the exam timetable has been announced you should make a firm plan on which subjects to revise and when.
- Plan your revision well. Remember the saying: Failing to plan is planning to fail!

What are you going to be asked in the exam?

- Lecturers often drop hints throughout the course as to what areas might appear on the exam.
- If your university runs revision lectures or seminars then make sure you go along to them. You may get an indication of the style of answers expected of you and you may be told about new cases or articles that have just been decided or published. You may even get some (further) hints about what might appear on the paper!
- Study as many past exam papers as you can and have a go at answering the questions under exam conditions.
- Even if you can't answer all questions it is worth preparing answer plans. Use this to inform your further revision.

Linking different subject areas together

- You should not look at an individual subject area in isolation as many are interrelated.
- Instead, you should consider the links between the different subject areas that have been covered in your course. This will improve your understanding of the subject generally and will also impress an examiner.
- Some examples of the links to consider in commercial law are set out below. It will be helpful for you to consider further links yourself as you work through the course and your revision. This is where past exam papers should help:
  - You will need to understand, and explain, which rules (for example, the statutory implied terms) apply to the question and whether they have been breached. If they have, then you will need to consider the remedies available to the innocent party.
  - **Exemption clauses** do not exist in a vacuum. Therefore, you will need to consider what the clause in question is seeking to exempt. If the exemption clause fails, then the provision it sought to exempt might well stand and you will need to explain the consequences of this.

Exam essentials
✷✷✷✷✷✷✷✷✷✷

- Questions on *nemo dat* might cross over with other areas, such as retention of title and agency.

- There is little point considering the relationships that have been created by agency without considering whether an agency relationship has in fact been created.

- There is a very close link between s 75 CCA 1974 and the terms of the contract with the supplier. This is because s 75 does not *create* a claim but merely enables the **debtor** to commence a like claim against the **creditor** which the debtor already has the right to commence against the supplier.

Tips and common mistakes to avoid

- The examiner cannot read your mind. You will not earn marks unless you write it down. For example, rather than writing that the goods were not of satisfactory quality, you should explain why you have reached this opinion, and you should support this, wherever possible, with key cases and other material.

- Don't forget to identify the legal principles involved. You should then expand on this by explaining the issues and supporting this by the use of appropriate legislation, cases, etc. You should, where possible, explain the reasoning behind the judgments and identify the key issues of any dissenting judgments. This should be supplemented by setting out key academic arguments. Finally, you should apply the law to the question and provide a reasoned answer.

- Don't assume that the examiner has inserted facts into a question for no good reason. For example, can you identify the reason for the following facts?

    - Why is Ian's delay in collecting the goods important? (Chapter 3, 'Problem question', p 44).

    - Why is it important for you to know that Dave's Bakeries also buys milk from several other suppliers? (Chapter 4, 'Problem question', p 56).

    - Why might it be important to consider Veronica's French connection? (Chapter 11, 'Problem question', p 170).

You will find out why these facts are important by looking at the Outline Answers in the book's Online Resource Centre.

- Don't just prepare for the minimum number of areas. If you have to answer four questions then don't just learn enough material to answer four questions. A question that you were banking on might not appear or it might be written in a way you don't like. Answering fewer questions than is required, no matter how well you have done so, will make it very difficult—or even impossible—for you to get decent marks.

- Read through the whole paper carefully before you begin and consider which questions you can answer best. There is nothing worse than beginning to answer one question only to realise that you could have produced a far better answer to an alternative question. Once you have identified the questions you are going to answer, you should then prepare a rough answer plan for each of them. Prepare an outline answer, noting relevant cases, sources, key arguments, articles, etc. Doing this should mean that your answer will be properly structured and you won't forget important cases.

- Make sure that you answer the question asked. This means reading the rubric of the question very carefully indeed. There is nothing more frustrating from an examiner's position than to find that the student has provided an excellent answer, but not to the question asked. If the question asks you to advise Fred, there is no point in advising Dawn. However, you should consider this in the wider context. For example, if you look at the problem question at the end of Chapter 11, p 170, where it asks you to advise Veronica of any rights she might have *against the credit card company*, you will need to explain that s 75 CCA 1974 does not create a claim but merely enables a **debtor** to commence a like claim against (in this case) the credit card company which the debtor already has the right to commence against the seller. This means that you will need to set out any claim that Veronica might have against the seller. Once you have explained this, then you should concentrate the remainder of your answer explaining whether a claim is likely to succeed against the credit card company.

- Spend roughly the same amount of time on every answer and don't lose track of the time. One thing that may help is to work out your timings at the beginning of the exam and write down the times at which you should be starting the next question.

- Finally, make sure your handwriting is legible. It is very difficult for the examiner to give you marks if they cannot read your writing. Legible handwriting also creates a better impression.

Glossary

Ab initio From the beginning (see 'Void contract')

Acceptance (1) An unconditional acceptance of all the terms of an offer

Acceptance (2) A buyer will be deemed to have accepted the goods when he does one of three things: (1) intimates to the seller that he has accepted them (s 35(1)(a) SGA); (2) when the goods have been delivered to him, he does any act in relation to them which is inconsistent with the ownership of the seller (s 35(1)(b)); (3) when after the lapse of a reasonable time he retains the goods without intimating to the seller that he has rejected them (s 35(4))

Actual authority A type of authority given by the principal to the agent authorising him to enter into arrangements with third parties on his behalf. This can either be express or implied

Agency of necessity An agency of necessity might arise in a case where, as a result of an emergency, an agent is compelled to exceed his authority to protect his principal's property

Agent A person who is authorised to act on another's (the principal's) behalf. An agent has the power to bind the principal in contracts with third parties

Apparent (or ostensible) authority Whereas actual authority derives from an agreement between the principal and the agent, apparent authority arises where the principal makes a representation so as to give an impression to the third party that the agent has authority to act on his behalf. Apparent authority arises where the third party has been induced into entering the contract with the principal by an agent who appears to have authority to act but in fact has no such authority. It is no more than an illusion of authority created by the principal's representation

Ascertained goods When the correct quantity of the goods has been set aside for delivery to the buyer

Bailee A person who takes possession of the goods with the owner's (bailor's) consent

Bilateral contract All parties to the agreement assume obligations under the contract

Condition The most important type of contractual term and typically goes to the heart of the contract. A breach of a condition is likely to cause significant consequences for the innocent party and if breached will usually entitle the innocent party to regard the contract as at an end. No further performance will be required and the innocent party will also be entitled to sue for damages

Consideration An act, forbearance, or promise by one party to an agreement that constitutes the price for which he buys the promise of the other party. Without consideration, a promise is not binding. With contracts of sale, the consideration must be money (s 2(1) SGA 1979)

Consumer credit agreement 'An agreement between an individual ("the debtor") and any other person ("the creditor") by which the creditor provides the debtor with credit of any amount' (s 8(1) CCA 1974). It includes a consumer credit agreement which is cancelled under s 69(1) or becomes subject to s 69(2) so far as the agreement remains in force

Consumer hire agreement 'An agreement made by a person with an individual (the "hirer") for the bailment or the hiring of goods to the hirer, being an agreement which is not a hire-purchase agreement and is capable of subsisting for more than three months' (s 15(1) CCA 1974)

Contra proferentem Where the court determines a contractual term to be ambiguous, it will be construed against the party that imposed its inclusion in the contract

Contract of sale 'A contract by which the seller transfers or agrees to transfer the property in goods to the buyer for a money consideration called the price' (s 2(1) SGA 1979)

Core terms Terms that either define the subject matter of the agreement or are concerned with the adequacy of the contract price

Creditor One to whom a debt is owed

Day certain Where the parties agree that payment will be made upon the occurrence of a specific event rather than on a particular date

Debtor One who owes a debt

Debtor-Creditor agreement (borrower–lender) Where the creditor is not also the supplier and has no business connection with the supplier. The creditor merely provides the credit for the transaction. The agreement is not made under pre-existing arrangements or in contemplation of future arrangements between the creditor and the supplier

Debtor-Creditor-Supplier agreement (borrower–lender–supplier) Where the creditor is also the supplier or has a business connection with the supplier. The agreement is made by the creditor under pre-existing arrangements, or in contemplation of future arrangements, between himself and the supplier, or which is financing a transaction between the debtor and the creditor. Typical D-C-S agreements are credit sales or where the payment is made by credit card

Declarator An action seeking to have some right, status, etc, judicially declared (Scottish law)

Del credere **agency** A type of agency where the agent undertakes to act as surety in respect of the performance of contracts that he has entered into on his principal's behalf. In return for acting as surety, the agent receives a specially agreed commission

Delivery The voluntary transfer of possession from one person to another (s 61(1) SGA)

Disclosed agency/principal Where the principal is named or where the agent indicates that he is acting on behalf of a principal rather than on his own behalf. The third party knows that the agent is acting as agent on behalf of a principal even if he doesn't know the exact identity of the principal

Exclusion clause A clause that seeks to exclude all liability for certain breaches of the contract or to exclude a contractual obligation

Exemption clause A term used to describe both exclusion and limitation clauses

Existing goods Goods that are either owned or possessed by the seller (s 5(1) SGA)

Express terms Terms that have been expressly agreed either orally or in writing

Fiduciary A person who acts on behalf of another in a position of trust

Fiduciary relationship Where the fiduciary is under a duty to act in good faith and with due regard to the best interests of the other party or parties

Fixed-sum credit Any other facility (other than running-account credit) under a consumer credit agreement whereby the debtor is enabled to receive credit (whether in one amount or by instalments)

Frustration An event, that is the fault of neither party, may render the contract impossible to perform or radically different from that agreed and which may lead to the contract being frustrated and the parties discharged from further performance

Future goods Goods to be manufactured or acquired by the seller after the making of the contract of sale (ss 5(1) and 61(1) SGA)

Hire purchase An arrangement where a person hires the goods on credit terms for a fixed term with an option to purchase them at the end of that term

Implied term A term that has not been agreed but may be implied in a number of different ways. One of these ways is by statute (see, for example, the statutory implied terms in the SGA 1979)

Innominate term A term where the consequences or seriousness of the breach determine whether or not it takes effect as a condition or a warranty. In this way, if the consequences of the breach are so fundamental that the innocent party has been deprived of substantially the entire benefit of the contract he will be entitled to treat the contract as repudiated and sue for damages. If the effects of the breach are only minor, it will be treated as a breach of warranty

Glossary

✳✳✳✳✳✳✳✳✳✳

Lien A party's right to keep hold of the property belonging to another until an obligation, usually payment, has been fulfilled

Limitation clause A clause where a party to the contract seeks to limit his liability for certain breaches of the contract

Misrepresentation A false statement of fact that induces another to enter into a contract

Nemo dat quod non habet 'No one can transfer what he has not got'

Offer An indication of willingness to be legally bound upon the other party's acceptance

Ostensible authority see 'Apparent authority'

Principal The person on whose behalf the agent acts

Quantum meruit A claim or an award of payment to reflect what a person deserves

Ratification If an agent carries out an act in the name of a principal for which he was not authorised, the principal may decide to ratify (approve and adopt) the transaction

Regulated agreement A consumer credit or consumer hire agreement that is not exempt under the provisions of the CCA 1974

Repudiate/Repudiatory breach Where a party to a contract acts in a way that demonstrates that he does not intend to be bound by the terms of the contract

Rescind To cancel the contract and relieve the parties of any further obligations under it

Rescission Where the contract is set aside and restores the parties to their original pre-contract positions

Reservation of title see 'Retention (or reservation) of title'

Res integra A point not covered by an earlier decision or by a rule of law

Retention (or reservation) of title A clause that allows a supplier to retain ownership over the goods supplied until such time as certain conditions (usually payment) are met, thus providing the supplier with a form of security against the buyer's default or insolvency

Romalpa **clause** A clause named after the leading case of *Aluminium Industrie Vaassen BV v Romalpa Aluminium Ltd* (1976)—see 'Retention (or reservation) of title'

Running-account credit A facility under a consumer credit agreement whereby the debtor is enabled to receive from time to time (whether in his own person, or by another person) from the creditor or a third party cash, goods, and services (or any of them) to an amount or value such that, taking into account payments made by or to the credit of the debtor, the credit limit (if any) is not at any time exceeded

Specific goods Goods that are identified and agreed upon at the time a contract of sale is made (s 61(1) SGA)

Specific performance A remedy that may be available when monetary damages are inadequate. The courts will usually be slow to make such an order although nowadays it is more readily available to enforce the additional rights of the consumer buyer (repair and replacement of the goods)

Unascertained goods Goods that are not specifically identified at the time of the contract of sale. Unascertained goods are not defined in the SGA but are, in effect, all goods that are not specific

Undisclosed agency/principal Where the agent doesn't reveal that he is acting on behalf of a principal. The third party, therefore, is unaware that the agent is acting as agent

Unilateral contract/offer Only one party assumes an obligation under the contract

Void contract A contract that has no legal force being void *ab initio* (from the beginning). No party can therefore enforce the agreement

Voidable contract A contract which is capable of being voided. It may be set aside by the innocent party but unless and until he does so, it has full legal effect. The innocent party can therefore choose whether or not to be bound by it

Warranty A contractual term that is less important than a condition. A breach of warranty is still a breach of contract but will not entitle the innocent party to terminate the agreement. He will only be entitled to sue for damages

Index

Index

✱✱✱✱✱✱✱✱✱✱✱✱

Index

✳✳✳✳✳✳✳✳✳✳✳✳

Index

****